New Risks, New Welfare: Signposts for Social Policy

Edited by

Nick Manning and Ian Shaw

BLACKWELL
Publishers

Copyright © Blackwell Publishers Ltd 2000

ISBN 0-631-22042-9

Blackwell Publishers Ltd
108 Cowley Road
Oxford OX4 1JF, UK

Blackwell Publishers Inc
350 Main Street
Malden Massachusetts 02148, USA

British Library Cataloguing in Publication Data has been applied for

Library of Congress Cataloging in Publication Data

New risks, new welfare: signposts for social policy/edited by Nick Manning and Ian Shaw.
p. cm.
Includes index.
ISBN 0-631-22042-9 (acid-free paper)
1. Social policy. 2. Social problems. 3. Public welfare. 4. Great Britain—Social policy—1979. I. Manning, Nick P. II Shaw, Ian. 1945–
HN28 .N49 2000
361-6'1-dc21   00-025850

Typeset at The Spartan Press Ltd,
Lymington, Hants
Printed and bound in Great Britain by
MPG Books, Bodmin, Cornwall

This book is printed on acid-free paper

Contents

Introduction: The Millennium and Social Policy

Nick Manning and Ian Shaw

This special edition has been organized to mark the millennium. Time is therefore an important theme, both in relation to the past, and perhaps more significantly for the future. Most of the chapters are concerned in one way or another with the likely developments in social policy and welfare states in the twenty-first century. However, in this introduction we shall look back both to the thoughts that social policy scholars might have entertained at the turn of the last century or two and, more speculatively, to what they might have thought in AD 999, at the end of the last millennium.

The main body of chapters has been selected in relation to a number of themes, which we have also adopted to analyse the earlier periods in this introduction. There are five themes. The first is social change. Social policy is in general the creature of social change generated elsewhere in society, and to which social policy is a response. At different times the nature and significance of key social changes will vary: sometimes social stratification, or political structure, at other times economic developments. However the scope of any particular society, often taken to be coterminous with the nation state, is not fixed. Hence a second theme is international or inter-regional change: social policy has never been simply national. There are a thousand years between the consolidation of England and that of Germany as national states. In the future the EU and global integration will change this again.

A third theme concerns the type of welfare system in place. This will after all be the key to understanding the social policies and welfare experiences of citizens in the twenty-first century. While the 1990s have been dominated by the analysis of unitary types of welfare system (regime), the proposed typologies have been shown to be less clear-cut once the types of social policy (for example health or social care rather than income support) and types of recipient (women, young people, disabled people, or ethnic minorities rather than white male workers) are taken as the focus. Hence the fourth and fifth themes are concerned with changes in work in all its aspects, not just paid work. The fourth is a response to the relative neglect of the study of industrialism and social welfare of late. Economic growth is often taken as a background to the creation of social problems and the funding of social policy, yet the relations of production, specifically industrial relations, are intimately related to the development of welfare regimes, and have changed significantly in recent years. The fifth extends the examination of work to include welfare work in its widest sense—the work necessary for the "production of welfare". This has of course always been centrally focused on households, particularly women, and mostly unpaid. Moreover with the growing individualism of the late modern era, individuals themselves have been urged to become their own chief carers —"risk society", we are encouraged to think, needs to be navigated with the aid of a kind of personal insurance bubble.

Post-Roman Society

The defining moment for the development of European welfare states was the withdrawal of Roman occupation—for Britain this occurred in 409. From this date on European states struggled towards separate nations: some, such as England, quite early (Egbert was first sole monarch from 827), and others, such as Italy or Germany, much later. By about 1000 there was a tangible start to the steady economic and social development in Europe that, despite a series of subsequent military conflicts, was to lead finally to the Renaissance and early capitalism. But between the fifth century and the end of the millennium, the direction and cumulative level of social development was not secure:

> The miseries of the ageing societies of the Roman Empire and the deficiencies of the young barbarian nations were a long way from cancelling one another out; rather than mutual regeneration, the result of Rome's collision with the barbarians was an accumulation of ills, the brunt of which fell on the powerless. (Mollat 1986: 15)

Evidence from early written histories and the Nottingham analysis of placenames shows for example that in Britain by the end of the first millennium, much of the population consisted of people from Ireland in the north and west, and from Germany in the south and east. The local British population had partly intermarried, but most often provided slaves for the invaders. By 600 there were ten independent Anglo-Saxon kingdoms covering most of modern England and Wales. Following a long period of relative peace, a further period of extensive invasion from Scandinavia took place from about 800, until a stable unitary English kingdom was established from 937. In other words, much of the first millennium was taken up with the consolidation of the first English state.

Social change over this period was thus heavily overshadowed by the effects of the international movement of people and armies, and the regional development of domestic political order. Social policy concerns, as conceived of today, such as health care or housing or education, were for the most part a private matter. Life expectancy was no more than 35 years, and housing rudimentary—the use of stone was not widespread. In Britain, poverty was the main private concern that extended into the public realm as a social issue, as it was throughout much of Europe, and the response was similarly shaped by European, that is Christian, ideas.

The collapse of Roman control across Europe had left behind a legacy of urban poor in the east of the empire, up to 50,000 "indigents" in Constantinople in AD 400, while in the more rural west peasants eked out a precarious existence at best, but fell into vagabondage at worst. They were particularly vulnerable to disease, and the class differences in disease rates were recognized at the time. The causes of poverty are entirely familiar to us today—lack of work (or land), sickness and disability (especially leprosy), inflation (leading to famine), and the absence of family support. In the sixth century a "tidal wave" of poverty inundated the eastern sector of the old Roman Empire, "in chronicles, laws, hagiographies, and sermons we find material that can be pieced together to form a picture of the poor" (Mollat 1986: 17). The poor were classified in an entirely familiar way, into *penes* (poor workers) and *ptochoi* (indigent people reduced to beggary). In the East, Byzantine law regarded the capacity to work as the critical issue: vagabondage and unemployment were political problems; physical and mental disability, abandoned children, and the hungry were moral problems.

Each of these types of poor people were helped through specific establishments, with specific names. The laws and welfare institutions from the East were in most respects reproduced in the West, where the charity principles and provisions of the Church were emphatically the most important. Indeed, Mollat records an assertion from historians that through the writings of the Church Fathers "everything had been said by the fourth century" (1986: 20). What did the Church provide? The obligation to be charitable was a central tenet of the Christian Church, and was the key to salvation. As early as AD 500, forty-one councils and synods had concerned themselves with the poor. Initially this concern consisted of the provision of food to those who were registered on a list drawn up to identify those entitled to help. This system, which predated the Church, gave way increasingly to hostel (or "hospital") provision, as the monasteries grew in wealth towards the end of the first millennium.

Archbishop Hincmar of Rheims laid down in 858 a social programme in which hospitality for the poor was central: one of the primary duties of a bishop, he stated, was "to receive the poor or other guests in hospitals kept open for the purpose and staffed with the necessary personnel" (Mollat 1986: 45). The main gatehouse was central to the monastery's welfare operation. The porter, often with many assistants, categorized the poor into types (whether sick—especially with leprosy—beggars, travellers, and so on), and status differences were acknowledged even though the same hospitality was to be offered to all: hostels for the poor and the wealthy were separate, as was the infirmary for the sick. By around 950 the growing number of claimants had resulted in a division between officers for the rich (*custos hospitum*) and for the poor (the almoner). Welfare provision was becoming a separate and institutional mechanism for the first time.

Towards the Second Millennium

By the tenth century, welfare ideology was being shaped by the two major types of social organization that continue to dominate it today: the church and the state. The Church had grown steadily in power and influence, and

3

the monastery system had secured education and learning, and the provision of both food and shelter for the poor: education, health, housing, and social security rolled into one. Political order was maintained by an increasingly complex set of obligations and rights between lords, farmers and peasants, closely defined by rights over different areas of land. Those who could not find their place in this system, the unemployed and vagabonds, were increasingly policed by the legal system.

State and church interests were pursued through military actions and the tradition of the crusades; but what were civil, political and social rights in 1999. Civil rights existed from an early date. The right to dispute-resolution through the local courts, concerning both property and divorce, was available, and relatively reliable, both for men and for women (Whitelock 1952: 150–1). This is a not inconsiderable social benefit, as yet still poorly applied in many countries in Eastern Europe at the end of the second millennium. Social rights were in the hands of the monasteries. For those poor who were registered, support was adequate in terms of the standards of the day. However, their numbers were to grow steadily in the early centuries of the second millennium, as economic growth generated growing inequality, and population growth resulted in widespread famine from time to time when agricultural production faltered. Mass protest resulted in many areas of Europe. Political rights, in other words, were highly restricted.

Looking out towards the new millennium, then, as we are now, what would a medieval social policy analyst think? We tend to look at the future in two ways: through the analysis and extrapolation of trends into the future, and through the re-classification of activities into new and enduring types. The former accentuates continuity, or "path dependency" as it is now called. The latter emphasizes the emergence of new eras, or new and qualitatively different constellations of social, political and economic relations.

The clearest path dependency that had appeared by AD 1000 was the emergence of a stable set of kingdoms. This, it might have been expected, would be enduring and would consolidate the classification and provision for poor people that the monastery system had devised. However, it must have been apparent that agricultural production was improving even at that early time, and the perspicacious analyst might reasonably have expected that the lot of the poor would steadily improve, and possibly that poverty might be expected to disappear. How wrong such an analysis would have been! Within 50 years of the end of the first millennium, a period of agricultural difficulty and population growth resulted in the regular outbreak of famine in Western Europe that was to last for nearly 150 years, and place great strain on the monastery welfare system. Poverty has made a periodic reappearance as a public issue since that time. Even now, at the threshold of the third millennium it is one of the central concerns of social policy analysis. Poverty in contemporary Europe—especially in the East—might serve as a warning to those of us tempted this year to speculate about the future convergence of welfare states towards a new positive global system.

Towards 1800

For most of the world's history, except for the very privileged, the most important problem has been that of survival. However, even with the reappearance of poverty, most people who live in an economically advanced country can now confidently expect to survive and achieve a basic level of comfort and security. This difference exists largely because the momentum for economic change has increased in many countries since the mid-eighteenth century. The kind of development that might formerly have taken thousands of years to accomplish has been achieved in a matter of decades. Britain was the first country to achieve a sustained increase in the rate of economic change, and this of course also brought social change.

The industrial revolution started in Britain in around 1760 at a time of population growth. By 1799 the population had risen to around 9 million (in 1750 it had been a mere 6.4 million). Birth rates were on the increase and death rates were beginning to fall. In the political arena it was a time of war and colonization. By 1799 these wars were making an impact upon economic and social life in Britain. The shortage of grain encouraged rapid enclosures and the utilization of waste and marginal land. This fuelled the agrarian revolution that served to release labour for early industrialization, and the population began to flow from the land and towards the factories in the emerging industrial centres. Other countries soon learned the ways of industrial manufacture. War demand created high levels of employment and stimulated industry. It was also a time of inflation, which aided the war, but adversely affected the welfare of workers as wages generally failed to keep pace with prices.

However, it was not individual need, but the fear of social disorder which gradually converted the maintenance of the poor from a work of personal Christian charity into a function of the state (Blaug 1974). In 1601 in England this was fear of disorder that had accumulated ever since the destruction of the monastery system. It was the Poor Law of 1601 that was still the bedrock of relief at the turn of the eighteenth century. Here public relief was largely confined to those too young, too old or too sick to work. However, in 1782 Gilbert's Act sanctioned the principle of relieving the "able-bodied" without requiring them to enter the workhouse. Then in 1795, the magistrates of Speenhamland, Berkshire, responding to the exceptional rise in wheat prices, decided to fix a "minimum standard" by supplementing earned incomes in proportion to the price of bread and the size of workers' families. Many other parishes quickly copied this initiative. This was the first time that earnings had been divorced from the productivity of labour and tied instead to an indicator of the cost of living.

Our eighteenth-century social policy analyst might well have seen this separation of work and income as resonant with the new vistas of social development that the revolutions in America and France appeared to have instigated. It is difficult to imagine today how radical the American States seemed in 1776 with the Declaration of Independence. A group of thirteen small colonies came together to wage war against the then most powerful nation on earth. That they won in 1783 was all the more remarkable because an unseasoned militia overwhelmed a professional army and the new American government was formed without an aristocracy. The American declaration that "all men are created equal" and the adopted Bill of Rights in 1789 had a deep resonance amongst populations who were experiencing economic and social change, autocratic rule and the hardships consequent on these. The first country to feel the effect of these ideals was the Americans' ally, France.

In 1789 France was seriously in debt, partly through the expenses incurred while fighting in the American War of Independence. These debts so weakened the crown treasuries that King Louis XVI was forced to seek assistance from the Estates-General, the French parliament, the first time they had convened in 175 years. They pressed for social and political reform and defied the king's attempt to disband them. The King yielded and adopted a constitution, but reformers were not satisfied and the Bastille was stormed that year. The events of the revolution followed quickly. A new revolutionary government was formed in Paris which abolished feudal privileges throughout France. Louis was arrested in 1791 and guillotined in 1793. By that time a reign of terror was sweeping France. Thousands of men and women identified with the old regime were executed. As the revolution grew more radical leaders once thought trustworthy (such as Robespierre) came under suspicion and were also guillotined. On 9 November 1799 an army officer named Napoleon Bonaparte seized power in a coup d'état and created a conscripted citizens' army. Within a few years he was to impose a French model revolutionary government over all of Western Europe with the exception of Portugal and Britain. He was, of course, eventually defeated by a coalition of Swedish, Prussian, Austrian and British troops at Waterloo in 1815. However, despite its relatively short duration and the horrible excesses, the revolution had been a step towards replacing hitherto-entrenched aristocratic forms of government with more open, elective systems. It was to inspire reformers throughout the Western world.

By 1799 the single nation state was widely established across much of the Western world, with the exception of Germany (created in 1871) and Italy (created in 1861). Technological, cultural, political and economic advances fostered the tendency towards nationalism. Improvements in communications extended the knowledge of people beyond their village or province. The spread of education in vernacular tongues to lower-income groups provided a feeling of common cultural heritage. Through education people began to identify themselves with the historical continuity of the nation. War and the struggle for political rights gave peoples the sense of sharing responsibility for the future of their nation. At the same time the growth of trade and industry laid the basis for economic units larger than traditional cities. The French and, to a lesser extent, the American revolutions were a turning point as loyalty to the king was replaced by loyalty to the nation. The French armies then spread this spirit of national identity. This "rise of nation(alism)" coincided generally with the spread of the industrial revolution, which would also promote national economic development, the growth of a middle class and popular demand for representative government into the new century.

The eighteenth century witnessed the growth of freedom of the individual.

Judges became more concerned for the rights of the accused and procedural fairness became a priority in law. The American and French revolutions both inspired, and were inspired by, writings that laid the foundations of modern civil liberties. The work of Voltaire, Rousseau, John Wilkes and Thomas Paine were all notable at the time. However, their impact upon Britain was only just beginning at the turn of the century, though in France the Revolutionary government had abolished the last semblance of the feudal system. Adam Smith even acknowledged the need for a stable social order for the successful pursuit of capitalism. He suggested that "no society can surely be flourishing or happy, of which the far greater part of the members are poor and miserable". This philosophical enlightenment led to a new sympathy for the poor. Religious enlightenment was also beginning to develop across much of Protestant Europe, with a relaxing of the puritan concepts of the shamefulness of poverty and the rise of Methodism.

The structure and role of the family were also beginning to change at the turn of the century. Historical studies suggest that family structure has been less changed by industrialization and urbanization than was once supposed (Fraser 1984). As far as is known, the nuclear family was the most prevalent pre-industrial unit and is still the basic unit of social organization in most modern industrial societies. The family in 1799, however, was beginning to differ from earlier traditional forms in its functions, composition, life cycle, and in the roles of parents and children. In the industrial era, employment became separated from the family group. Members of the family, including initially children, worked in different occupations and in locations away from the home. Families remained large. For example, the average number of children born to a woman was seven in 1800. The family unit was the basic form of welfare, from care during sickness to basic education, though some of this was starting to be provided in the workplace. However, poor families would often place some unproductive family members on to poor relief if they could not afford to support them (Fraser 1984).

Looking towards 1800, then, with early industrialism, revolution, and state-sponsored income support, there might, as in 999, have been cause for anticipation that the "treadmill of human existence" was due to change for the better. The policy analyst's expectations might well have been of a new welfare era, rather than the constraints of a path-dependent welfare system.

Towards 1900

The impact of electric power and the internal combustion engine after 1850 on economic development was no less spectacular than the impact of steam and coal during the initial industrial revolution. As a consequence, the period 1850–1914 is often known as the "second industrial revolution" (Smales 1975). This second revolution was associated with a leap in scientific knowledge and subsequent inventions. The relationship between science and technology began to move closer. Machine tools were developed which enabled the development of mass production. Shortly after the turn of the century Henry Ford would revolutionize the motor car industry by mass-producing a cheap car which could be sold to a much wider market.

Although standard assembly-line technology rapidly spread to some industries, management became more professional as specialized tasks also made other industries more differentiated. The specialization of labour brought with it recognition of the need to educate and train people for the economy. Equally, other aspects of human capital began to be considered, such as the need for illness provision and decent housing.

However the "needs of capital" were not the only stimulus to social policy. As both Bismark and Churchill were to observe, political elites would prefer social policy to the idea of socialism that was looming. The late nineteenth century saw the development of the organized labour movement following beneficial union legislation during the 1870s, and towards the end of the century pressure was mounting for better pay and work. The positive attitude of the new unions towards state intervention, symbolized by the campaign for an 8-hour day, was a cause of anxiety for commentators such as Herbert Spencer, who wrote "A plea for liberty" in 1891. The late summer of 1899 was notable because of a major dockyard strike that succeeded, in part, through public sympathy. It is difficult today to imagine the horror with which the middle and upper classes regarded every step towards the curtailment of laissez-faire. The key point is that resistance built up towards what we would now regard as elementary demands for social justice. This reached a head in 1901 when, as a result of the Taff Vale case, the unions found themselves stripped of the legal rights gained in 1870. This laid the unions open to being sued in the civil courts for acts committed on their behalf. In this particular case the Amalgamated Society of Railway Servants paid the Taff Vale Railway Company £23,000 in settlement of damages caused by the strike action. This pushed the unions towards seeking political remedies through parliamentary representation and legislation and, to this end, the development of the Labour party.

In fact a relatively autonomous space for debate about the development of social policy also gradually opened up in the nineteenth century, away from the clash of capital and labour. It derived from two sources. First was the emergence of middle- and upper-class charitable sensibilities. The 1834 Poor Law Act, with its punitive emphasis upon the work-shy and use of workhouses, began to decline in Britain from the 1890s. Social Darwinism, with its emphasis upon the survival of the fittest and natural selection still had strong roots, but began to be overshadowed by other concerns. The workhouses had become grim institutions based on the principle of deterring poverty and were beginning to be seen as inhuman. Much relief of poverty in London had begun to be taken over by the Charity Organization Society from 1869. This put the charities on a rational footing and developed casework for families, which became the foundation of modern social work. The extension of the franchise to the working class in 1884 made governments more sensitive to the wishes of the workers and political parties began to vie with each other in offering reforms which would increase their electoral standing. People were also becoming more knowledgeable about the nature and causes of poverty. Dickens and other literary figures highlighted the problems, and Charles Booth published his first work in 1889. There was also concern about the very poor physical condition of many recruits who volunteered for the Boer War in 1899. The scene was set for change in the new century and this started to happen from 1906—with a reversal of the Taff Vale decision, the Workmen's Compensation Act, provision of school meals and medical inspections, and state pensions in 1908. By the turn of the century it was clear that the Poor Law was in the process of breaking up, but it was unclear what would take its place.

The second source of social policy debate was the development of non-labour social movements. This was the period of action for the women's rights movements that were fuelled by the enfranchisement of women in New Zealand in 1893. The typical working-class mother of the 1890s, married in her teens or early twenties and experiencing ten pregnancies, spent around fifteen years in a state of pregnancy and in nursing a child for the first year of its life. She was tied, for this period of time "to the wheel of childbearing" (Titmus 1974: 278). This was not true of middle-class women, whose birth rates had begun to fall rapidly from the 1890s. The change between the situation then and today is largely due to a revolution in social attitudes, first fostered through women's movements, and the control women began to take over their own fertility. These early movements have been the inspiration for a whole raft of "new social movements" emerging towards the end of the twentieth century, and set to place gender, race, disability, ecology, therapy and many other issues on to the social policy agenda for the next millennium.

A final element in the context of late nineteenth-century social policy was the extent of colonialism. Britain was the most successful of the colonizing powers with the British Empire covering almost a third of the globe. Much of Africa, Canada, India, Malaya, Hong Kong, Australia, New Zealand and other scattered territories in Asia and the Americas were within the British sphere of influence. France, Belgium, Portugal, Spain, the Netherlands and Germany also controlled large parts of the world. In 1898 the United States acquired its first overseas possession, taking control of Puerto Rico and the Philippines after the Spanish–American war—which also marked the USA as a world power.

Patterns of colonization differed. In the "New World" Europeans provided the predominant population for their colonies. In Africa and Asia the pattern involved relatively small numbers of European traders/settlers who began to administer trade and ultimately the country on European administrative and legal lines, with soldiers and bureaucrats dominating much larger indigenous populations. Europeans of the day justified colonial rule on the basis of benefits allegedly conferred on the native populations. Thus European political, legal and administrative ideals were forced upon the colonies. During the twentieth century these countries have largely gained independence but the legacy of European styles of government remains. The effects on social policy included at the time a concern for the quality of British military personnel, but much more significantly the subsequent reverse migration of people from the colonies to Europe.

Towards the Third Millennium

How will these themes develop into the new millennium? Analysing the future is a risky business, if not self-contradictory, but nevertheless a task to which the authors of the chapters in this collection have devoted themselves in a variety of ways. It will be for the reader, and the passage of time, to judge the fruits of their work. We will confine ourselves to the briefest of guides as to their general approach. First, we could begin with the observation that social policy has historically followed social change, and that the engine of social change is economics. This is a theme in a number of the chapters in this edition. For example, Bob Jessop, although discussing useful trends in governance, focuses his chapter upon the transition to a common basic type of post-twentieth-century welfare state. Nicola Yeates discusses the impact on social policy of global economic developments and asks whether this serves to constrain policy-making within certain structural parameters.

However, although such broad-brush analysis is extremely valuable, there is also merit in a further fleshing-out of the proposal that the welfare state has reached a watershed. A more detailed pointer to the future would be to examine the development of different economic and industrial traditions across Europe. This is a theme picked up by Colin Crouch in his examination of the role of social partners, especially trade unions, in the management of national social insurance systems and, from a different point of view, Peter Abrahamson, who examines how welfare systems have varied even within advanced industrial states. Gáspár Fajth also examines variations on this theme in the policy emerging from some Eastern European post-socialist societies.

But external constraint does not automatically entail a common internal reaction from within welfare systems. There is an argument that the predicted trajectories and types of welfare discussed in these chapters are themselves also dependent on factors internal to welfare states. This is the argument put forward by Ian Shaw in his examination of financial, professional and familial resources, and by John Baldock's arguments on the cultural assumptions which underlie welfare states. It is also a theme picked up by Robert Dingwall in his chapter examining assumptions about risk.

In 1974, E. J. Hobsbawm wrote: ". . . the history of society is still being constructed" (1974: 20). It is clear from the chapters contained in this edition that profound changes are under way which will have significant implications for the future of social policy. We, as editors, hope that the chapters presented in this edited collection will assist readers in understanding those implications and in gauging the importance of both current and predicted developments.

References

Blaug, M. (1974), The myth of the old Poor Law and the making of the new. In Flinn, M. W., and Smout, T. C., *Essays in Social History*, Oxford: Clarendon Press.

Fraser, D. (1984), *The Evolution of the British Welfare State* (2nd edn), London: Macmillan.

Hobsbawm, E. J. (1974), From social history to the history of society. In Flinn, M. W., and Smout, T. C., *Essays in Social History*, Oxford: Clarendon Press.

Mollat, M. (1986), *The Poor in the Middle Ages*, New Haven: Yale University Press.
Smales, B. J. (1975), *Economic History*, London: Heinemann.
Titmus, R. (1974), The position of women: some vital statistics. In Flinn M. W., and
Smout, T. C., *Essays in Social History*, Oxford: Clarendon Press.
Whitelock, D. (1952), *The Beginnings of English Society*, Harmondsworth: Penguin.

I

The Changing Governance of Welfare: Recent Trends in its Primary Functions, Scale, and Modes of Coordination

Bob Jessop

The Keynesian Welfare National State

My main focus is the changing governance of welfare. But changes in this regard are inseparable from broader changes in the welfare regimes that emerged in advanced western capitalist states in the postwar Atlantic Fordist boom. Thus I will also discuss the social and economic functions that current welfare regimes are expected to perform and the scales on which these functions are undertaken. My analysis starts from the interest in more or less radical reform of postwar welfare states and relates this to the weakening of their governance structures as well as their policy effectiveness by the interaction of various economic, social and political factors.

A highly provocative claim in this regard comes from Claus Offe, who, writing as issues of crisis, crisis management and crisis resolution moved up the political agenda, argued that "while capitalism cannot coexist *with*, neither can it exist *without*, the welfare state" (1984: 153, italics in original). My concluding comments suggest a solution to "Offe's paradox". But this first requires a new analysis of welfare regimes going beyond what Offe and his neo-Marxist contemporaries, for all their acuity, could offer fifteen years ago, before the crises in and/or of welfare regimes had developed to the present extent (for a general critique of their position, see Klein 1993). Thus, building on the French regulation approach to political economy and recent institutionalist work on governance, I discuss the role of welfare regimes in economic and social reproduction, the scales on which welfare is organized, and the forms deployed in governing them.

An important step in clarifying Offe's paradox is to identify the form of welfare state said to be in crisis. This is the form that became dominant in Northwestern Europe, North America, Australia and New Zealand during the 1950s to 1970s, and that was closely linked with the Fordist growth dynamic. It can be described in ideal-typical terms as the Keynesian welfare national state (or KWNS). Each term in this fourfold construct highlights its *distinctive* features and ignores any *generic* properties the KWNS may share with other types of capitalist welfare regime. Thus, before presenting this ideal type, I justify the criteria used in constructing it and will thereby highlight some general features of capitalist economic and social reproduction.

The four criteria derive from features of capitalism as a mode of production. The first criterion is the state's distinctive roles in securing conditions for profitable private business. This is the broad field of economic policy. It is important because market forces alone cannot secure these conditions and are supplemented by non-market mechanisms. This insufficiency is grounded in generic tendencies towards market failure and in specific contradictions and dilemmas associated with capitalism. The second dimension refers to the state's distinctive roles in reproducing labour power individually and collectively over various timespans from quotidian routines via individual life cycles to intergenerational reproduction (on life cycles, see Falkingham and Hills 1995). This is the broad field of social policy. It matters because labour power is a fictitious commodity (Polanyi 1944; de Brunhoff 1968). For, although it is bought and sold in labour markets and may add value in production, it is not itself directly (re)produced in and by capitalist firms with a view to private profit. Labour power enters the market economy from outside and is embodied in individuals who have other identities than as bearers of labour power. This poses problems: economic problems as regards its individual and collective suitability to capital's needs and its own survival in the absence of a secure income or other assets; social problems regarding social inclusion and cohesion; and political problems regarding the legitimacy of state intervention in this area and its relation to other identities that workers may have. The third dimension refers to the main scale, if any, on which economic and social policies are decided—even if underpinned or implemented on other scales. This is important as economic and social policies are politically mediated and the scales of political organization may not coincide with those of economic and social life. The fourth dimension concerns the relative weight of the mechanisms deployed in the effort to maintain capitalist profitability and reproduce labour power by compensating for market failures and inadequacies. This is where issues of governance are most relevant—although governance also enters into the other three dimensions. Top-down state intervention is just one of these mechanisms; and, as is well known, states as well as markets can fail. This suggests the need for other supplementary mechanisms and, in so far as these also tend to fail, for attention to the balance among them (Dunsire 1996; Bochel and Bochel 1998).

I now define the KWNS on these four dimensions. First, in promoting the conditions for capital's profitability, it can be described as distinctively *Keynesian* in so far as it aimed to secure full employment in a relatively closed national economy and to do so mainly through demand-side management. Second, in reproducing labour power as a fictitious commodity, the KWNS social policy role had a distinctive *welfare* orientation in so far as it tried (a) to generalize norms of mass consumption beyond male workers in Fordist economic sectors earning a family wage so that national citizens and their dependants could all share the fruits of economic growth (and thereby also contribute to effective domestic demand); and (b) to promote forms of collective consumption favourable to the Fordist growth dynamic with its base in a virtuous national circle of mass production and mass consumption. Thus economic and social policies were linked to economic and social rights attached directly or indirectly to citizenship of a national territorial state—whether this citizenship was based on descent, acculturation, naturalization, political tests, or another criterion (on types of national state, see Jessop 1999a). Third, the KWNS was *national* in so far as economic and social policies were pursued within the historically specific (and socially constructed) matrix of a national economy, a national state, and a society seen as comprising national citizens. Within this matrix it was the national territorial state that was mainly held responsible for developing and guiding Keynesian welfare policies (de Swaan 1992). Local and regional states acted mainly as relays for policies framed at the national level; and the various international regimes established after World War II were mainly intended to restore stability to national economies and national states. And, fourth, the KWNS was *statist* in so far as state institutions (on different levels) were the chief supplement to market forces in securing the conditions for economic growth and social cohesion. It was the combination of market and state on different levels that prompted the use of the term "mixed economy" to describe the postwar system (classically, Shonfeld 1965). In addition to its role in facilitating and correcting the operation of market forces, the state also had a dominant role in shaping civil society and thus the identities held by its citizens.

There was never a pure form of KWNS. At best one finds particular welfare regimes that combine its four features (in one or other of its variant forms) with other functions, scales of action, or modes of governance. Nor is there a pure crisis of the KWNS—only specific, path-dependent, nationally variable crises. In some cases there has been greater continuity, linked to the dominance of the view that there was a crisis *in* the welfare state, with largely incremental shifts towards the new welfare regime (e.g. Denmark); in others there has been greater discontinuity—admittedly more marked in declared policy changes than actual policy outcomes—linked to a discursively constructed crisis *of* the welfare state (e.g. Britain).

The Importance of Governance

For present purposes "governance" refers to any form of coordination of interdependent social relations—ranging from simple dyadic interactions to complex social divisions of labour. Three main forms of coordination are usually distinguished: the *anarchy* of exchange (e.g. market forces), the *hierarchy* of command (e.g. imperative coordination by the state), and the *"heterarchy"* of self-organization (e.g. networks). Along with other commentators I refer to the third form of coordination as "governance in the narrow sense" in contrast to the broader concept that also encompasses market forces and organizational hierarchies (on governance and governance failure, see Jessop 1998; also Kooiman 1993; Dunsire 1996).

With the development of formally free labour markets, market forces became the chief mode of capitalist economic coordination. But the invisible hand, with its formal monetary maximands, impersonality (working, as Marx put it, behind the backs of the producers), procedural rationality, and *post hoc* operation, is supplemented through other modes of coordination that introduce more substantive objectives, elements of interpersonal or inter-organizational deliberation, orientation to collective goals, and *ex ante* concertation. It is in this context that welfare regimes can help to secure some of the key conditions for capital accumulation. For they are implicated in governing the economic, gender, ethnic, intergenerational (and many other) aspects of the division of labour—and indeed themselves contribute to the "labour of division", that is, the classification and normalization of individuals, groups and other social forces as a basis for differential treatment in the division of labour and for social inclusion-exclusion (on the labour of division, see Munro 1997). The concept of governance is very useful in analysing welfare regimes as it enables us to classify regimes in terms of their typical combinations of modes of coordination. The concept of the "mixed economy of welfare" (Titmuss 1963; Pinker 1992) captures aspects of this; but, because it focuses on mechanisms of redistribution (occupational, fiscal, welfare benefits), it neglects the ways in which welfare regimes govern production and reproduction more generally.

In this light one might consider three interrelated issues in the governance of welfare. These are the changing definitions of welfare; the changing institutions responsible for its delivery; and the practices in and through which welfare is delivered. These issues are closely linked. For it is a social scientific commonplace that governance practices (mediated by institutions) attempt to delimit, unify, stabilize and reproduce their objects of governance as the precondition as well as the effect of governing them. Moreover, as recent Foucauldian analyses have emphasized, governance practices also typically aim to create and reproduce the subjects needed for governance to operate effectively (Barry *et al.* 1996; Hunt and Wickham 1993). Thus, as the objects and modes of governance change, institutional mechanisms and actual practices change too—and so do the typical forms of governance failure. In this sense we should see welfare regimes as constitutive of their objects of governance and not just as responses to pre-given economic and social problems. Indeed this is one of the bases on which the welfare state is criticized—that it generates the problems it addresses. This also suggests that it will be self-expanding—always finding new problems to solve—and, perhaps, ultimately self-defeating as it becomes more complex, overloads itself with tasks, and eventually produces a crisis of ungovernability (e.g. Crozier *et al.* 1975).

Whether or not one subscribes to such criticisms, it was the purported failure of the KWNS as a mode of economic and social governance that prompted the search for new forms of governance. Its alleged crisis affected not only the modes of "governance-government-governing" in the KWNS but also its objects and subjects of social and economic governance. More specifically, the KWNS began to fail as a mode of governance when its coherence as an institutional ensemble became inconsistent with the objects it was governing, the practices being deployed to govern them, and the identities and interests of the active agents and/or "passive" subjects of the

15

KWNS regime. Thus, taking its four dimensions in turn, I would identify the following crisis-tendencies.

First, the primary object of economic governance in the KWNS was the national economy. The emergence and consolidation of Keynesian practices had helped to delimit and reproduce the national economy (Tomlinson 1985). They provided the means of measuring national economic performance, controlling economic flows across national borders, setting economic aggregates such as inflation, employment and growth as goals of national economic management, and creating the infrastructure for national economic development. But Keynesian economic management became increasingly problematic and generated stagflationary tendencies (stagnation plus inflation) that fuelled the emerging crisis of the Atlantic Fordist economy that the KWNS was supposed to manage (Boyer 1991). Economic internationalization exacerbated these problems. It undermined the national economy as an object of economic management and led to quite different conceptions of the economy and, *a fortiori*, its mechanisms of economic and social governance. States could no longer act as if national economies were more or less closed and their growth dynamics were primarily domestic (Teeple 1995). Replacing the national economy as the primary object of economic governance is the knowledge-driven economy in an era of globalization (Castells 1996). Its growth dynamic depends on how effectively a given economic space—not necessarily a national economy—is inserted into the changing global division of labour. This in turn has prompted concern with international economic competitiveness and supply-side intervention—initially to supplement national demand management, later as the primary objective and means of economic intervention.

The imagined scope and inclusiveness of the economy that needs governing have also expanded. This is no longer interpreted in narrow terms but has been extended to include many additional factors (deemed "non-economic" under the KWNS regime) that affect economic performance. This expansion is reflected in concepts such as "structural competitiveness" (Chesnais 1986) or "systemic competitiveness" (Messner 1997)—concepts that highlight the combined impact of diverse societal factors on competitiveness. State managers therefore intervene in a growing range of economically relevant practices, institutions, functional systems, and domains of the lifeworld to enhance competitiveness. This has two interesting and paradoxical effects on the state. First, whilst it expands the potential scope of state intervention for economic purposes, the resulting complexity renders postwar top-down intervention less effective—requiring that the state retreat from some areas of intervention and re-invent itself as a condition for more effective intervention in others (Messner 1997). And, second, whilst it increases the range of stakeholders whose cooperation is required for successful state intervention, it also increases pressures within the state to create new subjects to act as its partners. Thus states are now trying to transform the identities, interests, capacities, rights and responsibilities of economic and social forces so that they become more flexible, capable, and reliable agents of the state's new economic strategies—whether in partnership with the state and/or with each other or as autonomous entrepreneurial subjects in the new knowledge-driven economy (Barry *et al.* 1996; Deakin and Edwards 1993; Jones Finer 1997; Jones 1999).

Second, the generic object of social governance in the KWNS (as in other forms of national state) was a national population divided in the first instance into citizens of the national state and resident aliens. But this population was categorized and governed in distinctive ways suited to Atlantic Fordism and its mode of regulation. Above all, social policy was premised on conditions of full or near-full employment, lifelong employment—albeit not necessarily with the same employer—with a family wage for male workers, and the patriarchal nuclear family as the basic unit of civil society (Esping-Andersen 1994). The KWNS was also premised on a class compromise between organized labour and organized business in which responsible unionism and collective bargaining permitted managers to manage and workers to benefit from rising productivity as wage earners and welfare recipients. There were none the less some marginalized or overburdened social groups—most notably women as housewives, mothers and secondary participants in the labour force, and also immigrants or other workers (and their families) who worked in disadvantaged segments of the labour market (Lewis 1998). This pattern was undermined both economically and socially. The crisis of Atlantic Fordism undermined the assumptions of full employment, the family wage, and the gendered division of labour; and it also led state managers to see the social wage increasingly as a cost of international production rather than as a source of domestic demand. The KWNS was also affected by a weakening of the national identity and solidarity that shaped it in its formative period and helped sustain the coalition behind it. This is reflected in changes in the values, social identities, and interests associated with the welfare state. Indicators of this included rejection of the social democratic and/or Atlantic Fordist commitment to a class-based redistributive politics; a pluralistic identity politics and "politics of difference" that emphasizes mutual respect, authenticity and autonomy; increased concern for personal empowerment rather than for the bureaucratic administration of legal rights, monetized entitlements, and uniform public services; and expansion of the so-called "third" sector, which supposedly operates flexibly outside of the framework of pure markets and the bureaucratic state (but often in close conjunction with them as a "shadow market" and "shadow state"). These shifts have fragmented the KWNS coalition of forces, led to demands for more differentiated and flexible forms of economic and social policy, and led to concern with problems of social exclusion and ensuring lifetime access to the benefits of a restructured welfare regime (e.g. lifelong learning).

Third, the primacy of the national scale of economic and social governance depended on the coincidence of national economy, national state, national society, and the survival of the national state as a sovereign body. This structured coherence has also been weakened. The national economy has been undermined by internationalization, the growth of multi-tiered global city networks, the formation of triad economies (such as the European Union), and the re-emergence of regional and local economies in national states. This complex articulation of global-regional-national-local economies is related to the "hollowing out" of the national state as its powers are delegated upwards to supra-regional or international bodies, downwards to regional or local states, or outwards to relatively autonomous cross-national alliances among local metropolitan or regional states with complementary interests. There are also growing attempts to internationalize (or at least Europeanize) social policy. And, third, the unity of the nation state has been weakened by the (admittedly uneven) growth of multi-ethnic and multi-cultural societies, and divided political loyalties (with the resurgence of regionalism and nationalism as the rise of European identities, diasporic networks, cosmopolitan patriotism, etc.) (Jessop 1999a). Thus we see a proliferation of scales on which economic and social policy are pursued as well as competing projects to re-unify inter-scalar articulation around a new primary level—whether this be the industrial district, the city-region, wider sub-national regions, cross-border regions, the triads, or the global level.

Finally, the state's role in the mixed economy was undermined by several factors. These include: growing political resistance to taxation and the emerging stagnation-inflation; a crisis in postwar compromises between industrial capital and organized labour; new economic and social conditions and attendant problems that cannot be managed or resolved readily, if at all, through continuing reliance on top-down state planning and/or simple market forces; growing resentment about the bureaucratism, inflexibility and cost of the welfare state as it continued to expand during the late 1960s and 1970s; and the rise of new social movements which did not fit easily into the postwar compromise. Moreover, as society has become more complex and as new economic and social conditions emerge that cannot be managed or resolved readily, if at all, through the market and state as modes of governance, there has been increasing reliance on networks and partnerships as modes of coordination. Organizationally the Fordist period was one of large-scale, top-down hierarchical structures and this model spread to the state's economic and welfare roles. This paradigm is being challenged by a new "network paradigm" that emphasizes partnership, regulated self-regulation, the infor-mal sector, the facilitation of self-organization, and decentralized context-steering (Messner 1997). Overall, this involves a tendential shift from imperative coordination by the sovereign state to an emphasis on interdepen-dence, divisions of knowledge, reflexive negotiation, and mutual learning. In short, there is a shift from govern*ment* to govern*ance* in the narrow sense.

The Schumpeterian Workfare Postnational Regime

These changes are reflected in four general trends in the restructuring of the KWNS. The first is a shift from Keynesian aims and modes of intervention to Schumpeterian ones; the second is a shift from a welfarist mode of reproduction of labour power to a workfarist mode; the third is a shift from the primacy of the national scale to a postnational framework in which no scale is predominant; the fourth is a shift from the primacy of the state in compensating for market failures to an emphasis on networked, partnership-based economic, political and social governance mechanisms. These trends can be considered separately. Indeed, both severally and in combination, they have developed in quite different ways in the various Atlantic Fordist economies. They can nevertheless be summarized in terms of the suggestion that the Keynesian welfare national state (KWNS) is giving way to a Schumpeterian workfare postnational regime (SWPR). Moreover, whether viewed individually or in aggregate, these four changes are closely connected to the search for solutions to the Atlantic Fordist crisis.

The ideal-typical SWPR can be described as follows. First, regarding its functions for capital, it is *Schumpeterian* in so far as it tries to promote permanent innovation and flexibility in relatively open economies by intervening on the supply-side and to strengthen as far as possible their structural and/or systemic competitiveness. Complementing these new strategic concerns in economic and social policy has been the demotion or rejection of other, earlier policy objectives. Whilst the KWNS aimed to secure full employment, the SWPR demotes this aim in favour of promoting structural or systemic competitiveness. Second, regarding social reproduction, the SWPR can be described (at the risk of misunderstanding) as a *workfare* regime in so far as it subordinates social policy to the demands of labour market flexibility and structural or systemic competitiveness. Thus, whilst the KWNS tried to extend the social rights of its citizens, the SWPR is concerned to provide welfare services that benefit business and thereby demote individual needs to second place. This includes putting downward pressure on the social wage *qua* cost of international production. Concern with training and labour market functioning has long been a feature of state involvement in the social reproduction of labour power, of course, but the SWPR gives greater weight to flexibility and endows it with new connotations (Ainley 1997). It is for these reasons that there is also a major reorientation on the part of the state to the making and re-making of the subjects who are expected to serve as partners in the innovative, knowledge-driven, entrepreneurial, flexible economy and its accompanying self-reliant, autonomous, empowered workfare regime (for a recent illustration, see Blair and Schröder 1999).

Third, compared with the earlier primacy of the national scale, the SWPR is *postnational* in so far as the increased significance of other spatial scales and horizons of action (or "relativization of scale")[1] makes the national territory less important as a "power container". This is associated with a transfer of economic and social policy-making functions upwards, downwards, and sideways. International agencies (such as the IMF, World Bank, OECD and ILO) play an increased role in shaping the social as well as economic policy agendas; in Europe, moreover, the European Union also has a growing role (cf. de Swaan 1992; Deacon 1995; Leibfried 1993; Wilding 1997). But there is a simultaneous devolution of some economic and social policy-making to the regional, urban and local levels on the grounds that policies intended to influence the micro-economic supply-side and social regeneration are best designed close to their sites of implementation. In some cases this also involves cross-border cooperation among regional, urban or local spaces. In all three regards, welfare governance has become more postnational. Yet, paradoxically, this leads to an enhanced role for national states in controlling the interscalar transfer of these powers—suggesting a shift from sovereignty to a *primus inter pares* role in intergovernmental relations.

Finally, regarding the mode of delivery of economic and social policies, the SWPR has a regime form because of the increased importance of non-state mechanisms in compensating for market failures and inadequacies and in the delivery of state-sponsored economic and social policies. This provides a second important aspect to the apparent (but deceptive) "hollowing out" of national states, namely, the increased importance of private-private networks to state activities on all levels—from local partnerships to supranational neo-corporatist arrangements (e.g. Clarke and Gaile 1998; Falkner 1998).

Like all ideal-types, the SWPR has been formed through the one-sided accentuation of empirically observable features (in this case, in Atlantic Fordist societies) to construct a logically possible social phenomenon. This does not presuppose actual examples of the SWPR in pure form nor imply that any movement along its different dimensions occurs evenly and at the same pace. Indeed, there is significant variation in the search for solutions to the alleged problems of the KWNS. It involves neither a unidirectional movement nor a multilateral convergence across all national regimes.

Concluding Remarks

This chapter has presented an ideal-typical contrast between two forms of welfare regime—the Keynesian welfare national state and the Schumpeterian workfare postnational regime. My other work on these two forms deals mainly with their economic and social functions in reproducing private capital and labour power. This chapter addresses the governance of welfare regimes and the changing scales on which such governance occurs. It has argued that the national mixed economy of welfare (based on a combination of market and plan) is giving way to a new postnational mixed economy in which networks and partnership have become more important. I have also argued that the subjects as well as the objects of governance are being reconstituted. Since this involves far more than a simple technical fix, it is easy to see why the transition from KWNS to SWPR is always politically mediated and often difficult. Thus, although my entry point for analysing the transition is inspired by Marxist political economy, a critique of politics is also required. This would serve not only to interpret the political mediations of the transition (as well as any "conservation-dissolution" effects)[2] but also the constitutive role of politics in defining the problems to which the transition is a response and redefining both the objects and subjects of governance. This in turn helps to explain why, despite a tendential denationalization of the state and a shift from government to governance, national states still have major roles in shaping how the economic and social reproduction requirements of capital are met. For they try to determine which functions go upwards, downwards, and sideways and the conditions on which they stay there; and also seek both to design governance mechanisms and to politically organize self-organization.

Space limitations prevented me from identifying subtypes of KWNS and SWPR and from assessing how far the posited changes have occurred in particular cases. But, just as there were different forms of governance in the KWNS, so the SWPR also has variant forms (neo-liberal, neo-corporatist, neo-statist, and, as a supplement, neo-communitarian) (but see Jessop 1993,

1994, 1999b). While there are economic, political and intellectual forces that are closely identified with one or other mode of governance, these subtypes are best seen as poles around which different national solutions have developed (and are developing) during more or less extended periods of conflict and experimentation. Currently the neo-liberal form of SWPR is hegemonic on the international level, but important counter-currents exist in specific national and regional contexts. Each subtype and each welfare-workfare mix has different implications for welfare policy. The particular mix in individual cases will depend on institutional legacies, the balance of political forces, and the changing economic and political conjunctures in which different strategies are pursued. They will also be overdetermined by factors beyond those included within this particular approach to the political economy of welfare. There is certainly no reason to expect a multilateral convergence of welfare regimes around one subtype of the SWPR—let alone a rapid convergence.

Finally, I want to suggest a solution to "Offe's paradox". On the one hand, capitalism (in its Atlantic Fordist form) did coexist with the welfare state (in its KWNS form) for an extended period. Eventually the Fordist growth regime and its KWNS mode of regulation became mutually contradictory. This prompted a search for new economic and social bases for capital accumulation; and this involved a partial dismantling of the KWNS. In this sense the emerging post-Fordist capitalist regime cannot coexist with the KWNS. But this search extends to new forms of state (or, alternatively, extra-economic) intervention that might help to re-secure conditions for private profitability and the reproduction of labour power. One could perhaps label this a simple restructuring of the welfare state, but emphasizing policy continuities in this way actually hides as much (if not more) than it reveals (the problem in, for example, Klein's critique, 1993). For the core organizational principles of the KWNS are being superseded in favour of those of the SWPR as a condition for the renewed coexistence of capitalism and the welfare state. None the less, this has several possible forms and should not be reduced to the neo-liberal workfare state favoured by Thatcher and Major—and taken as the starting point for New Labour's "Third Way".

Notes

1. On the "relativization of scale", see Collinge (1996).
2. These effects occur when certain features of an earlier system are retained but acquire a new significance when inserted into an emerging system.

References

Ainley, P. (1997), Toward a learning society or towards learningfare? *Social Policy Review*, 9: 50–68.

Barry, A., Osborne, T., and Rose, N. (1996), *Foucault and Political Reason: Liberalism, neo-Liberalism and Rationalities of Government*, London: UCL Press.

Blair, T., and Schröder, G. (1999), Europe: The Third Way/Die Neue Mitte, http://www.labour.org.uk/views/items/00000053.html.

Bochel, C., and Bochel, H. (1998), The governance of social policy, *Social Policy Review*, 10: 57–74.

Boyer, R. (1991), The eighties: the search for alternatives to Fordism. In *The Politics of Flexibility*, ed. B. Jessop, H. Kastendiek, and K. Nielsen, Aldershot: Edward Elgar: 106–132.

Castells, M. (1996), *The Rise of the Network Society*, Oxford: Blackwell.

Chesnais, F. (1986), Science, technology and competitiveness, *STI Review*, 1: 86–129.

Clarke, S. E., and Gaile, G. L. (1998), *The Work of Cities*, Minneapolis: University of Minnesota Press.

Collinge, C. (1996), *Spatial Articulation of the State: Reworking Social Relations and Social Regulation Theory*. Birmingham: Centre for Urban and Regional Studies.

Crozier, M., Huntington, S. P., and Watanuki, J. (1975), *The Crisis of Democracy*, New York: New York University Press.

Deacon, B. (1995), The globalisation of social policy and the socialisation of global politics, *Social Policy Review* 7: 55–76.

Deakin, N., and Edwards, J. (1993), *The Enterprise Culture and the Inner City*, London: Routledge.

de Brunhoff, S. (1968), *The State, Capital and Economic Policy*, London: Pluto Press.

de Swaan, A. (1992), Perspectives for transnational social policy, *Government and Opposition*, 27, 1: 33–51.

Dunsire, A. (1996), Tipping the balance: autopoiesis and governance, *Administration and Society*, 28, 3: 299–334.

Esping-Andersen, G. (1994), Equality and work in the post-industrial life cycle. In *Reinventing the Left*, ed. D. Miliband, Cambridge: Polity: 167–85.

Falkingham, J., and Hills, J. (eds) (1995), *The Dynamic of Welfare: the Welfare State and the Life Cycle*, Hemel Hempstead: Prentice Hall.

Falkner, G. (1998), *EU Social Policy in the 1990s: Towards a Corporatist Policy Community*, London: Routledge.

Hunt, A., and Wickham, G. (1993), *Foucault and Law: Towards a Sociology of Governance*, London: Pluto Press.

Jessop, B. (1993), Towards a Schumpeterian workfare state? Preliminary remarks on post-Fordist political economy, *Studies in Political Economy*, 40: 7–39.

Jessop, B. (1994), The transition to post-Fordism and the Schumpeterian workfare state. In *Towards a post-Fordist Welfare State?*, ed. R. Burrows and B. Loader, London: Routledge: 13–37.

Jessop, B. (1998), The rise of governance and the risks of failure: the case of economic development, *International Social Science Journal*, 155: 29–46.

Jessop, B. (1999a), Narrating the future of the national economy and the national state? Remarks on re-mapping regulation and re-inventing governance. In *STATE/CULTURE: State Formation after the Cultural Turn*, ed. G. Steinmetz, Ithaca: Cornell University Press: 378–405.

Jessop, B. (1999b), From Keynesianism to workfarism. In *Rethinking Welfare Policy*, ed. Gayle Lewis, Open University Press: Milton Keynes (in press).

Jones, M. (1999), *New Institutional Spaces: TECs and the Remaking of Economic Governance*, London: Jessica Kingsley.

Jones Finer, C. (1997), The new social policy in Britain, *Social Policy and Administration*, 31, 5: 154–70.

Klein, R. (1993), O'Goffe's tale. In *New Perspectives on the Welfare State in Europe*, ed. C. Jones, London: Routledge: 7–17.

Kooiman, J. (ed.) (1993), *Modern Governance: New Government—Society Interactions*, London: Sage.

Leibfried, S. (1993), Toward a European welfare state. In *New Perspectives on the Welfare State in Europe*, ed. C. Jones, London: Routledge: 133–56.

Lewis, G. (1998), "Coming apart at the seams": the crises of the welfare state. In *Unsettling Welfare: the Reconstruction of Social Policy*, ed. G. Hughes and G. Lewis, London: Routledge: 39–79.

Messner, D. (1997), *The Network Society: Economic Development and International Competitiveness as Problems of Social Governance*, London: Frank Cass.

Munro, R. (1997), Ideas of difference: stability, social spaces and the labour of division. In *Ideas of Difference: Social Spaces and the Labour of Division*, ed. K. Hetherington and R. Munro, Oxford: Blackwell: 3–26.

Offe, C. (1984), *Contradictions in the Welfare State*, London: Hutchinson.

Pinker, R. (1992), Making sense of the mixed economy of welfare, *Social Policy and Administration*, 26, 4: 273–84.

Polanyi, K. (1944), *The Great Transformation: the Economic and Political Origins of Our Time*, New York: Rinehart.

Shonfield, A. (1965), *Modern Capitalism*, Oxford: Oxford University Press.

Teeple, G. (1995), *Globalization and the Decline of Social Reform*, Toronto: Garamont Press.

Titmuss, R. M. (1963), *Essays on the Welfare State*, London: Allen and Unwin.

Tomlinson, J. (1985), *British Macroeconomic Policy since 1940*, London: Croom Helm.

Wilding, P. (1997), Globalization, regionalization and social policy, *Social Policy and Administration*, 31, 4: 410–28.

2

Resources for Social Policy

Ian Shaw

Introduction

It may be expected that a chapter that purports to focus upon the resources required for social policy in the future may be fundamentally concerned with public expenditure issues. For example, in the UK the total taxes and social security contributions come to around 33.1 per cent of GDP. This could be compared to France at around 43.9 per cent, Sweden at 50.6 per cent and Germany at around 41.8 per cent (Glennerster 1997: 132). We are often told that taxes need to be as low as possible to enable the UK to compete on the world stage. However, at the time of writing both France and Germany enjoy higher rates of economic growth than the UK, which would seem to contradict such arguments. Even so, there are concerns that the increasing trends for globalization of commodity, capital and labour markets in a large number of fields have diminished the power of nation states. Technological developments affect patterns of work and employment and this has the effect of reducing security and opportunities for less skilled workers. There are also concerns that international competitive pressures are resulting in the transfer of jobs between countries according to the logic of markets. Some analysts argue that the capacity of national governments to control the impact of these changes is increasingly limited and politicians in many countries are convinced that state spending must be rigorously constrained, since higher taxes will increase production costs and render national industries less competitive (Taylor-Gooby 1999). As we move into the twenty-first century there are predictions that the Western invention of global capitalism will undermine the Western system of state welfare as a citizen right (Fukuyama 1989). Such concerns are real and would be a suitable focus for a chapter concerned with resources for social policy.

However, finance alone does not produce welfare. There are a number of underlying factors that will become increasingly important in the medium and long-term future, particularly as they will impact upon the financing framework. Three fundamental issues that will affect the future resourcing of social policy are discussed here. They are demographic factors and the changing role and nature of "the family"; environment constraints; and changing fundamentally public attitudes towards welfare. The argument of this chapter is that, for the future, these resources may well become critical for the future shape of social policy, particularly against a background of increasing demand.

Demand

The most important demand factors result from demographic change. There are three key issues here. First, the ratio of elderly people to those of working age has risen sharply in recent years and stands to increase dramatically in the first half of the coming century:

> In 1995 round 15 per cent of the population of the EU was aged 65 or over, equivalent to about 23 per cent of the working age population. By 2005 the number of those aged 65 or over will be equivalent to 26 per cent of the working age population, by 2015 30 per cent, and by 2025 36 per cent. The situation varies between countries. By 2025 the number of pensioners will be equivalent to 40 per cent of the working age population in Italy, and over 36 per cent in Belgium, Germany, France and Sweden. Only in Portugal will it be less than 30 per cent and in Ireland and Luxembourg less than 32 per cent. (EU 1996: paragraph 6)

Second, participation in the labour force by those of working age has fallen and appears likely to continue to fall. This is particularly true for those aged under 25 (who are likely to be in education or training) and those over 50 (who are more likely to be retired) (Vickerstaff 1999). Third, unemployment has risen and seems unlikely to fall significantly in the immediate future. At the same time the proportion of women in the population who enter the labour market has increased and this trend seems likely to continue. The combined effect of these factors is not easy to predict. Ellison and Pierson argue that this implies that "at some time in the new century the existing welfare state will become unstable because of the excess of (pensioner) demands over (worker) input" (1998a: 7). Other commentators argue that a positive outcome is possible. The European Statistics Office estimates that, if unemployment in EU countries were to return to the level of the early 1970s, before the oil crisis (3 per cent of the labour force), and the upward trend in labour market participation for women were to continue, the problem of financing pensions and other services for those over 65 would be resolved in most European countries (Taylor-Gooby 1999). However, if the situation remains much as it is at present the difficulties in achieving the necessary transfer of resources from those under 65 to those over 65 will be acute and the pressures to reform pensions and health and social services may become intense (EU 1996).

The rising numbers of the elderly as a proportion of the population pose two core problems. First, whilst there is not necessarily a strict correlation between increasing age and increasing frailty, the proportion of people with some disability rises sharply for those over the age of 75. For example, as Glennerster points out, the demands made upon the British National Health Service begin to rise significantly once one reaches the age of 44. The figures show that it is around 23 times as expensive to provide health care for those over 85 as it is for people aged between 16 and 44 (Glennerster 1997: 166). Moreover, Light argued that the NHS alone would have to have an increase of resources of 2 per cent per annum until 2020 just to maintain current levels of service in the face of this rising demand (Light 1997). Similar increases would be required in provision of social and related services. These arise from the demand generated solely from demographic factors. Second, there are concerns about both the supply and the funding of sufficient professional carers to meet the demands of an ageing population. If we take the case of the British NHS again as an example, around two-thirds of the total budget goes to pay staff salary costs. The government is having difficulty attracting and retaining nursing and other health care staff because of poor wage levels and cannot easily increase the level of services without increasing salaries and the taxation necessary to fund this. This is difficult given international competition factors in the global market.

Not surprisingly, there has been considerable debate surrounding the sustainability of present levels of state provision. European governments have tended to argue for retrenchment and for the substitution of state provision by other means.

Families as a Social Policy Resource

One "other means" which has been adopted is to shift responsibility for care on to families as a primary provider of welfare. A prime example of this is the development of community care policies. The development of these in recent years has firmly located the family at their hub. Indeed, although the idea of "the community"—encompassing family, friends and neighbours, backed up by statutory support—has achieved political consensus across most political parties in Europe, there is little agreement upon what this actually means in practice for the statutory services. This inevitably puts the emphasis upon families:

> Whatever level of public expenditure proves practicable and however it is distributed, the primary sources of support and care are informal and voluntary. These spring from personal ties of kinship, friendship, and neighbourhood. They are irreplaceable. It is the role of public authorities to sustain and where necessary develop—but never replace —such support and care. Care in the community must increasingly mean care by the community. (Wicks 1991: 173)

In 1985 the General Household Survey produced the first national data about people who give and receive care. When applied to the population as a whole the Survey estimated that some 6 million people were involved in some form of caring and that the different forms of care included:

- personal help with dressing, bathing, toileting and feeding;
- physical help with activities such as walking, getting in and out of bed, going up and down stairs;
- practical help with housework, meals shopping, etc.;

- other sorts of help such as giving medication, changing dressings, assistance with transport, etc.

The survey also showed that for a significant number of these carers such assistance involved them in providing care services for over 100 hours per week. Apart from the costs in time there are also financial, emotional, physical and opportunity costs to the carer (Glendinning and Millar 1992). These costs are also associated with poor health for the carer.

The family has long had a welfare role. Families can provide a means of redistributing income from those who earn to those who do not by ensuring that each family member is housed, fed and clothed. Children are reared within families and both minor illness and long-term disability are also usually cared for at home. Of course, whilst economists have used the family as a basic unit of analysis, it is individuals within families who actually produce welfare. In terms of the production of welfare, it is chiefly women who carry out the tasks and services associated with catering for the human needs within the family. One of the important consequences of the development of a welfare state is the move of many welfare tasks out of the home and into the public arena. This has had a significant impact upon women's lives. Welfare states have underpinned the rise in women's participation rates in waged labour as women moved from unpaid welfare activity within the home to paid welfare work in the public sphere, as nurses, teachers, social workers, etc. In 1997 the number of women in the UK workforce overtook the number of men for the first time. Of course, if women are engaged in the paid labour market it is bound to impact upon their availability to engage in unpaid welfare tasks within the family. This may ultimately lead to a reduction in "feminized" tasks within the family, though as Parker points out, women do combine the roles of carer, worker and mother, though the pressures involved in this are considerable (Parker 1990). There is no adequate framework of benefits and services to enable men and women to make rational choices about the balance between work and home responsibilities. Piachaud's study demonstrated at an early stage that families have only been enabled to enjoy a fair share of living standards because many wives go out to work (Piachaud 1982). The care of frail elderly people also provides an important example of the need to better integrate work and family life. There is little consideration of the role of workers as providers of care for their elderly relatives or elderly spouses. The children of the very elderly tend to be in their late fifties or early sixties when they take on a full caring role. Early retirement policies have meant that some of this group of potential carers are freed from paid work. Yet overall, the trend towards increasing numbers of very old people, together with the trend towards increasing female employment, makes this a key issue for the future resourcing of social policy.

Changing family patterns also affect the dependent population in that in previous generations there would have been three or four children to share the care of elderly parents, in future there will only be one or two. The increasing trends in divorce (1 in 4 marriages currently end in divorce) and remarriage may result in the blurring of family ties; thus the responsibility to care for elderly relatives may not be as clear cut or easy to meet. The nature of work has changed and family members may have to move away from the "extended family" locality to find employment. As families become more dispersed the "crisis support" and welfare role they can play may diminish. The increase in single-parent families may reduce the amount of time spent caring for elderly relatives, especially as income is likely to be low for these families.

In short, the family provides a very important welfare resource, but the nature of "the family" is changing and the amount of welfare it can be expected to provide certainly has its bounds, which are likely to contract rather than expand in the future. Cultural theorists argue that, because of increasing individualization, intimate relationships are changing away from the institution of marriage, with its structures of age and gender and towards the individually chosen relationship which can be broken when it ceases to satisfy (Giddens 1992).

The Supply of Professional Carers: the Example of Nursing

In the mid-1980s there was concern about the implications of demography upon the supply of nurses and the Institute of Manpower Studies was commissioned to examine the problem. Its report amassed clear evidence of what began to be called nursing's "demographic time bomb" (UKCC 1986). The contributing factor to this time bomb was seen to be not only demographic pressures but also the nature of nursing's manpower system.

> It would appear that in order to staff hospital wards, nursing has come to depend upon a high level of recruitment of learners to implement care and a low retention of qualified staff whose job it is to supervise rather than to give care. (Proctor 1986)

Given the wastage rates of trained staff, due to high work pressures, relatively low remuneration and status, nursing relied heavily upon recruiting 18-year-old school leavers. The pool of 18-year-olds, however, was rapidly diminishing as birth rates between 1964 and 1976 fell by 35 per cent. This is producing cohorts of 18-year-olds in the 1990s nowhere near the figure of the late 1960s. A 1985 report by the Centre for Health Economics in York pointed out that by the year 1993 the nursing profession would "have to recruit nearly a third of all school leavers in order to maintain intakes at the present level" (Bosanquet and Gerard 1985). This at a time when demand for healthcare, and consequently nurses and other professional carers, was set to increase because of the numbers of the very elderly in the population.

It was partly as a response to these demographic pressures that the United Kingdom Central Council for Nursing and Midwifery (UKCC) brought about the changes contained in Project 2000. This recognized that more weight would have to be put on trained staff as the "stock" became more important than the "flow" and student nurses became supernumerary.

However, the nursing "time bomb" failed to explode. This was because of the impact of an economic recession. Nursing is not "demand-led" and financial constraints led to a sharp reduction in the growth of nursing posts. Similarly the economic situation had an impact upon nurse retention rates:

> Nurses are increasing the hours they work and returning to the labour market in order to help sustain family incomes at a time of high mortgage rates and economic uncertainty. They are also moving jobs less frequently because there are fewer NHS posts to apply for. (Buchan 1992)

In the mid-1980s it was expected that the mid-1990s would see increased nursing demand and fewer nurses available. The change, from what was expected, in the number of posts available and the high retention rates had "thrown out" the data upon which training forecasts had been made. Consequently, by 1993/4 more staff had been trained than there were posts available and some newly qualified staff found themselves without jobs in the NHS. At the time of writing there is yet another "crisis" in nursing manpower. The economic situation has improved and retention rates amongst experienced staff have fallen back to, and in some cases below, the rates of the mid-1980s, resulting in a nursing shortage. The government has recently responded to this by reviewing and, for some grades, increasing salaries beyond the level of inflation.

The value of this example lies in the way it highlights the process by which the anticipated impact of demographic trends can be influenced by economic factors. Disney (1997) points out that the increased taxation derived from a modest growth rate in GDP of 2.5 per cent per annum over the next 25 years should enable most European countries to afford to finance the demand pressures generated by increased numbers of the elderly. However, such a growth rate would also impact upon the professional workforce, and services, as staff would have to be paid comparable salary increases if they were not to migrate to alternative better-paid employment elsewhere in the job market. Similarly, there would be fewer people, particularly women, available at home to care for dependent people in the community.

The Implications of Environmental Resources for Future Social Policy

However, those concerned about the environmental sustainability of economies have questioned the assumptions made by many policy analysts over the possibilities of funding increased levels of welfare out of increased levels of GDP.

It could be argued that social policies emerged as a result of the social problems created by the process of industrialization. Judged over time, industrialization managed to change society from one where life was relatively short and poverty was rife to an age of plenty—at least in the northern hemisphere. However, there were significant environmental costs:

> In order to achieve the levels of economic growth witnessed over the last

250 years, the environment has been pillaged: millions of hectares of forests have been removed, the seas and rivers have been used as dumps for chemicals, waste and other pollutants, and this in turn has meant that the habitats of marine life, birds, and most mammals other than man have been seriously damaged. The continuing world population growth, consequent upon the vast expansion in material wealth, has in turn produced yet greater pressures on the natural environment, leading to increasing demand for food and living space . . . during the last half-century the damage to the natural environment . . . has accelerated. (Cahill 1998)

It is consequently possible that, in the future, thinking about social policies may increasingly be informed by thinking upon sustainability. Indeed, government policy has been committed to sustainable development since 1992. The World Commission on the Environment in 1987 defined sustainable development as "development which meets the needs of the present without compromising the ability of future generations to meet their own needs". This is popular with governments as it accepts the importance of economic growth whilst acknowledging the aspirations of conservation. However, most "Greens" would argue that there are ecological limits to economic growth and that current levels of growth are unsustainable. The argument here is that the world economy and human society is dependent upon ecological systems. These systems are closed, and finite, and delicately balanced. It is therefore impossible for human economy and society to exceed the finite boundaries laid down by nature. This ecological critique, if it holds true, will have profound implications for social policy, as contemporary welfare states are dependent upon economic growth to provide the financial resources with which to deliver welfare goods and services. The welfare state as we know it is threatened if economic growth is limited. The Greens consequently argue that an alternative model will be required for the provision of welfare. Barry outlines this model as follows (1998: 220–1):

One of the central tenets of the "steady-state economy" is that the economy is geared towards optimising as opposed to maximising production and consumption, a central part of which requires the shifting of focus of social policy from welfare provision to being concerned with individual and collective well-being and quality of life. This transformation of social policy involves replacing welfare indicators, for example quantitative measures such as the standard of living, with qualitative indicators of well-being, a central aspect of which are non-material needs . . . ecological considerations would have to be integrated as a core factor in social policy planning and strategy.

Green social policy is focused upon decentralization of resources, a local orientation of services and that service should be located at the lowest possible level. It is also based upon the concept of the abolition of waged work and notions of self-provisioning. There are a diverse number of proposals and views within the Green movement. However, most would support policies whereby waged work would be replaced by a basic income scheme. This would be accompanied by a shift in the focus of taxation away from taxation on labour and on to use of environmental resources. It would also involve the introduction of a universal basic income to all citizens, regardless of whether or not they worked in the formal economy. There are benefits claimed for such a move—the end of means-testing, recognition of "unwaged work" in the home. Fundamentally:

> the implementation of a Citizens Income Scheme combined with an informal economy would free members of a community to help each other and to organise the provision of many services currently supplied by the state. (British Green Party 1997: 300)

Thus the Green welfare agenda separates the twin conventional priorities of full employment and rising living standards by redefining both the nature and value of work and by adopting wider quality of life measures (including quality of environment) in the place of economic living standards.

Although there are various forms of Green health policies they have some common threads and it may be useful to examine these in order to explore some of the issues. Wherever possible, all forms of medical assistance would take place at the community level. At the same time there is an emphasis upon the responsibilities which individuals have to take care of their own health with an emphasis upon preventative medicine (Irvine and Ponton 1998). There is an emphasis upon alternative and complementary medicine that, in part, reflects the desire to "empower" citizens to engage more directly in their own healthcare. This also reflects a restructuring of the relationship between healthcare professionals and citizens. Kenny and Little (1995) argue that this would imply that doctors would take on the role of "enablers" making individuals as self-reliant as possible in matters of health.

However, as Barry (1998: 230) points out, Green policy sees the ultimate abolition of waged work as an essential prerequisite to a healthy society:

> the link between health improvement and changes in the economic organisation of production, is . . . part of an argument for a basic income scheme and "self provisioning".

This has resonance with much of the literature that examines inequalities in health. Here the view is taken that social and environmental variables are key factors in determining health. For example, the link between childhood asthma and pollution such as traffic fumes is becoming better understood (Jacobs 1996), and Green policies would be concerned with improving the quality of the environment in order to improve individual and collective health.

In a sense, little of this thinking is different from mainstream social policy ideas on community development and it has been argued that Green perspectives offer little new to many areas of social policy. Cahill agrees, but argues that the important point is that new commitments to sustainable development and environmental taxation are moving the debate to examine the "how" rather than the "why" of sustainability (Cahill 1999: 482). The focus of government is also moving towards examination of the wider quality of life rather than just standard of living (cf. DH 1998). Even so, the Green agenda will still have to address the same policy agenda as we have now—housing, poverty, care of the disabled, etc. The difference will be a primary emphasis upon sustainable development first and social policy second.

Implications for the Future

In the late 1970s and early 1980s a number of writers were arguing that the welfare state was in crisis as low economic growth coupled with high levels of unemployment shook the then accepted view that growth in publicly financed services was both inevitable and desirable. Major changes in the way welfare was financed were deemed necessary (Gough 1979; Mishra 1983; Offe 1984). Both the political left and right believed that a mixed economy with a large publicly provided element of provision was incompatible with capitalist infrastructure. Either a financial crisis would result from the funding of welfare from taxation or a legitimacy crisis would result from attempts to dismantle it (Offe 1984).

The first of the current crises in resourcing welfare considered here is concerned with the problems of a high welfare demand brought about through demographics and the problems of meeting that demand from a comparatively smaller tax base. This would seem to echo some of the concerns voiced in the late 1970s and early 1980s, yet those predictions were not borne out by subsequent experience. Indeed, some commentators argue that too pessimistic a view is taken of the "dependent" population and that the whole debate takes place in the language of crisis and impending doom (Shaw and Shaw 1993). Two broad themes are apparent in this argument: first, that a larger proportion of the elderly population is healthier than most people imagine, and second, that much progress has been achieved in service provision for the elderly (though they admit that much remains to be done). They argue that resources should be diverted to those in greatest need within the elderly population but that negative stereotyping should not obscure the fact that large numbers of elderly people are fit and content with their lives.

Moreover, Walker (1991) argues that the concept of the "dependency" of elderly people has been socially constructed. He argues that some social policies, particularly retirement policy, have reduced the economic and social status of elderly people which in itself may have the "knock-on" effect of increasing their mental and physical dependence. Walker goes on to argue that the key to the dependent relationship between elderly people and the state is the labour market and meaningful work. Here there is a case for flexible retirement policies to enable elderly people to work longer (although he recognizes that this may be unlikely in times of high unemployment). Such a change in the social status of elderly people would be accompanied by increased incomes, better and more appropriate housing and by improved social services, as people were able to "shop around" as true consumers for the support they required.

The second "future crisis" concerns the sustainability of the levels of growth required to sustain contemporary models of welfare states. This seems a more intractable issue. Much of the Western world has seen the rise of individualism over the last 10–15 years. Accepting Green policy solutions would essentially mean restraining one's own consumption for the benefit of others. This means behavioural change would be required and this is likely to be politically unpopular. Indeed Field argued that new welfare measures should work with rather than against the grain of human nature (Field 1995). Field argues that self-interest is a far more powerful motivating force than selflessness. As such, he argues, the task for social policy is to ensure the pursuit of self-interest in ways in which do not undermine, and where possible enhance the common good. Smoking in public is an oft-quoted example. Smoking was seen as a matter for the individual until the links of passive smoking and cancer became more widely understood. Now smoking is generally seen as an anti-social habit that should not be undertaken in public because it impacts upon the common good. This links to communitarianism, which is perhaps one way forward as it stresses that communities need to be supported in enforcing their majority view on what constitutes acceptable behaviour (Etzioni 1997).

This emphasizes that the ultimate resource for social policy is people's willingness to support taxation and spending on welfare as well as volunteer their own time. Glennerster reports that:

> The number of British people saying that they wanted government to reduce taxes and spend less was never great—9 per cent in 1983, but it had fallen to only 3 per cent in 1990 and risen only slightly to 4 per cent in 1994. By contrast the number who said that they wanted to increase taxes and spend more rose in the same period from 32 per cent to 58 per cent. Health was the top priority, but with more people wanting to spend more on pensions and education as the decade passed. (1997: 297)

The welfare state has remained popular over the last 50 years and no doubt will continue to remain popular well into the future. Indeed, it could be argued that different European countries raise and spend different percentages of their GDP on welfare because there are different levels of expectation surrounding the role of the state, despite the pressures from globalization. However, as Glennerster and Hills (1998) argue, the paradox is that while welfare services are well supported by the public, policy makers (and not only those in the UK) seem to be continually seeking ways to reduce or restrict state provision. This has allowed the private market to move into areas that were traditionally the realm of the welfare state such as pensions, health and education. Anecdotal evidence, from my time as a Pensions Administrator, suggests that many of the very elderly see this as a disappointing watering down of the principles they fought for in the 1940s. However, the aspirations of one generation are not necessarily those of the next and circumstances change.

A fundamental concern is that unless public services keep pace with rising expectations and standards the middle class will vote with their feet and

33

move into alternative provision in the private sector. This is a strong argument for strengthened resourcing of health and education services (most used by the middle class) in particular. The withdrawal of middle-class support for any welfare service may well result in, at best, a two-tier system and at worst residual welfare provision that could only exacerbate societal inequalities. This would perhaps be the least promising situation for social policy to face in the next millennium.

References

Barry, J. (1998), Social policy and social movements: ecology and social policy. In N. Ellison and C. Pearson (eds), *Developments in British Social Policy*, London: Macmillan.

Bosanquet, N., and Gerard, K. (1985), *Nursing Manpower: Recent trends and policy options*, Discussion Paper 9, Centre for Health Economics, University of York.

British Green Party (1997), *A Manifesto*, London.

Buchan, J. (1992), The numbers game, *Nursing Times*, 88, 39: 19.

Cahill, M. (1998), Consumerism and the future of social policy. In N. Ellison and C. Pearson (eds), *Developments in British Social Policy*, London: Macmillan.

Cahill, M. (1999), The environment and Green social policy. In J. Baldock, N. Manning, S. Miller and S. A. Vickerstaff (eds), *Social Policy*, Oxford: Oxford University Press.

Department of Health (1998), *Our Healthier Nation*, London: HMSO.

Disney, R. (1997), *Can We Afford to Grow Older?* Cambridge MA: MIT Press.

Ellison, N., and Pierson, C. (1998a), *Developments in British Social Policy*, Basingstoke: Macmillan.

Ellison, N., and Pierson, C. (1998b), Contemporary challenges to welfare state development. In *Political Studies*, XLVI: 777–94.

Etzioni, A. (1997), *The New Golden Rule: Community and Morality in a Democratic Society*, London: Profile Books.

European Union (EU) (1996), *Social Protection in Europe: 1995*, Luxembourg: EU.

Field, F. (1995), *Making Welfare Work*, London: Institute of Community Studies.

Fukuyama, F. (1989), The end of history, *The National Interest*, 16: 3–8.

Giddens, A. (1992), *The Transformation of Intimacy*, Cambridge: Polity Press.

Glendinning, C., and Millar, J. (1992), *Women and Poverty in Britain—the 1990s*, Hemel Hempstead: Harvester Wheatsheaf.

Glennerster, H. (1997), *Paying For Welfare* (3rd edn), London: Harvester Wheatsheaf.

Glennerster, H., and Hills, J. (1998), *The State of Welfare: The Economics of Social Policy*, Oxford: Oxford University Press.

Gough, I. (1979), *The Political Economy of the Welfare State*, London: Macmillan.

Irvine, S., and Ponton, A. (1998), *Not 1986, A Green Manifesto: Policies for a Green Future*, London: Optima.

Jacobs, M. (1996), *The Politics of the Real World: Meeting the New Century*, London: Pluto Press.

Kenny, M., and Little, A. (1995), Gorz. In V. George and R. Page (eds), *Modern Thinkers on Welfare*, London: Prentice Hall.

Light, D. (1997), Embedded inefficiencies in health care, *The Lancet*, 338: 102–4.

Mishra, R. (1983), *The Welfare State in Crisis*, Brighton: Harvester Press.

Offe, C. (1984), *Contradictions of the Welfare State*, London: Hutchinson.

Parker, G. (1990), *With Due Care and Attention*, London: Family Policy Studies Centre.

Piachaud, D. (1982), *Family Incomes Since the War*, London: Study Commission on the Family.

Proctor, S. (1986), *The Effects on Patient Care of Reliance on Nurse Learners for the Provision of Hospital Services and its Implications for Manpower Planning*, London: South Bank Polytechnic.

Shaw, I., and Shaw, G. (1993), Demography, nursing and community care: a review of the evidence, *Journal of Advanced Nursing*, 18: 1212–18.

Taylor-Gooby, P. (1999), The future of social policy. In J. Baldock, N. Manning, S. Miller and S. A. Vickerstaff (eds), *Social Policy*, Oxford: Oxford University Press.

UKCC (1986), *Project 2000, A Report to the Council*, London: UKCC.

Vickerstaff, S. A. (1999), Work, employment and the production of welfare. In J. Baldock, N. Manning, S. Miller and S. A. Vickerstaff (eds), *Social Policy*, Oxford: Oxford University Press.

Walker, A. (1991), The social construction of dependency in old age. In M. Loney, R. Bocock, J. Clarke, A. Cochrane, P. Graham and M. Wilson (eds), *The State or the Market*, London: Sage: 41–57.

Wicks, M. (1991), Family matters and public policy. In M. Loney, R. Bocock, J. Clarke, A. Cochrane, P. Graham and M. Wilson (eds), *The State or the Market*, London: Sage: 115–29.

3

Social Politics and Policy in an Era of Globalization: Critical Reflections

Nicola Yeates

1. Introduction

This chapter critically examines the debate on the relationship between "globalization", social politics and social policy. Globalization, by some accounts, represents a paradigmatic shift in the dynamics of welfare state development. Global capital and international institutions possess an unprecedented amount of political power and are instrumental in eroding national policy autonomy and shaping, even determining, the content of national social policies. The prospects for welfare states and for social and economic justice are said to be bleak, and a restricted range of strategically possible policy options, the retrenchment, residualization and marketization of welfare states and the lowering of social standards are forecast.

In this discussion, I argue that the emerging debate on globalization and welfare states shares many of the flaws that can be found in globalization theory, notably with respect to the exaggeration of the strength and degree of unity of capital interests, the underestimation of the powers of the state and of both countervailing changes and oppositional political forces to globalization more generally (section 2). I suggest that the enduring power of "local" factors to impact on and mediate globalization suggests that national institutional, cultural and political differences are likely to prevail rather than be eliminated under the weight of global, "external" forces necessitating a particular course of action (section 3).

The discussion then moves on to propose an alternative way of approaching the relationship between globalization and social policy. I argue that a global governance perspective better captures the implications of globalization for social policy because, first, it permits recognition of the multiple levels and spheres (local, national, transnational, supranational and global) and the range of actors (state and non-state) in the social policy process, and second, it captures the dialectical relationship between global and local political forces in shaping globalization as a project and as a process (section 4). This global governance framework is applied to illustrate the relationship between social politics, social policy and globalization, and I show that a number of social dialogues and political strategies, of quite different types, are taking place with global capital (section 5). Overall, the chapter emphasizes a nuanced account of the dynamics of the relationship between globalization and social policy which recognizes the role of ideology and politics, the dialectical relationship between global and local, and the enduring resilience of local political forces.

2. Globalization: Global Capital Against National States?

Globalization is a highly contested term whose frequent usage has obscured a lack of consensus with regard to what it entails, explanations of how it operates and the direction(s) in which it is heading (Gordon 1987; Mittelman 1996; Amin 1997). It is often used inconsistently, at times to describe trends, at other times to explain them. It also contains normative overtones, being at once "a set of beliefs about how the world is and how it should be developing" (Wilding 1997: 411). In fact, it could be argued that even to ask whether "globalization" corresponds with a social reality at all, let alone analyse its implications for social policy, is possibly to participate in sustaining a myth. As Wilding has argued, "it may . . . not matter very much whether anything is actually happening or not, so long as key people believe it is happening or can convince other people that it is happening" (1997: 411). Despite these reservations, it is important to engage with "globalization" in order to comprehend and challenge the way it has been ideologically invoked to shape the political parameters of what is both socially and economically possible and desirable.

Broadly, globalization signifies qualitative changes in economic and political structures, trends and processes on a transnational and international scale. Economic globalization refers to changes in·capital flows, production systems, markets and trade in goods and services. Commonly used indicators of these changes are trends in international trade (imports and exports), foreign direct investment (FDI), international finance, and corporate alliances and networks. While the significance of these trends is disputable (Hirst and Thompson 1996), it is clear that with the exception of Cuba and North Korea, all economies are now a variety of market economy. Related to the "victory" of the market economy globally is the growth and spread of Western cultural forms, values and products that accompany it and which are spread by it. The global extension of Western culture results in some form of global cultural uniformity through the removal of indigenous ways of life and their replacement by Western products and Western methods of production. This is most obviously manifested in the spread of Western architecture, packaging, clothing (jeans), beverages (Coke), music and leisure, and Western consumerist values of individual acquisition, consumption and competition.

Political globalization refers to the changing global context of political awareness, political processes and political activity (Holton 1998: 109). Bretherton defines it as "a growing tendency for issues to be perceived as global in scope, and hence requiring global solutions; and to the development of international organizations and global institutions which attempt to address such issues" (1996: 8). Globalism refers to the growing awareness that social, economic and environmental issues are transnational and global in their nature and that they therefore require concerted action by states at the "collective" level of supranational and international institutions, organizations and agencies. Political globalization is also evident in the transnational and international forms of organization and mobilization by a range of non-governmental actors, such as charities, voluntary organizations, trades unions, professional associations and trade associations.

At the heart of what may be termed "globalization studies" lies the problematic nature, status and powers of the national state in the contemporary world political and economic order. A number of related questions stand out. One set of questions has focused on whether, and the extent to which, the balance of power between states and capital has shifted to the benefit of capital—and global capital in particular. Another set has focused on how significant the national state is as a sphere of social activity and how effective governments can be in economic management. States are locked into an unprecedented scale and depth of both interdependence and competitiveness, but their capacity to effectively manage both the global, "borderless" economy and their own "national" economies is said to be diminished. A third set of questions has focused on whether the state is being hollowed out, is withering away, or is "in retreat". Few predict the actual demise of the state, and the debate has focused more on the retreat of the state *relative* to other forms of authority in the global political economy and the extent that this will cause it to undergo transformation and adaptation.

One's position on the issue of the consequences of globalization for the state and for the welfare state is likely to hinge on the acceptance of a qualitative shift from the "old" international order based on inter-national relations primarily between nation states, to a "new", globalized order characterized by "global relations between organized capitals"under which relations between national states are subsumed (Teeple 1995). At its crudest, globalization theory views the world economy as dominated by uncontrollable global economic forces where the principal actors are transnational corporations which owe no allegiance to any state and (re)locate wherever market advantage exists (i.e. where profits can be maximized). Thus, Robinson argues that "transnational capital [is] being liberated from any constraint on its global activity"(1996: 13–14), while Meiksins-Wood argues that globalization is "another step in the geographical extension of economic rationality and its emancipation from political jurisdiction" (1997: 553). Closely associated with the supposed "uncontrollable" powers of transnational corporations is the notion that globalization represents a new stage in the development of capitalism:

The history of capitalism has ceased to be defined by and limited to national boundaries. It would be wrong to draw the conclusion that the world has entered a post-capitalist era. The ownership of capital still matters and it still remains the dominant factor of economic and socio-political power in the world. The great change that is occurring is not between a capitalist and post-capitalist society, nor between a "good" capitalism (the social market economy) and a "bad capitalism" (the jungle, or "casino" market economy). Rather, it is between a weakening of all aspects of a society founded on national capitalism and the growing power and dynamic of global capitalism. (Petrella 1996: 68)

Overall, "strong" globalization theories stress the primacy of global forces over national or "local" ones, and the primacy of economic forces over political ones. National states are deemed to have become instruments of global capital: international trade and investment bear a disproportionate amount of influence over the direction and content of national policy, so much so that governments are as sensitive or "accountable" to the requirements of international capital as to their electorates. It is important to note that those who advance claims of "strong" globalization come from both the right and left, politically; the former celebrate what the latter condemn.

A number of welcome counter-arguments have been made against "strong" globalization theory which cast doubt on predictions about the diminished capacities of the state as a "logical", inevitable outcome of the globalization process. "Strong" globalization theory is deemed to be wildly overstated, speculative and ahistorical, which is problematic in terms of its validity, accuracy and the degree of generalization from short-term, cyclical or local changes involved. A principal criticism has focused on the way in which "globalization" is depicted as something "new" and uncontrollable. Gray argues that "much current debate confuses globalization, an historical process that has been underway for centuries, with the ephemeral political project of a worldwide free market" (1998: 215). Indeed, much of the discussion on the contemporary world economy has "emphasized the complete 'globalization' of economic relations, so much so that there is sometimes an unquestioning certainty about the existence of a truly global economy" (Axford 1995: 94). Hirst and Thompson (1996) show that current levels of trade and investment are actually little higher than at the beginning of the twentieth century, that much of what is passed off as "globalization" amounts to no more than the intensification of existing exchanges between distinct national entities, and that capital flows have firmly remained within the Triad of Western Europe, North America and East Asia.

A further failing of "strong" globalization theory is its assumption of a predetermined economic "logic". This renders it vulnerable to accusations of being a totalizing theory and a crude form of economic determinism, particularly the representation of globalization as a homogeneous and unitary process (Hirst and Thompson 1996; Patel and Pavitt 1991; Green 1997). "Strong" globalization portrays capital as a unified force, whereas capital is as fragmented and fractured as the forces it faces globally. For example, foreign direct investment in a productive plant in a peripheral country has very different interests than speculative capital that flows into real estate and currency speculation. Domestic and global capital also have different interests; domestic capital has often been at the forefront of arguments for greater, not less, protectionism.

Furthermore, the economic determinism of strong globalization underestimates the continued importance of politics in the globalization process. The depiction of the huge resources of capital and its ability to leave the "bargaining table" and set up elsewhere has been exaggerated. Most "global" corporations are still decidedly national in their location and make-up (Ruigrok and Van Tulder 1995; De Angelis 1997). States continue to have strong regulatory powers over capital (Pitelis 1991; Pooley 1991). As Gordon argues, "it is not at all clear that they [multinationals] have already achieved new global structures of coordination and control which will *necessarily* enhance their power" (1987: 25), because the relationship between multinationals and governments is "both cooperative and competing, both supportive and conflictual. They operate in a fully dialectical relationship . . . neither the one nor the other partner is clearly or completely able to dominate" (1987: 61; Gray 1998). Capital is dependent on states to perform a range of functions that secure the conditions in which it can operate: the enforcement of property rights and the provision of infrastructure, education, training and the maintenance of social stability. Anyone who is in doubt of the powers of states need only look to their role in the downfall of the Multilateral Agreement on Investment (MAI). The MAI, if successful, would have significantly strengthened the powers of capital over states by allowing "investment rights" even where it was against national or broader social interests (Sanger 1998).

A related point about the importance of the state in shaping globalization, rather than merely "receiving" it, is the idea that much of the literature on globalization has focused on unifying economic and technological processes as evidence of greater global interdependence. In so doing, it has neglected the more fragmented political and social spheres which point to more moderate claims about the nature of "globalization" as well as offering importance evidence of resistance to it. Although recent economic trends may be correctly identified, it is not clear how these relate to long-term structural changes, or how they are moderated by counterchanges or opposing forces. On this point, Green argues that "the dialectic of history is missing . . . globalization theory has a strong tendency towards economism, reading the political off unproblematically from what it takes to be inevitable economic trends" (1997: 157). The neglect of these countervailing forces and counterchanges obscures decisive "local" factors and fragmentation that are associated with globalization:

> the conventional notion of globalization as an advancing force bulldozing the world around it is clearly at odds with the multiplicity of forms encountered or engendered in diverse contexts. Confusion occurs when one overlooks the way that centralizing elements of globalization fuse with distinctive local and regional conditions. (Mittelman 1996: 232)

Global economic forces, then, should not automatically be elevated above, or assumed to steamroll over, "local" factors and forces which are internal to states and which can restrict *both* the state's *and* capital's margin of operation. These "local" forces include the nature and strength of ideologies, social movements and traditions within countries which may resist or oppose "investment" by global capital and the implementation of the policies of international institutions. Neither have been unopposed, and inhabitants of affected countries have responded with civil and political unrest, with the result that "the new uprisings of the world's poor have altered the international political economy" (Walton 1987: 384).

Overall, globalization is not hegemonic or uncontested, nor does it steamroll over all areas of social life or trample over states as "strong" versions have portrayed. International economic processes are refracted through national institutions and mediated by local conditions. States and governments are far from being "victims" of globalization (even if they like to portray themselves as such), and although many have more than enthusiastically embraced the integration of their economies into the international economy they still possess substantial regulatory powers, both individually and collectively, over global capital. Whether they choose to exercise these or not is a different matter.

3. The Impact of Globalization on the Welfare State

The globalization literature has had relatively little to say about welfare states and social policy, while the social policy community has arrived relatively late to globalization studies (with the early exception of Navarro 1982). The emerging debate on globalization and social policy has been predominantly framed in terms of the *impact* of globalization on welfare states (Teeple 1995; Mishra 1996, 1999a, 1999b; Rhodes 1996; Perraton *et al.* 1997; Wilding 1997; Garrett 1998; Pierson 1998; Stryker 1998). This approach has emphasized the constraints that economic globalization places on states, public policy and welfare states. Although it is generally accepted that capitalism has always been a global system, that there was always the risk of capital flight, and that states' policies have historically been bound by parameters acceptable to international monetary institutions, there is none the less an assumption that state capacity and policy autonomy has been eroded by the "external" forces of the contemporary global economy.

International economic forces are said to have eroded the "domestic" economic (and political) basis and conditions that have historically underpinned the welfare state. The relocation of corporations from "high-cost" to "low-cost" countries impacts on the employment structure in the exited country, leaving behind unemployment and a fiscal deficit, while the transnational nature of economic activity makes its control and taxation much more difficult (Perraton *et al.* 1997). Stryker (1998) identifies a number of ways in which the structure and operation of the global economy may shape national social policy. First, financial globalization exacerbates the structural dependence of the state on all forms of capital (domestic and foreign). Second, globalized financial and productive capital increase the perceived risk, or the credibility of the threat, of capital flight. Third, financial integration reduces the possibilities for national states to pursue expansionary economic policies to cushion unemployment and encourages them to pursue fiscal austerity. Fourth, the global economy has severed the link between domestic economic growth and full employment in First World countries—the concerns for private profit do not sit easily alongside national economic and employment health (witness record profits alongside redundancies). The fifth factor that Stryker identifies is an ideological one, and is possibly the most important of all—the transnational diffusion of neo-liberalism. This stresses the "complete impotence or perversity of national level economic and social policy making", and encourages governments to believe they cannot change the structure, operation or outcomes of the global economy and must therefore conform with the requirements of international competitiveness (reduce or remove barriers to trade, reduce the size and cost of the state, taxation and welfare) (Stryker 1998: 8–9).

Contemporary globalization, it is argued, alters the internal dynamics of welfare state development and heralds the decline of social democratic reformist politics and projects upon which the welfare state was built (Teeple 1995; Rhodes 1996). The balance of "external", global influences to "internal", national ones (e.g. demography, labour markets, the balance of political forces) is held to have altered in favour of the former. As Ash Amin argues, "state policy *is* becoming more and more driven by external forces" (1996: 129, original italics). The range of "structurally viable" policy options has not only been narrowed by economic forces but state policy will be primarily oriented to supporting market forces and promoting economic competitiveness. Governments will increasingly stay clear of radical pro-grammes of redistribution, renationalization or other forms of intervention that capital does not "approve" of. The outcome will be "the retrenchment of national state intervention in spheres of social reproduction" (Teeple 1995: 5). Those that stray too far from these parameters will be punished electorally and economically due to loss of investment and employment and will leave themselves vulnerable to lower credit ratings, higher interest rates on borrowing, as well as currency speculation by international financial markets (Andrews 1994; Goodman and Pauly 1993; Stewart 1984).

The force of these "external" economic forces is such that it is said to impose a single model of development on countries: national welfare states will converge—they will all be "driven in the same direction by the imperatives of international competition" (Taylor-Gooby 1997; Wilding 1997; Mishra 1996). Geyer (1998: 77) summarizes the convergence thesis well:

> [D]espite varying national contexts and the policies of differing political parties, the welfare states of the advanced industrial countries should become increasingly similar as the forces of globalization squeeze them into a market-oriented welfare-state model. In essence it does not matter whether the national institutional contexts are conservative or social democratic, if the welfare state is conservative, liberal or social demo-cratic; or if a leftist or rightist party is in power, the constraints have become so extreme that only market-conforming welfare-state struc-tures will be allowed.

A major problem with these predictions about the power of the global economic forces, in particular global capital, to force a particular course of action is that they share many of the assumptions of "strong" globalization theories in so far as they regard globalization as an "external", naturalistic phenomenon; assume that capital interests are unified; assign a determinant degree of power to (global) economic forces over the course of (national) political action; and assume that globalization is a force primarily of unification. The criticisms levied against "strong" globalization theories in section 2 suggest that the political and economic resources of global capital to directly determine individual states' public policies have been exaggerated and that globalization is not homogeneous or unitary in process or effect, either within or across states. Indeed, the issue is far more complex than one of simple causality for the reasons I have just described, as well as for the reasons outlined below.

Of prime importance, first of all, is ideology. As Rhodes argues, "the nature of the contemporary welfare state dilemma . . . is difficult to disentangle from ideology" (1996: 307). Ideology is of particular importance here because it has been central to the advancement of globalization as a political project—through the diffusion of neo-liberalism (Stryker 1998). Neo-liberal ideology emphasizes the limited influence and effect that governments can exert over national economic performance or in subverting the "natural" outcomes of global markets, while stressing the costs of certain courses of political action: economic success (and prosperity) or failure (and hardship) in an interdependent and competitive global economy is seen as depending on maintaining a competitive advantage. From here it is but a short step to making explicit links between the extent and nature of state provision and delivery of welfare and national economic competitiveness. Stryker (1998: 11) argues that the impact of globalization on welfare states occurs *primarily* through ideological shifts *which in turn* cause national expenditure reductions, privatization and marketization in some social welfare programmes. However, even here, he asserts that the evidence over the past twenty years of left governments slowing welfare expansion and/or embarking on austerity programmes "does not prove the idea that financial globalization and global diffusion of market-oriented cultural ideals facilitate welfare state retrenchment. But it is consistent with these ideas" (1998: 11). On a similar line, Jordan (1998) also notes the consistency between the "new politics of welfare" of the British and American governments which put the wage-relation at the centre of welfare reform, and globalization which also hinges on the wage-relation. Ultimately, it seems, at best we may be able to demonstrate consistency rather than causality.

Ideology, rather than crude economic determinism, is important, therefore, in any explanation of the impact of globalization on welfare states. Policy-makers' beliefs, values and assumptions about the global economy are shaped by ideology: they may believe that particular interventions will prompt speculation on the national currency, mass capital flight abroad, or a downturn in investment by foreign firms. Moran and Wood (1996) refer to this framing of social policy by ideas and beliefs about national competitiveness in the global economy as "contextual internationalization". The contemporary welfare state "dilemma" can be attributed to the political power of economic ideas, in particular neo-liberal ideas, which have shaped perceptions of global economic "logics" and foreclosed "the parameters of the politically possible" (Hay 1998: 529). Jordan similarly argues that "the idea of a global market is probably even more powerful than global forces themselves; governments believe that they are competing for prizes in budgetary rectitude before a panel of international financial institutions, and this affects their actions" (1998: 9).

The second reason why it is not possible to establish causality is that states have other functions than economic ones and governments have to respond to a wider range of constituencies than just the international business community. These "local" factors are decisive rather than incidental in determining the content of public and social policy and how sweeping any reforms may be. These "local" factors include the political and institutional constellation of national welfare states, historical and cultural traditions, social structures, electoral politics, the partisan nature of government, the presence of strong "veto players", and the internal structure of the state (Esping-Andersen 1996; Rhodes 1996; Hallerberg and Basinger 1998; Garrett 1998). Other "local" factors mediating the way in which globalization is "received" also include the degree of integration of the national economy into the international economy and the particular species of capitalism that has developed nationally.

The emphasis on welfare retrenchment, residualization and marketization as an *inevitable* and *direct* outcome of globalization may also be somewhat misplaced for the reason that the attention to unifying forces of economic change masks counterchanges. Cerny (1997) argues that although states may indeed become oriented towards maintaining economic competitiveness—indeed, he predicts the rise of "competition states"—they may become more, not less, interventionist in certain spheres. They may become more authoritarian in policing the consequences of economic globalization —poverty, marginalization and crime. In fact, far from overriding pressures for the state to reduce its welfare effort, a range of pressures to expand the scope of public policy intervention may be placed on governments to counteract marginalization and promote social integration, equality and justice. Public (social) expenditure may increase as a direct consequence of policies that pursue economic competitiveness (Garrett and Mitchell 1996, cited in Wilding 1997), while social protection programmes may be extended to cushion individuals, households and communities against increased economic risk. It is not evident that the predominant theme, or the only way forward, is marketization, as the recent nationalization of care insurance in Germany has illustrated.

While the issue of whether the "embedded liberalism" of the international political economy imposes limits on redistributive justice (Rhodes 1996; Jordan 1998) is a pertinent one, economic globalization constitutes less of an objective constraint than it is often believed to be, while the convergence thesis is certainly exaggerated. The "constraints" arising from the global economy are to a large extent "imposed" by the political power of ideas about the logics and dynamics of the global economy. These constrain states and governments because they narrow the margins of what is believed to be possible and orientate them to the needs and exigencies of international competitiveness. Within these parameters, though, choices are still possible (Rhodes 1996: 309) and it is important to affirm that these choices have significant consequences for the distribution of resources, the quality, extent, and form of welfare provision, and the social rights of the population.

4. Global Governance and Social Policy

Although arguments that the state has been emasculated by international economic forces should be treated with a good deal of caution, it is equally clear that states operate in a markedly different economic and political environment than they did, say, forty years ago. Social policy making, implementation and provision takes place in a context in which states are no longer the exclusive subject of international politics, the sole mediators of domestic politics, or even the principal representative of their populations. Political globalization and associated institutional and organizational changes in the way that territories, trade and populations are governed means that "politics is becoming more polycentric" and that states are "merely one level in a complex system of overlapping and often competing agencies of governance" (Hirst and Thompson 1996: 183). This framework of "global governance", and the political processes associated with it, has implications for states' sovereignty and policy autonomy.

Gordenker and Weiss define global governance as "efforts to bring more orderly and reliable responses to social and political issues that go beyond capacities of states to address individually" (1996: 17). Global governance is predominantly associated with "the development of international organizations and global institutions which attempt to address such issues" (Bretherton 1996: 8). Governments collaborate with each other through cooperative arrangements in conjunction with, and through, international governmental organizations; they operate within a complex legal and political framework of international agreements, treaties, regulations and accords regulating economic exchange and accumulation between countries (Townsend and Donkor 1996). States have to take account of the international context in which they are embedded: they have to be increasingly "other-regarding", of other states and of the policies and actions of international agencies and transnational corporations which extol the virtues and efficiency of "free" markets (Mittelman 1996: 231).

International economic and trade institutions—notably the International Monetary Fund, the World Bank and GATT/WTO—have exerted a more tangible influence on states and national policies than has global capital. Government policies are legally bound to comply with the principles and regulations of international governmental organizations, international and supranational organizations (World Bank, IMF, UN system, EU, WTO). These institutions possess substantial financial and legal powers to regulate the international economy; they underwrite the conditions and patterns of international economic investment, production and exchange, set the parameters of national macroeconomic policy and, through this, largely determine the terms and conditions of social development (Townsend and Donkor 1996). They may override nation states' juridical sovereignty by, for example, legally obliging legislation of signatory states to conform with international principles. The economic and foreign-trade policies of states signed up to multilateral trade agreements are subject to enforceable WTO rules on "free trade". WTO rules restrict the range of policies that can be pursued nationally, even forbidding certain policies and courses of action if they present a barrier to the "free" trade of foreign capital locally (e.g. subsidies, social and environmental legislation) (Nader and Wallach 1996).

There is, of course, nothing new about international governmental institutions, which have been in existence for over a century and have coexisted with major periods of welfare-state-building in the advanced industrialized countries. What appears to differ now is that one species of capitalism—global "free trade"—is being sponsored by international institutions to compete with other species of capitalism (e.g. socially-regulated capitalism) that have historically developed at national level (Gray 1998). One notable example of this is the conditions attached to the receipt of economic aid from the World Bank and IMF. These include the implementation of economic and social reform ("structural adjustment"), common elements of which are the reduction of public sector debt, expenditure and subsidies, deregulation, and the reduction of public service provision. The policy autonomy of governments in such countries has been undermined by the imposition of a particular model of social and economic development which prohibits them from acting to protect the social cohesion of their societies.

Although global governance is predominantly associated with the institutional framework of national states and international bureaucracies, a far wider range of actors participate in global governance. In its broadest sense, global governance refers to *all* non-state sources of "authority" which have the power to allocate values and influence the distribution of resources: outlaw business organizations (such as drug cartels, the mafia); professional associations; transnational authorities in sports, art, music; transnational social, political and religious movements (Strange 1996). The Commission on Global Governance (1995: 3) also includes as actors in global governance non-governmental organizations, citizens' movements, multinational organizations, the global capital market and even the global mass media. Non-governmental organizations, for example, are increasingly seeking legitimacy, and justification for their rights claims, from the global as well as the national arena. They have helped raise the profile of social issues on international agendas (notably, social development, the environment, equality, poverty and population), and generally shape international responses to global problems. They also have formal channels of influence, working through bodies such as the UN Commission on Human Rights and the Commission on the Status of Women (Holton 1998; Gordenker and Weiss 1996). Whether or not NGOs' participation in global governance can be considered evidence of the existence of a "global civil society", it is certainly evidence of the globalization of political and social action.

The field of population and fertility illustrates these structures and processes of global governance. From the outset—the 1950s—"overpopulation" has been defined as a global issue requiring a global solution. The delivery of population control has involved a combination of both state and private-sector actors at the international, national, and local levels. The major push for this policy has been at the international level, and all the major international institutions have developed population policies: the UN and its various agencies, including WHO, UNICEF and even the ILO; and the World Bank. Also strongly involved in population control discourse has been that oldest of international institutions—the Catholic Church—as well as other, often fundamentalist, international religions and their institutions. At the level of policy implementation, global population control can be characterized as a hierarchy: the donor countries of the North at the apex and the women of the South as its base. Between these is an intermediate layer of international organizations (NGOs, UN agencies, development banks and private foundations), below which are the states of the South. On the national level are the government, the private (commercial) sector, the media (for "social marketing") and national NGOs; at subnational level are the hospitals, clinics and family planning providers and motivators, including local NGOs, that implement the policy (Bandarage 1997; Koivusalo and Ollila 1997).

The European Union is another example of the ways that the changing institutional and political processes affect social policy. The European Union has been characterized as a system of multitiered governance (Pierson and Leibfried 1995). Although its institutional architecture is predominantly intergovernmental, states are only one, if an important, player amongst other non-state authorities, such as the EU administrative, political and legal institutions, business organizations, trades unions and non-governmental organizations. Political action is "now having to be carried out through a web of common institutions, states, regional and local authorities and voluntary associations on the domestic front and simultaneously, in national and/or transnational alliances at the common level" (Meehan 1992: 159). Such alliances may consist of domestic interests, that may be antagonistic at times, against another state, or they may be bound by a "shared interest among civil associations in promoting a common policy against the wishes of their respective governments" (1992: 159; Streeck 1996). The consequences of European political integration are that social policy (agenda-setting, consultation, policy-making, policy implementation and delivery) is no longer confined and controlled within the national sphere. Transnational alliances and formalized channels of influence over the content and direction of supranational social policy have introduced new dynamics into social policy development nationally (Streeck 1995). "Sovereign" welfare states have been transformed into "semi-sovereign" welfare states, or parts of multitiered systems of social policy (Leibfried and Pierson 1995, 1996) through: "positive" social policy initiatives to construct areas of competence for uniform social standards at EU level (e.g. gender equality, health and safety); "negative" social policy reform via the imposition of market compatibility requirements (labour mobility and coordination, freedom of services, regional and sectoral subsidies); and indirect (*de facto*) pressures of integration that force adaptation of national welfare states (social dumping, tax harmonization, stages of EMU) (1996: 187).

5. Global Social Dialogues and the Social Regulation of Globalization

The European Union is one obvious forum where new institutional and political processes have tangibly impacted on social policy. Another forum may be seen in the formation of "global social policy" (Deacon *et al.* 1997). Just as global governance has predominantly been characterized in institutional terms, so is "global social policy":

Global social policy as a practice of supranational actors embodies global social redistribution, global social regulation, and global social provision and/or empowerment, and includes the ways in which supranational organizations shape national social policy. (1997: 195)

Global social policy has emerged as a consequence of two interrelated processes: global politics have become "socialized"—"the major agenda issues at intergovernmental meetings are now in essence social (and environmental) questions" (1997: 3); social policy has become "globalized"—international institutions are essentially preoccupied with issues such as poverty, employment, health and welfare, and with "the best way to regulate capitalism in the interests of social welfare East and West, North and South" (1997: 195). As in the EU where the social policy debate has focused on the choice to be made between Anglo-American-style welfare capitalism and continental Western European-style welfare capitalism, so the global political arena has also become a battleground over which contemporary ideological struggles about the role and the future of welfare states are fought out.

Deacon, Stubbs and Hulse argue that national social policy and social development are increasingly decided by international institutions: "the social policy of a country or locality . . . is increasingly shaped . . . by the implicit and explicit social policies of numerous supranational agencies, ranging from global institutions like the World Bank and the International Monetary Fund, through supranational bodies such as the OECD and the European Commission, to supranational non-government agencies like OXFAM" (1997: 10). However, even here, they acknowledge that much is still contingent on local factors. In the countries of Central and Eastern Europe, for example, international institutions have been instrumental in restructuring post-communist social policy, but the social policy prescriptions of the IMF have been accepted and implemented because they are consistent with the interests of national bureaucratic and political elites. In short, the national sphere is still a decisive site of struggle, and "external" forces—be they capital or international institutions—are dependent on the "ideological integration" of local political elites into the international economy.

Deacon's work on the social dialogue at the global level has been extremely useful in mapping the dominant political and ideological positions of different international institutions in the debate on how globalization should be socially regulated. Readers may refer to the work of Deacon and Hulse (1996), Deacon, Stubbs and Hulse (1997) and Deacon (1999) for a full account of this social dialogue. However, of notable importance in the context of the

Table 1

Global social policy discourse

Orientation	Welfare World	Agency Promulgating
Existing welfare as:		
Burden	Liberalism	IMF, OECD
Social cohesion	Conservative, Corporatist	EU, ILO, WB
Investment	(Southeast Asia)	OECD, WB
Redistributive commitment	Social Democracy	—
Emerging welfare as:		
Safety net	Social Liberalism	WB, EU
Workfare	Social Liberalism	IMF
Citizenship entitlement	Futuristic	ILO, COE
Redistribution	—	—

Source: Deacon and Hulse 1996: 52.
Note: WB: World Bank; EU: European Union; ILO: International Labour Organization; OECD: Organization for Economic Cooperation and Development; IMF: International Monetary Fund; COE: Council of Europe.

present discussion is that their work has showed that the "socialization of global politics" in no way signals the emergence of a unitary view about the role of welfare states or about their future development (see table 1). Competing discourses emerge from within the same institution, while institutional prescriptions vary according to the world-region in which they are embedded. Thus the prescriptions of the EU and ILO reflect their continental European origins, while those of the IMF reflect its US origins (Deacon *et al.* 1997). This very diversity warns us against apocalyptic interpretations of globalization as "the end of politics", or as a unifying, hegemonic force. However, Deacon *et al.*'s research also confirms that the range of welfare alternatives backed by these institutions is confined to variants of social liberalism, and there is a marked absence of any institution arguing a social democratic or redistributive welfare agenda.

The work of Deacon and his colleagues on the social policies of international institutions has been pioneering. Their focus can be explained by the fact that it is at this level that the most obvious attempt is being made to formulate global social policy; but it is also a result of the institutionalist tendency in social policy analysis itself. However, this approach must be supplemented to explain the complexity of levels at which global social policy occurs and operates as well as the dialectical relationship between these levels. The focus on social politics and policy at the level of international institutions draws attention to the more visible actors, but in its emphasis on the forces and initiatives to modify "globalization from above" the forces against "globalization from below" are neglected (Falk 1997). It confines our view only to the social dialogue that takes place at international level and excludes other "social dialogues" taking place at different levels and in various locations outside the boardrooms and bureaux of international institutions. A similar type of "global social dialogue" has been going on between social movements in the shadow congresses that now accompany meetings of the G8, such as the Other Economy summit. Nor is this dialogue purely reactive; the International Encounter against Neo-liberalism, for example, was brought together in response to calls from Zapatistas and social and political activists from a wide variety of countries. Another type of global social dialogue has been facilitated by the development of the internet; this technological factor makes global dialogue easier for highly disparate and isolated groups, many of whom cannot afford international travel.

In fact, a range of strategies and initiatives to regulate globalization can be identified, examples of which are presented in table 2 below. Some of these seek not to oppose globalization but instead seek negotiated reform, working with and through international institutions and/or corporations. The Trades Union Advisory Committee to the OECD has argued for more effective global social governance by strengthening the "social dimension" of globalization (Evans n.d.). Social clauses have been central to these attempts to strengthen the social regulation of global capital. They attempt to link trade agreements with minimum labour standards within the institutions and agreements that control international trade (Shaw 1996; Lee 1997). Shaw points out that a consensus exists amongst most participating parties in this debate that "free trade is to be welcomed and protectionism is undesirable" (1996: 3), but positions on social clauses are locally and politically rooted. While trades unions are generally in favour of social clauses, non-governmental organizations have ranged from qualified acceptance to outright opposition on the issue. Similarly, some governments of the South, as well as of the North, oppose social clauses on the grounds that they are a form of protectionism. Overall, attempts to seek to regulate the global economy by working with international institutions have not so far been phenomenally successful, particularly when compared with the scale, pace and social effects of international trade and investment agreements.

Other strategies which engage in a "social dialogue" with global capital take the form of direct action, often through the market mechanism. Market-based strategies include international campaigns by consumer groups and NGOs to bring about improved standards for groups of workers in particular industries by mobilizing consumers to redirect their spending power away from offending companies' products. Consumer, trade and labour boycotts and the social labelling of products have brought about corporate codes of conduct being adopted in global industries, such as in the baby foods market, pharmaceutical drugs industry and the textiles, garments and shoewear industries (Shaw 1996; Vander Stichele and Pennartz 1996). It is important to emphasize, though, that initiatives in the "market" and "political" spheres are not mutually exclusive forms of action. International institutions may be called on to back up local opposition: a labour union (OCAW) recently lodged a complaint against the German chemical company BASF with the OECD.

Table 2

Strategies and proposals to regulate globalization

Sphere	Social	Economic
Political-institutional (top-down)	Social (labour) clauses; human rights (Council of Europe, UN Declaration of Human Rights)	International Financial Commission (TUAC); Global Tax Authority; Toibin Tax
Market (bottom-up)	Fair (ethical) trade; social labelling; consumer campaigns; trade and labour boycotts.	Corporate codes of conduct; Ethical investment

Note: The Toibin Tax, proposed in 1974, is a tax levied on currency transactions.

Global social politics also includes strategies of outright opposition and disruptive action at the local level, for example against local branches of transnational corporations. Numerous examples of such action can be cited, for example, of various tribal and indigenous groups and NGOs which have taken their concerns to the AGMs of transnational companies such as RTZ (Rio Tinto Zinc), Shell, BP and Monsanto. With genetic engineering, for example, which can be expected to have far-reaching social, economic and environmental effects, the introduction of new technology by capital on a global scale, often aided by permissive state regulation of this technology, has encountered a range of popular opposition strategies. Just as globalization prompts a variety of national responses, so a variety of national opposition strategies have arisen in relation to genetically modified foods. Here, the types of resistance vary geographically: in England, consumer boycotts and activist attacks on test crops have been the principal forms of resistance; in Asia and Europe, opposition has developed on an ideological level, often with a religious basis; in India resistance has taken the form of attacks on companies by mass farmers' organizations.

Global issues are often fought out on a local level, and over what at first appear to be "local" issues. Local counter-struggles are fought by a range of groups and organizations: trades unions, women's groups, environmental groups, tribal and indigenous groups, consumer groups, civil liberties groups and anti-nuclear groups. Many of these struggles can be regarded as resistance to globalization in so far as they "have a cooperative element and a degree of social and political consciousness" (Teeple 1995: 149). In countries across the world, neo-liberal, deregulatory policies have prompted mass and public resistance in the form of demonstrations, strikes and riots. The 1995 strike protest by public sector workers in France in response to proposed cuts to income maintenance policies, specifically pensions, shows how the fate of globalization is often decided locally rather than globally, is mediated by class struggle and is dependent on the national balance of power. Thus, despite the fact that one in every twelve French workers was unemployed and one in every five was in a part-time or temporary job, a major popular mobilization prevented proposed pension reforms (Jefferys 1996; Bonoli 1997).

Demands and movements for local economic autonomy, self-sufficiency and economic nationalism may also be regarded as forms of resistance and opposition to globalization. At the local level, self-help and community groups, cooperative movements have mobilized to fill in the gaps left by the failure of capitalism to provide employment. In both the First and Third Worlds alike new forms of local economic organization and cooperation have emerged amongst the poor (Rowbotham and Mitter 1994; Norberg-Hodge 1996). Local exchange trading systems (LETS) and local currency schemes which strive to relocalize the economy can be regarded as a symbolic and practical "response to the local social and economic consequences of globalization", namely "the economic and political marginalization of people and places marginal or unnecessary to the capitalist development process" (Paccione 1997: 1179–80; Meeker-Lowry 1996).

The globalization process is a dialectical one in which "local" events will impact globally and will inform global political responses. The costs, for example, of the latest financial crisis—in Asia in 1997–8—were experienced both locally and globally (i.e. in the West) and prompted calls for reform to the IMF and World Bank and stricter regulation over international financial markets (although the eventual reforms have shied away from regulation in favour of the provision of emergency funds). In the same way, locally-expressed populist social dialogues have impacted on the more "elitist" social politics and policies of international institutions. The push for a change in World Bank policy to take better account of poverty came from local and national factors. It was forced to take account of the destabilizing effects of its policies by local food riots and the threat of local social unrest and disruption. The World Bank's strategic response to criticisms by international and national non-governmental organizations of the local social effects of structural adjustment programmes has been to include them in the policy process. Consultation with these organizations serves the useful purpose for the World Bank of testing the local social and political foundations before structural adjustment programmes are implemented; involving them directly in the implementation of social development programmes makes use of their grassroots links with "hard to reach" populations and with other local movements (Deacon *et al.* 1997).

6. Conclusions

This chapter has examined how the relationship between globalization and social policy has been approached within the academic literature. I have argued that this literature shares some of the assumptions—and the flaws—of "strong" globalization theory in so far as globalization is conceived of as a top-down, "external", naturalistic and unifying force. Consequently, some of the claims surrounding the process and impact of globalization on states, social policy and welfare states are simplistic and exaggerated. The "constraints" that are placed on social policy development are primarily ideological and thus susceptible to political manipulation. I have also highlighted the decisive role of the state and politics in shaping globalization and in mediating its effect on welfare states.

A global governance perspective offers a more nuanced framework for examining how social policy relates to globalization. Social policy now develops in a pluralistic and multi-levelled institutional framework of global governance which has altered the political dynamics of social policy. Social policy has been (partially) decoupled from the national sphere as a consequence of the greater involvement by supranational and international institutions in the political management of globalization. However, I have emphasized the decisive importance of "local" factors in shaping globalization—politics still matter. It is at this local level that non-geographically located global forces must "touch down" and be expressed. When they attempt to do so, they often meet with a range of mediating, regulatory and oppositional forces. These forces may be as instrumental in shaping the political management of globalization as the formal social policies and discourses of international institutions.

This recognition of the importance of local factors tempers the more apocalyptic accounts of the prospects for welfare states under contemporary globalization and elevates the importance of politics, rather than economics, as the driving force of national social policy reform. Consequently, it allows a re-evaluation of "traditional" factors such as class, ethnicity, race and gender politics in shaping social policy. From this perspective, "globalization" in the sense of international economic forces is just one factor amongst others that influence welfare state development. Ultimately, while it is necessary to recognize the global context of social policy development, global economic forces are contested and mediated by states whose political responses are conditioned by local, internal factors, such as historical and institutional arrangements, cultural and religious values and traditions, political and social forces and the balance of political power.

Acknowledgement

I would like to thank Tomas Mac Sheoin for his helpful comments and suggestions on early drafts of this chapter.

References

Amin, A. (1997), Placing globalization, *Theory, Culture & Society*, 14, 2: 123–37.
Andrews, D. (1994), Capital mobility and state autonomy: toward a structural theory of international monetary relations, *International Studies Quarterly*, 38.
Axford, B. (1995), *The Global System: Economics, Politics and Culture*, Cambridge: Polity Press.
Bandarage, A. (1997), *Women, Population and Global Crisis: A Political-economic analysis*, London: Zed Books.

Bonoli, G. (1997), Pension politics in France: patterns of co-operation and conflict in two recent reforms, *West European Politics*, 20, 4: 111–24.

Bretherton, C. (1996), Introduction: global politics in the 1990s. In C. Bretherton and G. Ponton (eds), *Global Politics: An Introduction*, Oxford: Blackwell.

Cary, W. L. (1974), Federalism and corporate law: reflections upon Delaware, *Yale Law Journal*, 83: 663–705.

Cerny, P. (1997), Paradoxes of the competition state: the dynamics of political globalization, *Government and Opposition*, 32, 2: 251–74.

Commission on Global Governance (1995), *Our Global Neighbourhood*, Oxford: Oxford University Press.

De Angelis, M. (1997), The autonomy of the economy and globalization, *Common Sense*, 21: 41–59.

Deacon, B. (1995), The globalization of social policy and the socialization of global politics. In J. Baldock and M. May (eds), *Social Policy Review* 7, Social Policy Association.

Deacon, B. (1999), *Towards a Socially Responsible Globalization: International Actors and Discourses*, GASPP Occasional Papers, STAKES: Finland.

Deacon, B., and Hulse, M. (1996), *The Globalization of Social Policy*, Leeds: Leeds Metropolitan University.

Deacon, B., with Stubbs, P., and Hulse, M. (1997), *Global Social Policy: International Organizations and the Future of Welfare*, London: Sage.

Esping-Andersen, G. (ed.) (1996), *Welfare States in Transition: National Adaptations in Global Economies*, London: Sage.

Evans, J. (n.d.), *Economic Globalization: the Need for a Social Dimension*, discussion paper, TUAC, Paris.

Falk, R. (1997), Resisting "Globalization-from-above" Through "Globalization-from-Below", *New Political Economy*, 2, 1: 17–24.

Garrett, G. (1998), *Partizan Politics in the Global Economy*, Cambridge: Cambridge University Press.

Geyer, R. (1998), Globalization and the (non-)defence of the welfare state, *West European Politics*, 21, 3: 77–102.

Goodman, J., and Pauly, L. (1993), The obsolescence of capital controls? Economic management in an age of global markets, *World Politics*, 46.

Gordenker, L., and Weiss, T. G. (1996), Pluralizing global governance: analytical approaches and dimensions. In T. G. Weiss and L. Gordenker (eds), *NGOS, the UN, and Global Governance*, London: Lynne Rienner.

Gordon, D. M., (1987), The global economy: new edifice or crumbling foundations, *New Left Review*, 168: 24–64.

Gray, J. (1998), *False Dawn: The Delusions of Global Capitalism* (2nd edn), London: Granta.

Green, A. (1997), *Education, Globalization and the Nation State*, Basingstoke: Macmillan.

Hallerberg, M., and Basinger, S. (1998), Internationalization and changes in taxation policy in OECD countries: the importance of domestic veto players, *Comparative Political Studies*, 31, 3: 321–52.

Hay, C. (1998), Globalization, welfare retrenchment and the "logic of no alternative": why second-best won't do, *Journal of Social Policy*, 24, 4: 525–32.

Hirst, P., and Thompson, G. (1996), *Globalization in Question: the International Economy and the Possibilities of Governance*, Cambridge: Polity Press.

Holton, R. J. (1998), *Globalization and the Nation-State*, Basingstoke: Macmillan.

Jefferys, S. (1996), France 1995: the backward march of labour halted, *Capital and Class*, 59: 7–21.

Jordan, B. (1998), *The New Politics of Welfare*, London: Sage.

lied to the East Asian countries and a Radical regime applied to Australia
New Zealand. With the ongoing discourse on globalization, the welfare
ologizing business is bound, as a tendency, to be applied worldwide, as we
with Gøsta Esping-Andersen's *Welfare States in Transition* of 1996.
his chapter tries to give a kind of state-of-the-art review of the welfare
ologizing business that has caught on within the social sciences since 1990
which seems to be occupying a prominent position within welfare state
arch here at the turn of the millennium.

oticed Beginnings

yone even remotely familiar with social science discussions of welfare
during the 1990s will know that the publication of Gøsta Esping-
rsen's *The Three Worlds of Welfare Capitalism* in 1990 made the tripolar
re regime typology very well known and somewhat contested; but the
e about whether welfare states cluster around distinctly different
e types had started long before 1990 in social policy literature. To the
we consider the welfare state to be a post-World War II phenomenon,
ps the earliest distinction applied was the one developed by Harold
sky when he and Lebaux talked about *residual* versus *institutional* welfare

conceptions of social welfare seem to be dominant in the United
es today: the *residual* and the *institutional*. The first holds that social
are institutions should come into play only when the normal
tures of supply, the family and the market, break down. The
d, in contrast, sees the welfare services as normal, "first line"
ions of modern industrial society . . . In our view, neither ideology
in a vacuum; each is a reflection of the broader cultural and social
itions . . . and with further industrialization the second will prevail.
138, 140)

nsky, residual and institutional denote two ends of a continuum with
lual welfare state as the least developed and the institutional as the
veloped. This way of arguing has been labelled the modernization
d it anticipates a move from residual to institutional welfare state
ng. We can say that the explanatory variable is maturity or degree of
lization, and the most commonly used measure was welfare state
ated by total social expenditure relative to GDP. As we shall see
ese two concepts are still very much alive in the social science
on welfare state regimes, but the modernization thesis has been
by most scholars and only lives in the form of expectations of
ce of particular welfare states, still expressed by some scholars
and Quintin 1992).

re lasting influence is the discussion introduced by the late
professor of public administration at the London School of
, Richard Titmuss. In a keynote address delivered to the Interna-
ference of Social Welfare in the Hague, August 1972, Titmuss

Koivusalo, M., and Ollila, E. (1997), *Making a Healthy World: Agencies, Actors and Policies in International Health*, London: Zed Books.

Lee, E. (1997), Globalization and labour standards: a review of issues, *International Labour Review*, 136, 2: 173–89.

Leibfried, S., and Pierson, P. (1995), Semisovereign welfare states: social policy in a multitiered Europe. In S. Leibfried and P. Pierson (eds), *European Social Policy: Between Fragmentation and Integration*, Washington DC: Brookings Institution.

Leibfried, S., and Pierson, P. (1996), Social Policy. In H. Wallace and W. Wallace (eds), *Policy-Making in the European Union*, Oxford: Oxford University Press.

Meehan, E. (1992), *Citizenship and the European Community*, London: Sage.

Meeker-Lowry, S. (1996), Community money: the potential of local currency. In J. Mander and E. Goldsmith (eds), *The Case Against the Global Economy and For a Turn Toward the Local*, San Francisco: Sierra Club Books.

Meiksins Wood, E. (1997), Modernity, postmodernity or capitalism?, *Review of International Political Economy*, 4, 3: 539–60.

Mishra, R. (1996), The welfare of nations. In R. Boyer and D. Drache (eds), *States Against Markets: the Limits of Globalization*, London: Routledge.

Mishra, R. (1999a), *Globalization and the Welfare State*, Cheltenham: Edward Elgar.

Mishra, R. (1999b), Beyond the nation states: social policy in an age of globalization. In C. Jones Finer (ed.), *Transnational Social Policy*, Oxford: Blackwell.

Mittelman, J. H. (1996), How does globalization really work? In J. H. Mittelman (ed.), *Globalization: Critical Reflections*, London: Lynne Rienner.

Moran, M., and Wood, B. (1996), The globalization of health care policy? In Philip Gummett (ed.), *Globalization and Public Policy*, Cheltenham: Edward Elgar.

Nader, R., and Wallach, L. (1996), GATT, NAFTA and the subversion of the democratic process. In J. Mander and E. Goldsmith (eds), *The Case Against the Global Economy and for a Turn Toward the Local*, San Francisco: Sierra Club Books.

Navarro, V. (1982), The crisis of the international capitalist order and its implications for the welfare state, *Critical Social Policy*, 2, 1: 43–61.

Norberg-Hodge, H. (1996), Shifting direction: from global dependence to local interdependence. In J. Mander and E. Goldsmith (eds), *The Case Against the Global Economy and for a Turn Toward the Local*, San Francisco: Sierra Club Books.

Paccione, M. (1997), Local exchange trading systems as a response to the globalization of capitalism, *Urban Studies*, 34, 8: 1179–99.

Patel, P., and Pavitt, K. (1991), Large firms in the production of the world's technology: an important case of non-globalization, *Journal of International Business Studies*, First Quarter: 1–21.

Perraton, J., Goldblatt, D., Held, D., and McGrew, A. (1997), The globalization of economic activity, *New Political Economy*, 2, 2.

Petrella, R. (1996), Globalization and internationalization: the dynamics of the emerging world order. In R. Boyer and D. Drache (eds), *States against Markets: the Limits of Globalization*, London: Routledge.

Pierson, P. (1994), *Dismantling the Welfare State? Reagan, Thatcher and the Politics of Welfare Retrenchment in the US and UK*, Cambridge: Cambridge University Press.

Pierson, C. (1998), *Beyond the Welfare State: the New Political Economy of Welfare*, 2nd edn, Cambridge: Polity Press.

Pierson, P., and Leibfried, S. (1995), Multitiered institutions and the making of social policy. In S. Leibfried and P. Pierson (eds), *European Social Policy: Between Fragmentation and Integration*, Washington DC: Brookings Institution.

Pitelis, C. (1991), Beyond the nation state? The transnational firm and the nation state, *Capital and Class*, 43: 131–52.

Pooley, S. (1991), The state rules, OK? The continuing political economy of nation states, *Capital and Class*, 43: 65–82.

Rhodes, M. (1996), Globalization and West European welfare states: a critical review of recent debates, *Journal of European Social Policy*, 6, 4: 305–27.

Robinson, W. (1996), Globalization: nine theses on our epoch, *Race and Class*, 38, 2: 13–31.

Rowbotham, S., and Mitter, S. (eds) (1994), *Dignity and Daily Bread: New Forms of Economic Organizing Among Poor Women in the Third World and the First*, London: Routledge.

Ruigrok, W., and Van Tulder, T. (1995), *The Logic of International Restructuring*, London: Lawrence and Wishart.

Sanger, M. (1998), *MAI: Multilateral Investment and Social Rights*. Paper presented to the GASPP seminar on International Trade and Investment Agreements and Social Policy, Sheffield, December.

Shaw, L. (1996), *Social Clauses*, London: Catholic Institute for International Relations.

Sklair, L. (1998), *Competing Conceptions of Globalization*. Paper presented to World Congress of Sociology, Montreal, July.

Stewart, M. (1984), *The Age of Interdependence: Economic Policy in a Shrinking World*, Cambridge MA: MIT Press.

Strange, S. (1996), *The Retreat of the State: The Diffusion of Power in the World Economy*, Cambridge: Cambridge University Press.

Streeck, W. (1995), From market making to state building? Reflections on the political economy of European social policy. In S. Leibfried and P. Pierson (eds), *European Social Policy: Between Fragmentation and Integration*, Washington DC: Brookings Institution.

Streeck, W. (1996), Neo-voluntarism: a new social policy regime? In G. Marks, F. W. Scharpf, P. C. Schmitter and W. Streeck (eds) (1996), *Governance in the European Union*, London: Sage.

Stryker, R. (1998), Globalization and the welfare state, *International Journal of Sociology and Social Policy*, 18, 2/3/4: 1–49.

Taylor-Gooby, P. (1997), In defence of second-best theory: state, class and capital in social policy, *Journal of Social Policy*, 26, 2: 171–92.

Teeple, G. (1995), *Globalization and the Decline of Social Reform*, Toronto: Garamond Press.

Townsend, P., and Donkor, K. (1996), *Global Restructuring and Social Policy: the Need to Establish an International Welfare State*, Bristol: Policy Press.

Vander Stichele, M., and Pennartz, P. (1996), *Making it our Business—European NGO Campaigns on Transnational Organizations*, London: Catholic Institute for International Relations.

Walton, J. (1987), Urban protest and the global political economy: the IMF riots. In *The Capitalist City*, Oxford: Blackwell.

Wilding, P. (1997), Globalization, regionalism and social policy, *Social Policy and Administration*, 31, 4: 410–28.

4

The Welfare Modelling Bu

Peter Abrahamson

Introduction

Though Peter Baldwin has it that "typologizing . . . intellectual endeavour" (1996: 29), parallel to the work bookkeepers, it has nevertheless become very popul issues are being studied and debated. Of course, ther about which typologies to apply; yet the assumption th around certain distinct regimes has become commor it is taken for granted. In particular, when *Europe* is three typologies is usually utilized. One makes a universal state-centred approach named Beveridg one stressing the social insurance and corpora Chassard and Odile Quintin put it: ". . . the contra tradition, which relates proportionally each wag contributions that he has paid or his employer ha the Beveridgean concept of a general insurar population of a country" (1992: 104). Another tyr regimes or traditions as expressed by e.g. Jos European model, however, three distinct traditic Scandinavian, the Atlantic and the continen Compared to the former distinction, Berghman Beveridgean tradition into an Atlantic one and maintained that Southern Europe does "not so n distinct model, but rather a less developed cc tripolar typology has been challenged by (European) welfare state classification where guished from the Continental or Bismarckian t example, in Anthony Giddens's latest pamph can be divided into four institutional grot Scandinavian or Nordic welfare states . . . Iv [and] Southern systems" (1998: 6–7).

Moving beyond Europe, but mostly stayir countries, scholars are discussing whether typologies is applicable or whether new ones their specificity. So the existence is suggestec presented three "broad . . . and very rough approximations to variants of the real world of social policy" in the form of three welfare models of social policy. In the posthumously published book *Social Policy* (1974) we find them again. This distinction between what he labelled the *residual* welfare model of social policy, the industrial *achievement-performance* model of social policy, and the *institutional-redistributive* model of social welfare has had a major influence on students of welfare state issues ever since (1987 [1972]: 261–6; 1974: 30–2). Let us recall what Titmuss told the audience in the Hague:

> The residual model of social policy . . . is based on the premise that there are two "natural" (or socially given) channels through which an individual's needs are properly met; the private market and the family. Only when these break down or fail to function effectively should social welfare institutions come into play and then only temporarily.

What Titmuss describes here is a marginal role for social welfare based on "organic-mechanical constructs of society" advanced early in the development of social policy in the West. He makes a specific reference to the British Poor Law Amendment Act of 1834 with its principles of self-reliance, less eligibility and restrictive intervention. Developed in a time when poverty was viewed as a crime (Disraeli)[1] the function of social welfare became very much a question of control and management, based firmly in liberal ideology and its belief in the superiority of free-market forces. This poverty-oriented approach to social welfare is still very influential in a number of contemporary welfare societies, e.g. in the anglophone world and Switzerland. Titmuss uses the concept given by Wilensky and is apparently inspired by some of his formulations.

> The industrial, achievement-performance model of social policy . . . incorporates significant roles for social welfare institutions, particularly education, public health provisions and social security (or social assistance) as adjuncts of the economy. It holds that social needs should be met on the basis of merit, achieved status differentials, work performance and productivity . . . In short, this is the functional, technocratic-servant role for social welfare.

This model aims at maintaining differences of social status and thus focuses on income substitution. It is comprehensive and conforms to a conservative ideology of preserving *status quo* and existing privileges. Social insurance is the form this model utilizes. It leaves a large space for the social partners of the labour market regarding administration and financing of social welfare. A number of Continental European nations subscribe to this model, and Germany is very often quoted as a prime example.

> The institutional-redistributive model of social welfare . . . sees social welfare as a basic integrated institution in society providing both universal and selective services outside the market on the principle of need. Universal services, available without distinction of class, colour,

sex or religion, can perform functions which foster and promote attitudes and behaviour directed towards the values of social solidarity, altruism, toleration and accountability.

Here social policy has a role as identity-creator—fostering integration, stressing universalism and redistribution of resources. The role of the public sector is substantial. In retrospect one would be led to make a historical reference to the Scandinavian welfare societies, but Titmuss's own reference is to the voluntary cooperative action among the "Ujamaa Villages" in Tanzania.

The categories of residual and institutional we know already from Wilensky; but while he treated them as less and more developed forms of welfare organization indicating a general move from residual to institutional forms over time, Titmuss described a simultaneous but distinctly different way of organizing welfare. What determines which models apply is not development but ideology. Already in 1955 Titmuss had developed a distinction with respect to social welfare:

> Considered as a whole, all collective interventions to meet certain needs of the individual and/or to serve the wider interests of society may now be broadly grouped into three major categories of welfare: social welfare, fiscal welfare and occupational welfare. (1987 [1955]: 45)

However:

> These three systems of social service [can be interpreted] as separate and distinctive attempts to counter and to compensate for the growth of dependency in modern society. Yet, as at present organized, they are simultaneously enlarging and consolidating the area of social inequality. (1987 [1955]: 54)

What we learn here is, first, that social welfare interventions take on different forms, and second, that each of them can act as both regressive and progressive with regard to redistribution and equality. If we connect these two pieces of work it suggests that the achievement-performance model emphasizes occupational and fiscal welfare and thus "divides loyalties, nourishes privilege and narrows the social conscience", while the institutional-redistributive model emphasizes social welfare in a comprehensive way and hence produces a more equal resource distribution, while the residual model emphasizes social welfare in a restricted way when dealing with the poor, and emphasizes fiscal welfare when dealing with the middle and upper classes, and in this way accomplishes two different results for the two major groups of citizens in modern society.

Table 1

Typology of institutional settings for welfare state development

Parliamentary regime	*Liberal democracies* Public assistance as disqualifying alternative to political (and civil) rights	*Mass democracies* Social rights as political corollary of political rights and as a consequence of party competition for votes
Non-parliamentary regime	*Constitutional-dualistic monarchies*	
	Poor relief as paternalistic responsibility for poor "subjects"	Social welfare as authoritarian defence against (full) political citizenship and as consequence of a competition for loyalty
	Limited (manhood) suffrage or estate representation	Extended (manhood or adult) suffrage

Source: Flora and Alber (1981): 46.

In the understanding of welfare states in modern society presented by Titmuss above, it seems that given the same basic issues of structural differentiation and democratic governance, nation states can choose freely among the three ideologically different models. On the Continent the trend has been somewhat different. Here, the emphasis has been on the different historical origins of welfare states, in terms of economic, demographic, political and cultural (religious) development. Regarding the material side of things, industrialization and urbanization including their class relations are viewed as important determinants of welfare development. On the side of ideas, political mobilization and political/constitutional development are viewed as determining. Based on Stein Rokkan's scheme for political development, Peter Flora and Jens Alber (1981) reach a distinction taking into consideration the forms of enfranchisement, parliamentarism and social rights.

Four hypotheses are formulated:

1. Constitutional-dualistic monarchies with a limited suffrage or an estate representation are likely to develop relatively undifferentiated and localized systems of poor relief in the paternalistic tradition of bearing responsibility for needy and obedient subjects. Benefits are based on charity, not entitlements . . .

2. Liberal democracies with a limited suffrage based on property, tax or social status tend to restrict government intervention in general and public assistance in particular . . . They oppose obligatory schemes but may subsidize voluntary mutual benefit and other associative efforts . . .

3. Mass democracies are more likely to develop extended, differentiated and centralized welfare systems based on social rights and obligatory contributions . . . Within mass democracies, however, great variation may

result from differences in the party system (strength and coherence of working-class movement), as well as from differences in the development of state bureaucracies.

4. Constitutional-dualistic monarchies with extended suffrage are most likely to develop more extended, differentiated and centralized welfare systems based on obligatory contributions and entitlements . . . They face greater organized pressure from the working class that leads to the development of welfare institutions as a defence against full participation rights and as a means to strengthen working-class loyalty for the authoritarian state.

"This fourfold classification thus produces a simple typology of institutional settings that may promote or retard the development of welfare states and produce specific variations in public welfare institutions" (Flora and Alber 1981: 47).

If we follow conventional wisdom and locate the maturation of welfare state society in the period immediately following World War II, different nation states had a very different background according to Flora and Alber's scheme. Greece and Spain would fit nicely with category (1) above, and the Anglo-Saxon world of the USA and Australia fits equally nicely with category (2). The Scandinavian nations could be examples of category (3); and Germany and Italy fit category (4).

Obviously, the Stein Rokkan-inspired scheme sees the welfare state (redistribution) as a fourth stage in political development following state formation, nation building, and participation. While state formation and nation building are viewed as processes moving from the centre to the periphery the two latter (participation and redistribution) are viewed as originating in the periphery and moving towards the centre. The centre/periphery distinction is, therefore, another important conceptual demarcation in the Rokkan-inspired welfare discussion. Looking ahead, Peter Flora later suggested that the industrial base of Western societies has diminished since the 1960s for core countries, while it has continued to grow in the European periphery (1993: 15).

The geographical or geopolitical element in welfare typologizing can be read out of the work revolving around Peter Flora in the sense that a nation state cannot easily escape its historical inheritance. Hence, the Catholic church plays a major role for understanding the development of the core or Continental European countries, while the peripheral nation states like the Scandinavian ones are more influenced by a secular development having strong influence on the local government level (municipalities). According to such a way of thinking both the Finnish social scientist Pekka Kosonen, and the Danish economist Bent Rold Andersen operate a scheme in which the Scandinavian nations are viewed as one regime, the *Scandinavian* or the Nordic model of welfare, and Continental Europe clusters around what they label as the *Continental* model of welfare. This is the least differentiated regime typology. The normative position of a *we* (the good guys) versus a *them* (the bad guys) is quite strongly felt in those writings that consider Scandinavia as the best of all worlds while welfare provision on the Continent, in the words of Titmuss, "divides loyalties, nourishes privilege and narrows the social conscience". In a more played-down manner we can describe the differences as opposites. The application of the term Continental is typically made as a contrast to what the regime or model is not, or what it is the opposite of. So, if the Beveridge or social democratic model is universal then the Continental is not; it is reserved for those contributing. Whereas the Beveridgean model is based on flat-rate provisions, the Continental model is not; provisions mirror performance. When the Scandinavian or the Anglo-Saxon model favours tax financing of social provision, then the Continental favours the opposite, namely contributions from the labour market actors.

Setting the Scene for the 1990s: Three or Four Regimes?

Comparative welfare research was taking shape during the 1980s with scholars making reference to profound distinctions between different welfare state developments such as a Scandinavian model (Andersen 1984; Korpi 1983), a specific French way (Ashford 1986), or a particular German experience (Alber 1982). One illustrative example is Gøsta Esping-Andersen's characteristic of the three Scandinavian countries in *Politics against Markets* (1985): "The thrust of social legislation in all three countries was to establish what Titmuss (1974) terms the 'institutional welfare state'" (1985: 159); but it was with the publication in 1990 of his relaunching of Titmuss's three-model scheme that the welfare modelling business really took off. In his *Three Worlds of Welfare Capitalism* Esping-Andersen renames Titmuss's models into the *Liberal* (residual) the *Conservative/Corporatist* (performance-achievement) and the *Social Democratic* (institutional-redistributive) regime by using the names for the ideologies supporting the three distinctly different social policy models. This exercise has proven exceptionally popular, and whether in agreement or disagreement, every scholar writing on the contemporary welfare state has made a reference to Esping-Andersen's tripolar scheme since then. First published in 1989 under the title "The three political economies of the welfare state", we get acquainted with the viewpoint critical towards both the modernization thesis promoted by Wilensky and the uneasy convergence thesis which seems to follow from Flora's work; a viewpoint which holds that welfare states cluster around the identified three distinct regimes. In the 1990 book Esping-Andersen specifies what he under-stands by a welfare regime:

> . . . the concept of welfare state regimes denotes the institutional arrangements, rules and understandings that guide and shape concur-rent social policy decisions, expenditure developments, problem definitions, and even the respond-and-demand structure of citizens and welfare consumers. The existence of policy regimes reflects the circumstance that short-term policies, reforms, debates, and decision-making take place within frameworks of historical institutionalization that differ qualitatively between countries. (1990: 80)

In one cluster we find the "liberal" welfare state, in which means-tested assistance, modest universal transfers, or modest social insurance plans predominate. Benefits cater mainly to a clientele of low-income, usually working class, state dependants. (1990: 26)

A second regime-type . . . the historical corporatist-statist legacy . . . [was] predominated by the preservation of status differentials; rights, therefore, were attached to class and status. This corporatism was subsumed under a state edifice perfectly ready to displace the market as a provider of welfare. (1990: 27)

The third . . . regime-cluster is composed of those countries in which the principles of universalism and decommodification of social rights were extended also to the new middle classes. We may call it the "social democratic" regime-type . . . (1990: 27)

The three regimes are distinguished by the degree of so-called decommodification and the kind of stratification they produce in society. By decommodification is understood "the degree to which individuals, or families, can uphold a socially acceptable standard of living independently of market participation" (1990: 37). The highest such degree is experienced in the social democratic cluster and the least in the liberal cluster. As regards stratification, the social democratic cluster is the one that changes the stratification determined in the outset by the class structure of the capitalist economy, the corporatist cluster focuses on status maintenance; and the liberal cluster supports a pure market distribution of resources against all historically established privileges.

As already mentioned in the introduction, at the time of publication this three-regime typology was challenged by a four-model approach. Two Danish social scientists, Sven Bislev and Henning Hansen, presented a paper in 1989 arguing that European welfare states could be distinguished according to the following four ideal types:

The first type is the *catholic* social policy—a principle of residual public support for individual responsibility in a family framework; and assistance for the needy. The emphasis of supporting paternalistic family patterns, individual thrift and responsibility and private charity is essential.

The second is *corporatist* social policy—social insurance as part of the worker–employer relationship, tailored to the needs and traditions of each particular sector, mandated and supported by the state in the interest of upholding orderly labour relations [it will be] financed through contributions from workers and employers.

The third is *liberal* social policy—universal, mandatory social insurance protecting employers and the public purse against claims and demands from distressed people. Low, flat-rate benefits are provided to ensure incentives to seek work.

Social democratic social policy is the fourth principle—universal, preventive, protecting living standards and labouring abilities, and emphasizing services rather than benefits. (Bislev and Hansen 1990)

When compared to Esping-Andersen, we can see that this scheme is identical except for the important addition of a fourth, Catholic, model. What has happened is that the original Titmuss scheme has been enlarged by differentiating the achievement-performance model into a corporatist/ conservative one and a Catholic one. One of the inspirations for Bislev and Hansen was Jon Eivind Kolberg (1991, 1992a, 1992b), who cooperated closely with Esping-Andersen and who in a paper from 1990 had suggested the following three welfare regimes: the liberal regime, the conservative/catholic regime, and the Scandinavian model (Kolberg 1990: 9–12). Here we see that the Bismarckian regime is open to differentiation and that it can be viewed either as Catholic (and Southern) with reference to the principle of subsidiarity, or status-preserving (and modern) with reference to a high level of extension and coverage.

A similar extension of the Titmuss scheme was also presented in 1989 and 1990 at several EC seminars by German lawyer Stephan Leibfried and published for the first time in 1991 as "Towards a European welfare state: on integrating poverty regimes in the European Community". His first category is labelled *modern* welfare state, which refers to a Scandinavian experience, and it signifies that men and women are both treated as workers. He argues that modern is a better term than Titmuss's institutional-redistributive model which he found was essentially modelled on the working of the British National Health Service where women were treated independent of their work status. Such a system resembles a Bismarckian system and they are therefore allotted the label *institutional*. Again, Leibfried is aware of the fact that Titmuss would have categorized Bismarckian countries such as Austria or Germany as achievement-performance model. Nevertheless, "I abandoned this terminology because: (1) in the 1960s and the early 1970s the Bismarck countries have 'universalized' their 'performance model' to a 'male citizenship model', which was backed (2) up by a (male) full employment promise" (1992: 18). When characterizing the anglophone world, Leibfried sticks with Titmuss's *residual* welfare model, and describes it in terms of selectivism and compensator of last resort. Finally, Leibfried adds on the fourth model which he names *rudimentary* welfare state, which is a characteristic of the Latin Rim countries and could include Ireland also. He sums up the distinctions in table 2:

Table 2

Types of European welfare states

	Scandinavian	Bismarck	Anglo-Saxon	Latin Rim
Type of Welfare Regime	Modern	Institutional	Residual	Rudimentary
Characteristics	Full employment; welfare state as employer of first resort and compensator of last resort	Full growth; welfare state as compensator of first resort and employer of last resort	Full growth; welfare state as compensator of last resort and tight enforcer of work	Catching up; welfare state as half institutionalized promise
Right to	Work	Social security	Income transfers	Work and welfare proclaimed
	Backed up by an institutionalized concept of social citizenship		No such backup	Only implemented partially

Source: Leibfried (1992): 23.

Leibfried goes to some length in constructing a citizenship understanding of the Bismarckian experience which is quite different to conventional interpretation. In doing so he downplays the status maintenance elements of the model.

It is, hence, established that since 1990 welfare state research has made reference either to the Titmuss/Esping-Andersen three regime types or to the four-model approach of Leibfried *et al*. What these typologies have in common is that they view welfare ideology as the explanatory variable, at the same time maintaining a spatial distinction or arguing that welfare ideology is spatially distributed. Some references have been supportive and have utilized the developed typologies (see e.g. Gustafsson 1994; Papadopoulos 1998), while others have been critical and partly rejected or have substantially altered the typologies; but very few have totally ignored the typologies. We shall now consult some of the critical voices.

Subdividing Regimes and Moving (Again) Beyond Western Europe

The three- and four-model typologies have been criticized on a number of grounds. One kind of criticism centres around the appropriateness of a specific clustering of nation states into one of the regime types. While most British scholars seem to have accepted the label of residual or liberal as a characteristic of their welfare regime, some representatives of "the old commonwealth of nations" e.g. Francis Castles and Deborah Mitchell (1990) are not very satisfied with this typology. Castles and Mitchell (1990: table 4) add what they term a *radical* model of welfare regime to Esping-Andersen's typology in order to distinguish their Australia (plus New Zealand and the UK!) from the liberal regimes. They state, however: "Esping-Andersen's operationalization makes absolutely no sense in terms of a Socialist principle of stratification, and only makes sense in the case of de-commodification, if that principle is absolutely unrelated to redistributive outcomes" (Castles and Mitchell 1990: 12). Hence they criticize that Esping-Andersen attaches low scores to means-tested programmes. That they find to be a "somewhat idiosyncratic decision" (Castles and Mitchell 1993: 103) since they may very well offer relatively generous replacement ratios. As mentioned, in conclusion they identify a "fourth world of welfare capitalism" which they label *radical*: "A radical world, in which the welfare goals of poverty amelioration and income equality are pursued through redistributive instruments rather than by high expenditure levels" (1990: 16). In the 1993 paper they specify what is implied by the term radical: "radicalism being interpreted here in terms of the equalizing potential of a given policy instrument" (1993: 105). Parallel to this discussion we find the differentiation between Bismarckian and Southern welfare provision.

A key difference between the Titmuss/Esping-Andersen and the Leibfried *et al.* typology is, of course, the specification of the Latin-rim countries or the catholic realm. Others talked about a Southern model of welfare (Ferrera 1996), while some are critical of the extension of the tripolar scheme, and suggest that the southern countries are, in fact, examples of the achievement-performance/corporate-conservative model (Kastrougalos 1994a, 1996). George Kastrougalos maintains that

In the framework of this classification [the Esping-Andersen typology] and from an institutional point of view, i.e. regarding the scope, the financing and the underlying organizational features it is difficult to perceive a fundamental, structural difference of Greece (or the other South-European countries . . .) from the standard of the Continental model. (1994b: 2)

. . . Spain, Portugal and Greece lack the specific institutional and organizational features that could constitute a distinct fourth ideal-typical regime. They form rather a subgroup, a variation of the Continental model, with immaturity and weakness being the main characteristic. (Kastrougalos 1994a: 6–7)

An absence of substantial social services, and a paternalistic and centralist state tradition are further characteristics. Kastrougalos embraces my suggestion from 1992 to characterize the Southern European countries as a "discount edition of the Continental model" rather than a regime in its own right (Abrahamson 1992).

In contrast to this view, Maurizio Ferrera is open to the understanding of the southern European countries forming a cluster of a particular welfare state type although he finds it misleading to talk about rudimentary or Catholic welfare regimes (1996: 18). Ferrera found the following to be characteristic of the "Southern model":

1. a highly fragmented and "corporatist" income maintenance system, displaying a marked internal polarization: peaks of generosity (e.g. as regards pensions) accompanied by macroscopic gaps in protection;
2. the departure from corporatist traditions in the field of health care and the establishment (at least partially) of national health services based on universalistic principles;
3. a low degree of state penetration of the welfare sphere and a highly collusive mix between public and non-public actors and institutions;
4. the persistence of clientelism and the formation—in some cases—of fairly elaborated "patronage machines" for the selective distribution of cash subsidies (1996: 17).

"The southern welfare states do not only share similar characteristics and a similar genesis, but also are currently confronted by similar developmental challenges of both external and internal nature" (Ferrera 1996: 31).

A similar debate is taking place regarding the Southeast Asian societies. Do they constitute a regime of their own (Kwon 1997) or are they rather hybrids of the tripolar typology (Esping-Andersen 1997)? Catherine Jones has tried to forward the phrase *Confucian* welfare state. According to her understanding, the "Tiger economies" of Southeast Asia cannot be accounted for as conservative-corporatist, though that would be the one of Esping-Andersen's regimes to which they are closest. Instead she describes them as follows: "Conservative corporatism without (Western-style) worker participation; subsidiarity without the church; solidarity without equality; laissez-faire without libertarianism; an alternative expression for all this might be 'household economy' welfare states—run in the style of a would-be traditional, Confucian, extended family" (1993: 214). The same argument is put forward by Arthur Gould (1993).

A fourth example, following the Antipodes, Southern Europe and Southeast Asia, is the case of former communist Eastern Europe. Here we find the same debate about whether to understand the development as an emergence of a new particular welfare regime or as a variation of an already existing regime type. Bob Deacon maintains that both are correct, depending upon which country is in question. Hungary, Slovenia and Croatia are seen to develop as variations of the liberal regime, while East Germany overnight joined the conservative-corporatist model. However, regarding parts of the former USSR, Bulgaria, Romania and Serbia, he finds it appropriate to develop a new regime type, labelled: *post-communist conservative-corporatist*. This expression ". . . captures the ideological and practical commitment to socialist values, the maintenance in power of some of the old guard, and the social deal struck with major labour interests" (Deacon 1993: 195–7).

Esping-Andersen has summed up the problem of subdividing the regime clusters. That kind of methodological dialectics "is almost certain to result in a world composed of 18 distinct 'worlds of welfare capitalism'" (1993: 136). That is, if we allow subdivision of the original regimes we might end up with as many types as we have numbers of nations, in this case 18 OECD countries. Esping-Andersen felt compelled to stick with the original three regimes when he took on, if not the entire globe, then most of the world in a study presented to the UN Social Summit in Copenhagen in 1995. In order to accommodate what he called the "embryonic welfare state evolution in the new industrial democracies of Asia, South America and Eastern Europe" he constructed a division of the world into Scandinavia, Anglo-America, Continental Europe East-Central Europe and South America, and East Asia. The last group of countries are viewed as hybrids borrowing from both the liberal and the corporatist regime types. Countries such as Brazil and Costa Rica can be seen to take on board elements of a social democratic regime; while Chile, East-Central Europe and Argentina follow a liberal route. He puts the question:

> Are the nations of East-Central Europe, East Asia, or Latin America in the process of emulating the Western model, or are they following qualitatively new trajectories? If by "new" we mean models that deviate markedly from existing welfare states, the answer is essentially no. (1996: 20)

So, Esping-Andersen maintains that there are more geographical clusters than there are welfare state trajectories. He is, hence, implicitly critical of purely spatially defined regime clusters, whether of the *centre/periphery* or the *East-West-North-South* type (Flora 1993; Therborn 1995). But, as we have just seen, he is perfectly willing to include more areas of the world than Western Europe. Thus, the criticism of Eurocentrism is wasted on him.

From a methodological point of view the conflict demonstrated here is one of perspective on comparative welfare state research. With distance from the object the perspective changes, as Simmel taught us, and as we have been reminded by Commaille and de Singly (1997: 7). If one wishes to maintain a very broad, "world", view of welfare-state development the above-mentioned cases of Southern Europe, Southeast Asia, Australia etc. are merely variations of the basic regimes. Hence, Esping-Andersen argued as follows in a workshop at the Madrid World Congress of Sociology in 1990: "Seen from New Zealand the Scandinavian countries look pretty much the same" [with respect to welfare arrangements] (quoted from memory). Likewise, viewed from South Korea or South Africa this could be equally true for France and Germany. So, in such an encompassing perspective it makes sense to stick with the "original" regime typology. However, when narrowing down the perspective, either to compare nations within regions or when the perspective is narrowed down to a particular policy area, it makes sense to subdivide the regime categories to capture specific qualities.

Another effort along the same lines is the typology developed by Korpi and Palme (1994, 1998), which is not just an extension and reshuffling of the Titmuss/Esping-Andersen scheme. Although they find Esping-Andersen's exercise valuable because it points to the multidimensional nature of welfare state variation, they maintain: "Yet, because of the diffuseness of underlying ideologies, the complicated ways in which they have interacted in social policy development, and the relative heterogeneity of social policy programs within each country, as many have pointed out such an undertaking meets formidable difficulties" (Korpi and Palme 1994: 6). Analytically they instead distinguish between the following five "institutional types of social insurance programs", *targeted, voluntary, corporatist, basic security,* and *encompassing* as shown in table 3.

Table 3

Ideal-typical models of social insurance institutions

	Bases of entitlement	Benefit level principle	Employer-employee cooperation in programme governance
Targeted	Proven need	Minimum	No
Voluntary state-subsidized	Membership, contributions	Flat-rate or earnings-related	No
Corporatist	Occupational category *and* labour force participation	Earnings-related	Yes
Basic security	Citizenship *or* contributions	Flat-rate	No
Encompassing	Citizenship *and* labour force participation	Flat-rate and earnings-related	No

Source: Korpi and Palme (1998): 666.

However promising this may seem at first glance, it is limited because it only considers welfare states as transfer arrangements, and only sick pay and old-age pensions, following the tradition of focusing on pensions, unemployment and sick-pay. And at the end of the day it is not that much different from the regime typologies discussed above. What has happened in comparison to Titmuss's typology is that a Beveridgean regime has been differentiated out from the residual and the institutional. When the usual 18 OECD countries are placed in the typology the three Nordic countries of Finland, Norway and Sweden end up in the encompassing model while Denmark finds itself together with Great Britain and Ireland in the basic security model. The other models hold the same countries as in the Esping-Andersen and Leibfried discussion; hence Australia, New Zealand, Canada and the USA are said to fit the targeted model; the Southern European countries of Portugal, Spain and Italy are said to fit the voluntary model;

while countries such as the Benelux, France and Germany are said to fit the corporative model. Furthermore, this typology reflects data from 1980 and—at best—1985, which makes it dubious with regard to developments in Southern Europe, for instance Spain, which has experienced something like a revolution in social policy development during the last decade. Finally, civil societal dimensions of welfare provision cannot be thematized within this approach.

So far, it must be concluded that the Titmuss/Esping-Andersen and Leibfried *et al.* regime typologies have proven rather robust in the sense that it is widely recognized that indeed there are rather few basic regime types, and although the names differ widely, comparative social science research has, in all practical terms, accepted a welfare regime approach. This is evident when e.g. Catherine Jones Finer considers "the fortunes of the original agglomeration of the Western welfare states". She writes:

> There are two main, in a sense rival, groupings to bear in mind, based on geography and cultural affiliation: the anglophone world of the British "old commonwealth" of nations (which can include the USA in this context), versus the Western-Continental-European world of French and especially German acculturation. In addition there are two "peripheral" groupings of contrasting import: the supermodel welfare states of Scandinavia (the "Scandinavian rim") versus their so-called rudimentary counterparts of Southern Europe, "the Latin rim". (1999: 18)

This is a split image of Stephan Leibfried's (1992) scheme, which is the extension of the Titmuss/Esping-Andersen "classic" typology, and one we have elaborated suggesting that the Scandinavian model is the luxury edition of the Beveridge model and the Catholic model being the discount edition of the Bismarckian model (Abrahamson 1992). The four-model scheme has become self-evident to the extent where it is seldom questioned, but referred to as common knowledge, parallel to, e.g., the evolution of citizenship developed by Thomas Marshall. In his book on *The Third Way* (1998), Anthony Giddens reproduces the four-model welfare state scheme with a slight change of wording with reference to German social scientist Fritz Scharpf, as already mentioned.

All the above approaches have considered welfare policy as merely income transfers and often exemplified as covering only the risks of sickness, old age and unemployment in this respect; furthermore, they seem to neglect the existence and importance of family and networks as institutions of welfare provision and are said to be insensitive to women's issues. The latest generation of comparative studies have added on the case study so that particular sectors or policies are studied in selected countries representing this or that regime.

From Social Security to Welfare Services and to Cases

From a gender perspective, perhaps particularly within feminist writing, the integration of gender into the analysis of welfare state regimes has led to a modification of the concept. Julia O'Connor wrote:

> In addition to recognizing the gender composition of mainstream political organizations, the institutional legacy must be evaluated in terms of its conduciveness to facilitating or hindering the incorporation of women into the political system and to effecting change through corporatist institutions, policy bodies such as Pay or Employment Equity Agencies, and client representative associations. Furthermore, the influence of new social movements, such as the feminist movement, must be assessed in terms of their ability to influence the policy agenda and form coalitions with mainstream political organizations. (1993: 511)

The major problem identified with the kind of analyses coming out of the power resource-school (Esping-Andersen, Korpi, etc.) is, from this point of view, the undifferentiated citizenship status with which they operate. However, women's relationship with the welfare state cannot be understood only as organized workers; but must be expanded to include their roles as "needs-bearing clients and rights-bearing consumers of services . . . and political citizens" (O'Connor 1996: 3). When developing a gender-sensitive approach to welfare state regimes the role of *care* becomes central; and through the focus on care the other half of social policy, namely *personal social services*, becomes important.

It is obviously a good idea to take on board analyses of social care services in this discussion of welfare models and regimes, but if we apply the correlational method the result does not seem much different to what has already been established with regard to the analyses of transfer systems. Hence, Anttonen and Sipilä (1996) found that three of the four clusters discussed by Leibfried were consistently constructed:

> By and large our description of social care services seems to fit together with the welfare state typologies presented by Esping-Andersen and Leibfried. Service systems seem largely to reflect the general principles of social security provision. (1996: 24)

Only the conservative/corporatist regime lacked coherence. This problem was then solved by Anttonen and Sipilä by splitting it into two regimes which were labelled the Dutch-German subsidiary and the French-Belgian model of family policy.

One type of case study focuses on one policy area, e.g. Baldwin's study on pensions or Pedersen's study on family policy, and limits the analyses to a smaller sample of countries; by doing so either specifications of the regimes re-occur, or new concepts are framed. With Susan Pedersen's comparison of Britain and France she found that in the case of France we can talk about a *parental* model of welfare state. She defines it thus in contrast to the well-known label of *male bread-winner*: "Put simply, while male bread-winner policies compensate men for dependent women and children during legitimate interruptions of earnings, states with parental policies compensate adults for dependent children irrespective of earnings or need" (Pedersen 1995: 18).

Furthermore, the countries do not necessarily cluster the same way when other transfer schemes than the major ones are analysed. Ditch *et al.* (1998) have analysed the value of what they define as a child benefit package and compared it to the cost of having children in the 15 European Union countries. Based on this the clusters look like this:

- Luxembourg, France, Belgium and Germany with the most generous provision;
- Denmark, Finland, Sweden, Austria and the UK with middling provision;
- Ireland, Portugal, Netherlands, Spain, Italy and Greece with low levels of provision.

They conclude: "Clearly the groupings of countries that we have found are rather different from the welfare regimes proposed by Esping-Andersen" (Ditch *et al.* 1998: 68). If we add the provision of childcare services to the child benefit package, we get yet another cluster, as shown by Gornick *et al.* (1997). They found that the United Kingdom, Germany and the two Scandinavian countries (Denmark and Sweden) belong to the same cluster, but they fitted France into the same group as these Scandinavian countries. This indicates that when it comes to family policy and the various kinds of social services involved here we are bound to change the standard typology.[2]

This case-centred approach seems to be the most promising development of the application of welfare typologies. There seems to be developing the beginning of a consensus about abandoning the cluster analysis approach and a move to various case studies exemplifying the workings of the regimes. Even Esping-Andersen recommends this in his "reply to his critics" (1993: 127–9):

> The great advantage of the case-centred approach is its capacity to examine welfare states holistically and relationally. It can show us how relations of citizenship or relations between family, markets and state crystallize . . . Indeed, the comparison of particular welfare state components seems to be emerging as a fruitful and dynamic new third-generation approach. (Esping-Andersen 1993: 127–8)

What some of the previous studies failed to address, such as the role of *civil society*, especially family and networks, is now more commonly integrated into welfare analyses. These issues were never excluded because of the regime typology approach but they have been subject to the understanding of welfare *state* development in the "classic" anglophone way of state/justice versus market/liberalism (Briggs 1961).

Conclusion

At the turn of the millennium a number of conclusions can be reached about the use of ideal-typical regime models within comparative welfare studies. First, the substantial growth in this welfare modelling business is closely related to the emergence of debates over globalization and, especially, European integration illustrated by the Single Market. When these processes are studied it becomes relevant and fruitful to apply a regime typology and try to cluster welfare state nations around a limited and qualitatively different set of models. Hence, the typologizing of welfare regimes has been facilitated by the ongoing discussions of globalization and Europeanization. In particular, the debates over convergence and even harmonization of European social policy and the development of the so-called social dimension of European cooperation have spoken to the utilization of welfare models, as recognized recently, although not elaborated, by e.g. Sylvia Walby (1999: 128). It is obvious that, for instance, the effort towards developing a common agenda of employment policy as an important issue within the Union sits very differently with the different models.

Second, the perspective on, or the distance to, the object of study, i.e. the cluster of welfare states, determines whether differentiation or simplification is applied. Taking my own region of Scandinavia as an example, it is clear that from far away—ideologically, institutionally, culturally—the Nordic countries cluster around some common welfare traits, even though Esping-Andersen could not easily fit Finland into this cluster, and likewise Korpi and Palme excluded Denmark from this company. However, on a closer look it can also be argued that there are some profound qualitative differences between Denmark and Norway on the one side and Finland and Sweden on the other side. In such a perspective there is a distinct Western and Eastern Scandinavian experience (see e.g. Abrahamson 1999). The same could be said to be the case for the Southern European countries; at a closer look they are not just variations of the Bismarckian model. So, when single nations are discussed they are often viewed as not fitting into the regime typology (see e.g. Cousins 1997 regarding Ireland). Nevertheless, as an organizing principle for comparative studies of welfare states the distinction of Bismarck versus Beveridge, or its differentiation into corporatist, residual and institutional, or even adding a Catholic model, has proven to be a very robust and convincing tool.

Third, there is certainly some disagreement as to what can be said to be the ordering principle in the welfare modelling business. The majority of contributions treat welfare ideology as the explanatory variable while a minority refer to historical development of state-formation as determining. Rather few contributions stick with simple accounts of expenditure level or geographical position. There is, however, a tendency towards an emphasis on institutional features in a more narrow sense than political welfare ideology within the welfare modelling business, which points to the last point of *programme sensitivity*.

Fourth, in different ways the development of discussions around welfare models emphasizes context dependency. This means that analyses of different welfare programmes such as unemployment insurance and child-care warrant different regime typologies. However, not to the point where "anything goes", i.e. there still seems to be a very limited number of regimes at play in connection with the same kinds of welfare provisions; but when we change focus from one set of policies to another set we may have to alter (some of) the regime definitions. In other words: context matters![3]

Acknowledgements

A draft version of this chapter was presented at the 20th Nordic Congress of Sociology, Bergen, Norway, June 1999. The author wishes to thank the participants in the workshop on The Welfare State in Comparative Perspective, and specially its convenor and the discussant on this chapter Eero Carroll, for instructive comments and criticism. This research was, in part, supported by a grant from the Danish Social Science Research Council.

Notes

1. Disraeli described the Poor Law thus: "it announces to the world that in England poverty is a crime" (quoted in Piven and Cloward 1971: 35).
2. With respect to a current comparative study on reconciliation of family and working life in the European Union we have chosen to operate with the following four models: the *residual-poverty oriented* model (the liberal) exemplified by the UK, the *male bread-winner* model (Bismarckian) exemplified by Germany, the *parental welfare* model (the family supportive) exemplified by France, and the *local social service* model (the Scandinavian) exemplified by Denmark and Sweden (see Abrahamson *et al.* forthcoming).
3. Paraphrasing the dictum of the Stockholm school of welfare state understanding: "Politics matter."

References

Abrahamson, P. (1992), Europe: A Challenge to the Scandinavian Model of Welfare? Paper contributed to the First European Conference of Sociology, University of Vienna. A revised version is published in Bruno Amoroso and Jesper Jespersen (eds), *Welfare Society in Transition. Annals 1994*, Roskilde: Department of Social Sciences, Roskilde University (1995): 135–51.
Abrahamson, P. (1999), The Scandinavian model of welfare. In Denis Bouget and Bruno Palier (eds), *Comparing Social Welfare Systems in Nordic Countries and France*, Paris: MIRE.
Abrahamson, P., Boje, T., Greve, B., and Schmid, H. (forthcoming), Welfare and solidarity in post-modern Europe: new models for provision of social welfare and social citizenship in Europe.
Alber, J. (1982), *Vom Armenhaus zum Wohlfahrtsstaat*, Frankfurt am Main: Campus Verlag.
Alber, J. (1995), A framework for the comparative study of social services, *Journal of European Social Policy*, 5, 2: 131–49.
Andersen, B. R. (1984), Rationality and irrationality of the Nordic welfare state, *Daedalus*, 113, 1: 109–39.
Andersen, B. R. (1991), *Velfærdsstaten i Danmark og i Europa (The Welfare State in Denmark and in Europe)*, Copenhagen: Fremad.

Anttonen, A., and Sipilä, J. (1996), European social care services: is it possible to identify models?, *Journal of European Social Policy*, 6, 2: 87–100.

Ashford, D. (1986), *The Emergence of the Welfare States*, Oxford: Blackwell.

Baldwin, P. (1991), *The Politics of Social Solidarity*, Oxford: Oxford University Press.

Baldwin, P. (1996), Can we define a European welfare state model? In Bent Greve (ed.), *Comparative Welfare Systems*, London: Macmillan: 29–44.

Berghman, J. (1997), Can the idea of benchmarking be applied to social protection?, *Bulletin Luxembourgeois des Questions Sociales*, 4: 119–29.

Bislev, S., and Hansen, H. (1990), The Nordic welfare states and the European single market. In Lise Lyck (ed.), *The Nordic Countries in the Internal market of the EC*, Copenhagen: Handelshøjskolens Forlag.

Briggs, A. (1961), The welfare state in historical perspective, *Archives européennes de sociologie*, 2, 2: 221–58.

Castles, F. G., and Mitchell, D. (1990), *Three Worlds of Welfare Capitalism or Four?* Australian National University, graduate program in public policy, discussion paper no. 21.

Castles, F., and Mitchell, D. (1993), Worlds of welfare and families of nations. In Castles, F. (ed.), *Families of Nations: Patterns of Public Policy in Western Democracies*, Aldershot: Dartmouth.

Chassard, Y., and Quintin, O. (1992), Social protection in the European Community: towards a convergence of policies. In *Fifty Years After Beveridge*, vol. 2, York: University of York: 103–110.

Commaille, J., and de Singly, F. (1997), Rules of the comparative method in the family sphere: the meaning of comparison. In Jacques Commaille and François de Singly (eds), *The European Family: the Family Question in the European Community*, Dordrecht: Kluwer: 3–22.

Cousins, M. (1997), Ireland's place in the worlds of welfare capitalism, *Journal of European Social Policy*, 7, 3: 223–35.

Deacon, B. (1993), Developments in East European social policy. In Catherine Jones (ed.), *New Perspectives on the Welfare State in Europe*, London: Routledge: 177–97.

Ditch, J., Barnes, H., Bradshaw, J., and Kilkey, M. (1998), *A Synthesis of National Family Policies*, Brussels: DGV.

Esping-Andersen, G. (1985), *Politics against Markets*, Princeton NJ: Princeton University Press.

Esping-Andersen, G. (1989), The three political economies of the welfare state, *Canadian Review of Sociology and Anthropology*, 26, 2.

Esping-Andersen, G. (1990), *The Three Worlds of Welfare Capitalism*, Cambridge: Polity Press.

Esping-Andersen, G. (1993), The comparative macro-sociology of welfare states. In L. Moreno (ed.), *Social Exchange and Welfare Development*, Madrid: Consejo Superior de Investigaciones Científicas.

Esping-Andersen, G. (1995), Europe's Welfare States at the End of the Century. Paper, University of Trento, April.

Esping-Andersen, G. (1996), *Welfare States in Transition: National Adaptations in Global Economies*, London: Sage.

Esping-Andersen, G. (1997), Hybrid or unique?: the Japanese welfare state between Europe and America, *Journal of European Social Policy*, 7, 3: 179–89.

Ferrera, M. (1996), The "southern model" of welfare in social Europe, *Journal of European Social Policy*, 6, 1: 17–37.

Finer, C. J. (1999), Trends and developments in welfare states. In Jochen Clasen (ed.), *Comparative Social Policy: Concepts, Theories and Methods*, Oxford: Blackwell: 15–33.

Flora, P. (1993), The national welfare states and European integration. In L. Moreno (ed.), *Social Exchange and Welfare Development*, Madrid: Consejo Superior de Investigaciones Científicas.

Flora, P., and Alber, J. (1981), Modernization, democratization and the development of welfare states in Western Europe. In Peter Flora and Arnold Heidenheimer (eds), *The Development of Welfare States in Europe and America*, New Brunswick, NJ: Transaction Books: 37–80.

Giddens, A. (1998), *The Third Way: The Renewal of Social Democracy*, Cambridge: Polity Press.

Gornick, J., Meyers, M., and Ross, K. (1997), Supporting the employment of mothers: policy variation across 14 welfare states, *Journal of European Social Policy*, 7, 1: 45–70.

Gould, A. (1993), *Capitalist Welfare Systems: A Comparison of Japan, Britain and Sweden*, London: Longman.

Gustafsson, S. (1994), Childcare and types of welfare states. In Diane Sainsbury (ed.), *Gendering Welfare States*, London: Sage: 45–61.

Jones, C. (1993), The Pacific challenge. In C. Jones (ed.), *New Perspectives on the Welfare State in Europe*, London: Routledge: 198–221.

Kastrougalos, G. (1994a), The South-European Model of Welfare State and the European Integration. Mimeo. Roskilde: Department of Social Sciences, Roskilde University.

Kastrougalos, G. (1994b), The Greek Welfare State: in Search of Identity. Mimeo. Roskilde: Department of Social Sciences, Roskilde University.

Kastrougalos, G. (1996), The South-European welfare model: the Greek welfare state in search of an identity, *Journal of European Social Policy*, 6, 1: 39–60.

Kolberg, J. E. (1990), Velferdsmodeller i Europa. Forelesning på Nordisk Seminar 1990, Svendborg, Danmark, 24 September.

Kolberg, J. E. (1991), *The Welfare State as Employer*, New York: M. E. Sharpe.

Kolberg, J. E. (1992a), *Between Work and Social Citizenship*, New York: M. E. Sharpe.

Kolberg, J. E. (1992b), *The Study of Welfare Regimes*, New York: M. E. Sharpe.

Korpi, W. (1983), *The Democratic Class Struggle*, London: Routledge and Kegan Paul.

Korpi, W., and Palme, J. (1994), *The Strategy of Equality and the Paradox of Redistribution*, Swedish Institute for Social Research, Stockholm University, Sweden.

Korpi, W., and Palme, J. (1998), The paradox of redistribution and strategies of equality: welfare state institutions, inequality and poverty in the Western countries, *American Sociological Review*, 63, 5: 661–87.

Kosonen, P. (1992), European Welfare State Models: Converging Trends. Paper presented at the 1st European Congress of Sociology, Vienna, August.

Kwon, H.-J. (1997), Beyond European welfare regimes: comparative perspectives on East Asian welfare systems, *Journal of Social Policy*, 26, 4: 467–84.

Leibfried, S. (1992), Towards a European welfare state? In Zsuzsa Ferge and Jon Eivind Kolberg (eds), *Social Policy in a Changing Europe*, Frankfurt am Main: Campus Verlag. First published (1991) as *ZeS Arbeitspapier*, nr. 2/91. Bremen: Zentrum für Sozialpolitik, Universität Bremen.

Marshall, T. H. (1950), *Citizenship and Social Class*, Cambridge: Cambridge University Press.

O'Connor, J. (1993), Gender, class and citizenship in the comparative analysis of welfare state regimes: theoretical and methodological issues, *British Journal of Sociology*, 44, 3: 501–18.

O'Connor, J. (1996), From women in the welfare state to gendered welfare state regimes, *Current Sociology*, 44, 2: 1–127.

Papadopoulos, T. N. (1998), *Welfare Support for the Unemployed: a Comparative Analysis of Social Policy Responses to Unemployment in Twelve European Union Member-States*, York: PhD dissertation, Department of Social Policy and Social Work.

Pedersen, S. (1995), *Family, Dependence, and the Welfare State*, Cambridge: Cambridge University Press.

Piven, F. F., and Cloward, R. (1997), *Regulating the Poor: the Functions of Public Welfare*, New York: Vintage.

Therborn, G. (1995), *European Modernity and Beyond: The Trajectory of European Societies 1945–2000*, London: Sage.

Titmuss, R. (1974), *Social Policy*, London: Allen and Unwin.

Titmuss, R. (1987), *The Philosophy of Welfare. Selected Writings*, ed. S. M. Miller, London: Allen and Unwin.

Walby, S. (1999), The new regulatory state: the social powers of the European Union, *British Journal of Sociology*, 50, 1: 118–37.

Wilensky, H., and Lebaux, C. (1958), *Industrial Society and Social Welfare*, New York: Russell Sage Foundation.

5

Social Security in a Rapidly Changing Environment: The Case of the Post-communist Transformation

Gáspár Fajth

Introduction

The collapse of the communist states and the market-oriented transition in Central and Eastern Europe and in the former Soviet Union has been one of the most important events of the twentieth century, provoking a rich descriptive and analytical literature. This great interest has been fully justified by the sudden, drastic and systematic changes affecting all areas of human life in this particular part of the industrialized world since 1989. In a process which has not always been peaceful, the number of countries has grown from 8 to 27. Since 1990 Albania and five newly independent states of the former Soviet Union have found themselves among the low-income countries (World Bank 1996), and even the middle-income countries have found it difficult to finance the social sector. In some places the State has collapsed or ceased to exist. Over the 1990s GDP has fallen in a range between 15 and 70 per cent in the 27 countries, with real wages falling even more (UNICEF 1999a). Full employment ceased to exist; unemployment soared and full basic education enrolment and health service coverage rates eroded. Income inequality has grown (in many countries it has exploded), and hardly any economic or social indicators have remained unaffected.

This chapter follows up the transition story from the viewpoint of social security: it investigates what main cash social programmes were available at the outset of the transition and what major changes occurred as the political, economic and demographic environment rapidly changed during the 1990s. The chapter does not include an in-depth theoretical or statistical analysis; it aims to focus on the big picture and highlight some interplay and synergy among the various social programmes as they have changed and affected people.

The chapter is organized as follows. The section after this introduction sums up the inherited situation regarding cash and non-cash social programmes; the second section reviews arguments and pressures for radical changes in these transfers after 1989; and the third section describes the emerging new patterns of social security and related programmes.

The Inherited Situation: Social Security and Other Transfers

When the state socialist regimes collapsed in Central and Eastern Europe around the end of the 1980s and the beginning of the 1990s they left behind a social security system that in many ways resembled those of the developed world. Screening through international handbooks such as the *Social Security Programs throughout the World* of the US Department of Health and Social Services, or the *Cost of Social Security* published by the ILO, Ferge concluded that in this regard the great dividing line has never been between "socialism" and "capitalism", but rather between both of them and the Third World: in contrast to North American, Western or Eastern European industrialized societies, most Asian or Latin American countries had limited programmes which reached only a few (3 to 4 per cent) of workers with some noted outliers such as Chile (Ferge 1991: 70).

The emergence of a comprehensive social security system took decades in the postwar period in capitalist and the state socialist countries alike; Gordon notes that linkages to full employment and rapid economic growth rates in the 1950s and 1960s in both groups of countries played a significant role in the expansion of social security (Gordon 1988: 2). In the centrally planned economies entitlement to social security benefits was used as an important incentive tool to swell employment in the state-controlled sectors; and high employment rates of both genders resulted in wide access to pension and other benefits. In fact, these countries often reached relatively high expenditure levels earlier than their capitalist adversaries; but from the mid-1960s this rapid growth in social security expenditure decelerated while in Western Europe and North America expansion continued until the troubled 1980s (Gordon 1988: 10–19).

Central and Eastern Europe devoted about 15 per cent of their Net Material Product on cash social transfers by the end of the 1970s (Ferge 1991: 70) and the 1980s saw in many countries an extension of entitlements and programme coverage. Even if data availability problems and measurement issues blur such comparisons it is clear that relative to their economic output the social security effort of the communist countries broadly fitted with that of the developed market economies. In 1990 OECD member countries spent on average 16 to 17 per cent of their Gross Domestic Product (GDP) on income transfers such as old age, sickness, occupational injury, unemployment and family benefits (Barr and Harbison 1994: 18).

Social security available for Eastern Europeans had three big "pillars" (old age pensions, health-related transfers and family benefits); these were supported by two other big systems each of them comparable in importance and in dollar terms to the sum of social security cash transfers: employee benefits and consumer subsidies. The main arrangements were as follows.

Pensions

As in the West, most public cash social expenditure went to the old age pension system, which absorbed about 5 to 9 per cent of their national income (UNICEF 1997: 137). The pension systems were based on social insurance; through linear earmarked taxes on wages (levied in most cases on both employers and employees) annual contributions fed current expenditures without any direct links between individual contributions and benefits. Such pay-as-you-go systems feature also in Western European countries; however, in Eastern Europe boundaries between the state budget and social security budget were symbolic and expenditure was not only exposed to day-to-day political decisions but these decisions lacked any public control and transparency.

As Ferge put it: "the concept of social rights was absent from the political vocabulary" (Ferge 1991: 76). Some countries (like Czechoslovakia or Romania) provided a means-tested minimum benefit. However, the aim of the Soviet pension system (that all Eastern European communist states took as a model when expanding their prewar social security systems) was not to guarantee a minimum income to all aged citizens, but to reward long service records in the state-controlled economy. Provisions that particularly benefited long-service workers were a distinctive feature of pension formulas in the Soviet bloc (Gordon 1988: 52).

The pensionable age (55 for women and 60 for men) was lower than is the norm in the West; when calculating entitlement, the total employment record and earnings in the pre-pension period (typically the last five years) were considered. Representing an important career incentive in these bureaucratically organized societies, these rules could secure individual pensions as high as 55 to 65 per cent of wages after twenty to twenty-five years of service and 70 to 75 per cent after forty years (these are high maximum values by Western standards). In reality, however, pensions tended to be significantly lower: in 1989 national pension–wage ratios ranged within the USSR between 33 per cent in Russia and 41 per cent in Lithuania; Poland and Czechoslovakia had ratios of 40 to 50 per cent, and only Hungary and Slovenia achieved relatively high ratios (63 and 75 per cent respectively) (UNICEF 1997: 142).

One reason for the discrepancy between the relatively generous pension rights and the often meagre benefit values was the lack of adjusting mechanism for wage and (crawling) price rises over decades of the planned economy. (This was true also for deposits in national savings bank accounts, which, apart from cash, were the only place where people could accumulate their own savings.) Moreover, as coverage was extended to agricultural labour relatively late, some population groups—chiefly rural women—tended to have short service records. This situation placed the elderly at high risk of relative poverty, and contributed to their generally weak income position by international standards.

However, it is important to point out that as a consequence of full employment rates, almost all elderly people possessed some pension rights by the end of the 1980s; and the low pension age favoured access to additional earnings, work in the household economy or care for grandchildren. Social security had strong child- and maternity-related components; even in some countries, such as Czechoslovakia, women's retirement age was differentiated according to the number of children born (in the

Soviet system only mothers of five and more children could retire earlier, see Baskakova 1999).

Family allowances and child-related leave

As in the West the different programmes have shown considerable variance across countries (see Fajth 1996; UNICEF 1997: 94), but generally the Central and Eastern European countries tended to spend significantly more on child- and family-related programmes than Western nations. While countries such as Sweden, Germany and the USA spent 2.1, 1.3 and 0.3 per cent of their GDP on cash family benefits respectively, Poland spent 2.3 per cent, Czechoslovakia 3.1 per cent and Hungary 4.4 per cent (OECD 1996: 28; Fajth 1996: 3).

In most cases the greater expenditure reflected more programmes and generous benefits rather than just bigger child populations. In Czechoslovakia, for example, family allowances amounted to 10.4 per cent of the average wage, in Hungary 20.5 per cent, in 1989. In the Soviet Union (where, however, no universally available cash child allowances existed), 112 days' maternity leave was paid at full rate. In Hungary, either parent could take parental leave to care for children up to the age of 3, with a sick-leave benefit rate (Fajth 1994: 32–41). In Bulgaria, as in other countries, sick pay for child care was generous: 60 days annually at 50 to 100 per cent wage replacement rate (Noncheva 1995).

Eligibility for these benefits was usually pegged to an employment record, but most parents had access to maternity benefits; in many countries family allowances were also close to being universal. Observers concluded that the system promoted rather than discouraged women's employment and was effective in reducing child poverty rates (see Sipos 1994: 227–33). These functions were important as the command economy needed an expanded labour force, and families with many children faced a high risk of relative poverty (Sipos 1992: 21–44; UNICEF 1994: 7–12). The effectiveness of the poverty-alleviation capacity of family benefits was confirmed by studies using comparable survey micro-data and relative poverty lines. For example, Bradbury and Jäntti found that children of single parents in the Czech Republic, Hungary or Poland—unlike children in most Western market economies—did not face a significantly higher risk of poverty than those living with couples (Bradbury and Jäntti 1999).

Disability benefits and sick leave

These classic social insurance arrangements also formed an important part of social security of employees and working parents; and the source of financing was the same public fund as in the case of regular benefits. In the case of invalidity pension the wage replacement rate was 55 per cent (with 1 to 15 years of service record required depending on actual age); in some countries like Bulgaria, level 2 and 3 invalids were entitled to only 25 to 40 per cent replacement.

Poor occupational safety and health standards at work (Preker and

Feachem 1994) increased demand for invalidity pensions. Moreover, as Szalai and others have pointed out, these programmes were frequently misused. Beneficiaries of disability benefits have also increased rapidly in market economies over recent decades, but this has been more associated with high unemployment and a demand for social assistance than with higher sickness rates or changes in eligibility conditions (Gordon 1988: 128). In the planned economies illegal use was frequently associated with work in the "second economy" (e.g. sick leave from the main job could allow work on private plots or farms) (Szalai 1986). In Poland in 1990, one-third of expenditure on old age pensions benefited individuals below the normal pensionable age (World Bank 1993, quoted by Barr 1994: 196).

Child-related sick leave was, again, generous (e.g. in Poland 100 per cent of the wage was paid while caring at home for sick children) underlined by high female employment rates. Children with disabilities had increased family allowances: for example, the mother of these children received double allowances in Hungary. However, long-term assistance for parental care of children with disabilities was either not available or was a meagre flat-rate benefit—the state favoured institutional care.

The emergence of comprehensive social security systems and full employment went hand in hand with wider access to health services. Yugoslavia followed the classic German "sickness insurance" model, with employment-related coverage where the system operates through sickness funds. However, the Soviet Union has had a national health service since 1926 (Gordon 1988: 203) covering all residents in providing medical and hospital services free of charge (and prescribed drugs at a reduced price); a model most Eastern European countries (and also many in Western Europe) adopted later (1988: 203). Despite a basically full coverage of the entire population and high rates of doctors per capita, public health expenditures tended to be lower in Central and Eastern Europe than in Western countries, as professional wages were low and because infrastructure development lagged behind staff expansion.

Other work-related benefits

The most striking difference from market economies was the complete lack of unemployment insurance/compensation in the planned system (partly responsible for the emerging gap in social security expenditures—since the mid-1970s high unemployment rates became persistent in Western countries). However, outside the social security system a wide range of work-related benefits existed, most of them in kind rather than cash.

A World Bank survey of 439 firms throughout Russia found that 79 per cent of enterprises offered subsidized childcare, 71 per cent a health facility (some big firms even owned hospitals), 59 per cent housing subsidy and 57 per cent transportation and holiday resort or subsidy in 1990/1 (Commander and Jackman 1997: 96–8). Although occupational welfare (called also "social wages" by some authors) was less important in early-reform state socialist countries, such as Hungary or Poland, it was still important at the end of the 1980s or early 1990s. Analysing the 1992 Labour Cost Survey that closely followed the standard Eurostat surveys Rein and Friedman found that customary expenditures in Hungary amounted to 14 per cent of the total wage costs, considerably higher than the 7 to 12 per cent that French, German or UK firms with more than 20 employees secured for their staff (Rein and Friedman 1997: 143).

Universal transfers

Despite the many cash transfer programmes, truly universal programmes existed more in kind than in cash (although in the late 1980s Hungary introduced universal child allowances on citizenship grounds and Bulgaria secured a maternity benefit also to women out of the labour force). Consumer and housing subsidies were far more widespread in the planned economies than in their market economy counterparts. While in Western Europe government subsidies were basically limited to mortgage and public transport, in Central and Eastern Europe they were almost as important in dollar terms as total cash benefits from social security. Consumer subsidies amounted to 11 per cent of GDP in Poland in 1987 (Atkinson and Micklewright 1992).

In Hungary, even discounting support for pre-schools and similar in-kind services, 8 per cent of the GDP went to consumer and housing subsidies (1 per cent on public transport and medicines, 4 per cent on supporting access to housing, the rest on food, energy and some consumer services). A study of the incidence of these transfers concluded that higher-income households and families with children benefited most from these (Kupa and Fajth 1990; KSH 1990, 1991). On the other hand, some types of non-cash support, such as child tax allowances, which in the USA, for example, similarly reward mostly middle-class families with children (Esping-Andersen and Micklewright 1991) had little role or did not exist at all (as comprehensive personal income taxes were introduced only during the reform period).

Arguments and Pressures for Radical Changes in Social Transfers after 1989

Observers and policy-makers agreed that the complex system of social transfers described above should be adjusted along with the institutional changes and ownership reforms associated with the transition to a market economy. It was clear that the role of the state should be reduced in general; that state-owned enterprises dominating the economy should be privatized; that people should be empowered to seize new opportunities. However, there was controversy about how to do all these. In particular there was little agreement about how to radically reduce the role of the state, how to sequence reforms, and how to adjust social transfers in the immediate and longer term.

The system of consumer subsidies was the first obvious target of liberalization. Most analysts—especially those associated with the International Monetary Fund—saw these non-cash transfers as a particular feature of the planned system (see, for example, Kopits 1991; Ahmad 1992), and macroeconomic stabilization and full price liberalization as a stepping stone to institutional reforms. Indeed, radical reformers in Poland, Hungary and Russia were quick to eliminate or reduce state subsidies on basic necessities. Some of those who worried about inflation shocks, sudden rises in poverty and inadequate nutrition urged a more cautious and gradualist approach to the removal of these subsidies (see, for example, Cornia 1995). Others, placing the stress on the importance of maintaining political support for reforms, argued for using wide-scale cash compensations. The idea of transforming non-cash benefits into cash compensations, which dominated the early transition literature, favoured a rise in social security revenues and expenditures.

In fact, in the early transition years social security expenditures tended to fall less sharply than economic output; that is, despite falls in real terms countries spent more on cash benefits in relative terms. UNICEF reported that while consumer subsidies were reduced at a sharp rate, social security expenditures (including unemployment compensation and also health services) grew in the early transition years in relative terms. Between 1989 and 1993, the ratio of expenditure to GDP grew in the Czech Republic from 22 to 26 per cent, in Poland from 20 to 29 per cent, and in Romania from 14 to 16 per cent (UNICEF 1995: 123–6). However, in those countries where GDP fell particularly sharply the share of social expenditures to GDP did not rise (or rose only modestly, such as in Lithuania, for example, from 15 to 18 per cent). In Russia pension and health expenditures remained proportionate to GDP, but in Armenia or Azerbaijan they fell even more than output (which had shrunk to 36 and 42 per cent) between 1989 and 1995 (UNICEF 1995).

Certainly, the existing social security systems were a very important asset to the reforms: they offered a market-friendly institution and infrastructure to buffer the impact of reforms on households in general and on vulnerable groups in particular. Nevertheless, controversies emerged regarding the role and capacity of social security programmes.

The first concerned the longer-term effects that termination of subsidies (and employee benefits) would have on the structure of existing social security programmes and how the aggregate expenditure would change. It was obvious that the aggregate cost effect had to be moderate and that social security benefits could not be augmented/extended to fully absorb former non-cash transfers; also, many strategy papers stressed the need for fiscal saving. Full-scale compensation in many countries would have doubled already-substantial social security outlays—a wholly unrealistic scenario. The fact that aggregate cash expenditure could rise little made adjustment more difficult.

Second, the existing system reflected the needs of the planned economy and the ways these regimes were operating. It certainly had some important programme gaps (or, as some commentators put it somewhat inadequately "holes in the safety net"). In Western social security systems there are some built-in mechanisms to counter the impact of economic cycles. Eastern European systems, however, were not designed to adjust entitlements for inflation or to compensate for unemployment. In particular, as noted above they did not explicitly aim at securing a basic income for the needy. The system described above had three "pillars" (old age pension, family benefits and transfers associated with sickness and disability). It seemed, therefore, reasonable to start adjustments by putting in place two further "pillars" from Western welfare states (Esping-Andersen and Micklewright 1991: 35): labour market measures (unemployment support and "active labour market policies") and social assistance.

As overt unemployment appeared and started its upward course, Central and South-eastern European countries reacted by introducing strikingly generous compensation regimes and a wide array of active labour market policies from scratch (apart from Yugoslavia). Typically, early cash compensation imitated social insurance-type systems with earnings-related benefits: they accepted former employment, even if short, as a contribution record. (Financing mostly came from general tax revenues, and later from payroll taxes.) Poland started the transition with an open-ended unemployment benefit system in 1989, and virtually anyone who did not have a job could register and claim benefit; this triggered a rise in labour force participation (Gora 1994: 205; Gora *et al.* 1996: 152). In Hungary the 1991 Act on "Employment Promotion and Provision for the Unemployed" offered a 70 per cent wage replacement rate for a year, and 50 per cent for a second year; moreover, anyone who had been receiving compensation since the introduction of the first scheme in 1988 could enrol into the new system (Fajth and Lakatos 1994: 170–5). From mid-1992 Bulgaria introduced a one-year regime securing 60 per cent of the previous wage (Bobeva 1994: 92).

As market reforms and the collapse of the Eastern European trade system (COMECON) wiped out much of the industrial capacity built under the planned system these new regimes underwent a hard test: while in 1990 there were 1.4 million people registered as unemployed in Poland, Czechoslovakia, Hungary, Romania, Bulgaria and Albania, in 1993 there were 6.1 million (UNICEF 1999b). As a consequence expenditure has risen rapidly. Significant amounts were spent on active labour market policies as well; the aggregate labour policy expenditure approached 3 per cent of GDP in Poland and Hungary (Boeri 1996: 58). This did not include the costs of early pension schemes which were widely used as a labour market tool to reduce unemployment rates among those aged over 50, contributing to rises in the number of pensioners and pension expenditures. In most countries of the former USSR, GDP fell by 50 to 70 per cent, making it impossible politically and practically that layoffs (and not real wage losses) could absorb the bulk of the impact as they had in Central Europe (UNICEF 1999: 5–7).

Third, there was and has remained much controversy about what role social security should have in the middle and longer term in these emerging market economies. As Esping-Andersen and Micklewright warned, per capita GDP in the Eastern European countries (including the USSR) in 1990 was estimated to be little more than a quarter of that in developed market economies, with agriculture securing as much as 12 to 30 per cent of the jobs (Esping-Andersen and Micklewright 1994: 36).

The large falls in economic output after 1990 highlighted the vulnerability of these economies once barriers to free trade and international competition were removed: using GDP in purchasing power parities as a development measure, the full transition region appeared amongst the developing countries. In 1997, for example, the per capita GDP of Slovenia, which had the highest income expressed in comparable prices in the region, was similar to that of Argentina or Barbados (but lower than that of Chile); Russia, which was in the middle range among the transition countries had less per capita income than Brazil or Turkey (but still more than Paraguay or Bolivia, UNDP 1999: 134–6).

By coining the term "prematurely-born" welfare states, János Kornai has suggested a strong link between per capita social expenditures and per capita GDP (or labour productivity) that no country could break without risking longer-term development (Kornai 1992). Nicholas Barr, on the other hand, claimed that "the state in Central and Eastern Europe has a continuing and substantial role to play in cash benefits, as it does in the highly industrialized countries", in the semi-official World Bank book on labour market and social policy strategies in the region (Barr 1994: 193). However, Bank officials shared serious concerns about the affordability of the existing benefit systems; and Barr himself noted that "under the current fiscal crisis poverty relief should be given priority over the other aims of cash benefits such as insurance and income smoothing [over the lifecycle]" (ibid.). Barr's remark makes an implicit reference to pensions, universal family allowances (and perhaps to generous unemployment benefits, maternity and childcare-related leave) highlighting some areas for predictable cuts. It is clear that the neo-liberal, "residual" welfare state is emerging as an appealing model from these arguments; although authors may have different views on why and how drastically the social security system should move in that direction.

Arguments for dismantling or downsizing social programmes received ammunition from the growing fiscal crisis (also referred to in Barr's comment) and from the need to improve the savings–consumption ratio for financing investments needed for economic recovery. The tax reform centred on shifting from profit to personal income and consumption taxes, and improving tax collection (a persistent problem mainly in the CIS, see EBRD 1998). As regards social security, initially the separate funding of expenditures was set as a goal; however, that did little to improve financial stability. Contributions built on wage costs suffered from shrinking employment, growing self-employment and employers' efforts to avoid paying high social security contributions. In Hungary, for example, the number of social security beneficiaries increased or stayed flat while employment declined between 1989 and 1997 by as much as 30 per cent and a further third of the workforce found jobs in the small-enterprise sector (UNICEF 1999a: 7).

None the less, on the other side of the coin, social security and other wide-scale public transfers contributed greatly to the overall development of these countries; this gave them a comparative advantage, over countries at a similar level of economic development, on social indicators for women and children. A study carried out recently (UNICEF 1999a) found that by the mid-1990s the post-communist countries still enjoyed a comparative edge in the international field when the so-called human capabilities-based indicators (such as life expectancy and educational attainment) were looked at rather than their GDP; the best result came when the so-called "gender-related development index" (GDI) or child-health related indicators formed the basis of the countries' ranking in the international arena. Ranking by per capita GDP Hungary or Poland had a position similar to that of Chile or Argentina, but shifting to the GDI (which also considers inequality between genders) the transition countries overtook their Latin American counterparts. By this measure the best-performing post-communist Slovenia or Czech Republic (despite their flagging economic output) have approached the levels of the weaker-performing EU nations, such as Portugal or Greece. However, the study concluded that, nevertheless, in the mid-1990s the transition countries are faring worse than in 1990 (UNICEF 1999a).

Arguments for strengthening social programmes and developing a new infrastructure of family support received attention because of the increasing evidence of breakdown in social cohesion, rises in social exclusion, adult male mortality, violence, and child abandonment (UNICEF 1994, 1995, 1997, 1998). In Russia between 1989 and 1995, 1.5 million people died because of rises in mortality; in Estonia after 1994 the number of divorces exceeded that of marriages; in Latvia the number of children aged 0–3 declined by 50 per cent between 1989 and 1997; and in 10 out of 14 countries on which data were available the rate of young children left in children's homes has grown, often substantially (Cornia 1998; Harwin and Fajth 1997; UNICEF 1999a).

Changes in Old Age Pension Systems and Benefits

During the transition years most social transfers underwent massive changes; however, the inherited pension system has remained basically intact despite the fact that its comprehensive reform has been on the agenda in most countries since the beginning of the transition. Inflation hikes focused most attention on the indexation of existing entitlements; decisions about major adjustments in the pay-as-you-go public insurance systems, or a radical shift from these to mandatory or voluntary pension savings regimes that are privately managed (and offer annuities based on individual contribution records) were regularly postponed. However, some countries have allowed voluntary private pension schemes to exist and recent years have seen more fundamental reforms.

One main advantage of the social insurance system noted in the literature is that benefits are defined, so individuals know with a fair degree of certainty what replacement income they will receive at the moment of retirement (Gillion 1997: 34). For policy-makers and for those already receiving a pension, however, the pay-as-you-go system has another important feature: that it raises no technical problems in adjusting current benefit payments, for example to link them to changes in the living standards of the active population. This feature, normally regarded as an advantage (1997: 35), could, however, become a major disadvantage under unstable economic and political conditions. For example, it entails no insulation from short-term economic problems, and offers little transparency or guarantee that could protect the system from day-to-day political considerations or even corruption.

There is evidence that the pay-as-you-go state pension systems in the transition countries have been highly vulnerable to the impact of the economic crisis and to political influence. In the Czech Republic, between 1990 and 1996, pensions were raised eight times; and not just the actual size but also the way of adjustment was different in each case. Solutions have shown swings between adjustments with a fixed amount (strengthening solidarity with those with low benefits), and linear adjustment (respecting "acquired rights" better). In many countries, however, a maximum cap has been used for adjustments, and pensions established earlier often received a better treatment with the goal of poverty alleviation.

Hungary introduced wage-based indexation in 1992 (when real wages were falling sharply) and changed this system to a gradually introduced wage-and-price related indexation from 1997, when real wages started to rise (Simonovits 1998: 697). The considerable amount of redistribution in the system is indicated by the low level of inequality in "old" pensions in comparison to wages and new pensions: in 1994 the so-called decile ratio (those belonging to the 90 and 10 per cent) was 2.8 for the earnings used for setting the new benefits; then this was immediately reduced to 2.5 as new pensions were set and this compares to the ratio of 1.8 in the full stock (1998: 693).

Benefits have lost a considerable part of their real value in all countries (reduced, in several, to a small portion of the value in 1989) and pensioners have had every reason to be disappointed in presumed state guarantees regarding their old-age income. Still, the new democratic political system that most countries managed to create and maintain despite economic difficulties has brought important results to pensioners in economic terms. Observers have noted that under the new political conditions pensioners have excelled in using their voting power to influence decisions regarding social security, and have often achieved preferential treatment in comparison to other population groups.

Commander found, for example, that in Russia the real income of pensioner households improved by 6 per cent while that of families with three and more children deteriorated by 34 per cent between mid-1992 and late 1996 (Commander 1998). Average pension and wage data suggest that on a 1990 or 1991 basis the same calculation would have resulted in a big decline in real income for both groups; but the relative advantage of pensioners would still be true. The ratio of average pensions to wages has risen also in Poland, Slovenia and Lithuania, but in many other countries including Romania, Bulgaria and Azerbaijan pensions have fared worse than wages (UNICEF 1997: 142).

A further noted advantage of social insurance systems is that they can help to enhance the benefits of the less well-off, by crediting periods off work due to unemployment, sickness and maternity, or by establishing a regressive benefit formula or a minimum pension. As the Czech example has illustrated, those with low pensions often benefited in relative terms; while in some countries, such as Azerbaijan, differentiation became meaningless because of very low purchasing power anyway or, as in Armenia, benefit values converged towards a uniformly low value (about a quarter of the average wage, which also collapsed in real terms) (UNICEF 1997). The latter arrangement follows the recommendation of the World Bank, which suggested that the transition countries should shift to flat-rate pensions in their social insurance system, to focus on poverty alleviation (World Bank 1994). In most countries, however, separate means-tested and parsimonious social assistance programmes were introduced that operate outside the pension system and involve the discretion of local-level public administration.

Despite its achievements, the state social insurance system has lost credibility among most of its customers: the system could not protect people with low pensions from poverty, while those with higher benefits could feel their entitlements, accumulated through a life's work, becoming devalued. In the light of higher poverty rates among families with many children, Commander argued that the Russian pension system actually redistributes from the poor to the rich (Commander 1998). Exposure to politically motivated adjustments embarrassed those with a social-rights approach (as the pay-as-you-go system confirmed patriarchal images of state power), while those agreeing with classic insurance principles saw little evidence that "you pay for what you get". A survey in Hungary found that only 20 per cent of the people supported "the pension system as it is" in 1996 (Csontos *et al.* 1998). Young people saw the entitlements of their parents collapse in real terms; people getting older saw no certainty about the replacement income they would receive at retirement. Middle- and high-wage earners saw little incentive for participation, while low-wage earners increasingly missed social security when working in the informal sector. (The size of this sector has been estimated as from 7 to 60 per cent of countries' GDP across the region, see Johnson *et al.* 1997.)

The comprehensive reforms initiated in recent years in most transition countries centre around the idea of adopting a Chilean-type pension system. This has been at the core of the reform proposals in Hungary, Poland, Slovenia and Russia; some countries, however, like the Czech Republic decided on the German-type pay-as-you-go model. Latvia opted for a US-type social security system by mixing public redistribution with individual contribution records ("accounts"); Slovakia introduced a complementary pension scheme on a voluntary basis (Council of Europe 1999).

While the new and reformed regimes reflect a variety of solutions, they tend to employ higher retirement ages, strengthen the insurance and weaken the solidarity features of the pension system. Most often, 62 years is proposed for both genders implying a 2-year rise for men and 7 for women, who will lose their considerable advantage under the old system; Latvia raised only women's pension age to be implemented gradually between 1996 and 2004 (Council of Europe 1999).

The Chilean model replaces the government pay-as-you-go system by a mandatory retirement savings programme managed by highly regulated private institutions and a mechanism that converts the fund accumulated in an individual savings account into indexed annuities upon retirement (Cortezar 1997: 123). The system offers more predictable costs, a high degree of transparency and better incentives. Moreover, it could help to strengthen the financial market (and even civil society—in Chile, for example, trade unions also run such funds). However, critics claim that benefits are unpredictable because of investment risk and because variables affecting annuity rates (such as individual life expectancy and the current interest rate) are difficult to forecast. Administrative costs absorb a significant share of contributions (in Chile 30 per cent) in contrast to pay-as-you-go systems (which run with 3 per cent cost in the transition countries). Moreover, there is no risk-pooling and solidarity (there is no redistribution to those with lower earnings or shorter contributions) (Gillion 1997: 35; Simonovits 1998: 703). Finally, state redistribution is not fully excluded: the state offers guarantees in any case of insolvency of private pension funds, and secures a minimum pension to the needy (Cortezar 1997: 128).

Many of the features of the Chilean pension system—that it adapts automatically to change through market forces and not through the political process, that redistribution is more difficult and transparent, or that it assigns a crucial role to the private sector and civil society—are certainly appealing to Eastern Europeans who have been traumatized by seeing what happened to their former "insurance". Still, even those countries that introduced mandatory retirement savings schemes have maintained a long-term, albeit reduced, role also for the public social insurance system.

Hungary, for example, introduced a three-tier system in effect from 1998, where the first (and biggest) tier is a reformed social insurance system, the second is a new mandatory private savings scheme (that broadly follows the Chilean model), and the third, and by far the smallest, tier is the voluntary private old age insurance (available since 1992). Although the change is towards "privatization" of old age security, the role of the state remains important; for example, considerable tax relief supports the private schemes. In the reformed social insurance, minimum pensions are replaced by a means-tested old age benefit and each service year will have the same weight, unlike the old system where those with shorter work records had relatively higher benefit. For those who start work after 1998 it is compulsory to participate in the first two tiers; those who have participated in the old system can decide whether they want to shift (a part) of their contribution to the second tier, although planners have built in only moderate incentives to do so because of fears of destabilizing the first tier. The Russian system, which was due to start in 1998 but which is still under discussion by the State Duma, is similar in its main thrust in shifting away from social insurance to a mixed system (Baskakova 1999).

While many things are similar in the position of the transition countries and Chile (or other countries in Latin America that introduced similar reforms), including a fiscal crisis that was relieved with help from international organizations (1981 in Chile), there are also many differences. First, in Chile (unlike in the transition countries) not all employees were covered pre-reform, and coverage—despite compulsory participation—has remained around 60 per cent as the new system has been building up (Cortezar 1997: 124). This fact undermines hopes that the new system could eliminate growing exclusion in the transition countries; rather, by weakening the solidarity character of the full system, exclusion will increase. Young people appear to be at particular risk: studies in Hungary and Russia have shown that this group pays hardly any attention to their entitlements (Csontos *et al.* 1998), and has particularly low awareness about the features of the new pension systems (Baskakova 1999).

Second, female labour force participation is much lower in Latin America than in Central and Eastern Europe (including Russia) where despite declines since 1989 it is nearer the pattern of Germany or Sweden (UNICEF 1999a). In Chile fertility, although declining, is still considerably above the population replacement rate. In Hungary, Bulgaria or Belarus pre-transition fertility was already below the population replacement threshold (2.2 children per woman). Since 1989 the full transition region has posted plunging fertility; now even Azerbaijan is below the replacement rate (UNICEF 1999a: 46). In Central Europe the total fertility rate now is getting close to that which forecasts the halving of the population from one generation to the next. These statistics suggest that policies should avoid any reduction in incentives for women to work *and* to have children.

Many of the new features of the reformed systems are gender-blind and act against women in their multiple roles as workers, mothers and caregivers (often even as wives and grandmothers). Baskakova, for example, estimated that the exclusion of the period of maternity and parental leaves could reduce women's retirement savings by 7 to 11 per cent for one child and 14 to 21 per cent for two children in Russia (Baskakova 1999). Even in Latvia, where such periods will be credited by the state (Council of Europe 1999), the use of the minimum wage as the basis for the state's contribution entails lower entitlements. Moreover, the new systems extend women's pay gap—which is according to UNICEF about 10 to 30 per cent in the region and is little related to job and human capital differences—also into old age (UNICEF 1999a: 33–6). For women who divorce after a long marriage the old-age pension earned will not be shared between the spouses, unlike all other property acquired during the years of marriage (Baskakova 1999). Individual women will be penalized when they purchase a life annuity from their accumulated fund, as insurance companies will consider women's better average life expectancy.

The main aims of the new pension regimes—such as solvency of public funds, greater transparency, building capital and insurance markets, strengthening individual responsibility and the civil society—should be respected. However, it does not need a demagogue to conclude that there is a risk that the considerably higher operational costs of the new system will be financed from savings made by curtailing the current entitlements of those—sick, widows and orphans—for whom social insurance was originally invented. Protecting these particular groups and ensuring that women do not bear—unequal—new burdens is important also for the long-term sustainability of the old-age income security systems.

It is important to stress that gender-related problems are not confined to the new tiers of the pension system, but appear also in the reformed pay-as-you-go systems as well—without adding the marked advantages of the private solutions. Finally, the implications of the ongoing changes are rarely discussed along the dimensions of family solidarity, intergenerational ties and early childhood development. UNICEF found that early childbearing is a particular feature of these countries: the first child is born at the age of 22 for women on average, about five years earlier than in Western countries (UNICEF 1999a). With a 5–9 year rise in women's retirement age, grandmothers will have less time to care for and play with their children's children—a significant loss for early childhood development in these ageing societies where the primary caregiver parents are often engaged in multiple jobs and grandfathers are scarce because of high mortality rates.

Recent Changes in Other Social Programmes

As the above discussion has illustrated, old-age income security and other social programmes influence each other; a change in one may affect another and transformations in the demographic, work or political environment may impact on all of them. During the transition period these changes have been considerable and interactions have been strong. It is necessary, therefore, to look at the main thrust of adjustments in other public transfer programmes before concluding with the relationship between the transition and social security.

Unemployment compensation

The systems that were created to buffer the impact of the sharp fall in employment following market reforms (mainly in Central and South-eastern Europe) have gradually been curtailed. The maximum duration of insurance benefits was cut in Czechoslovakia to 6 months, and Poland added a 12 months' cap in 1992 when moving to a flat-rate benefit regime (Scarpetta and Reutersward 1994). Hungary did not index benefits (Micklewright and Nagy 1997) and cut the benefit period to 18, then to 12, then (from 1999) to 6 months. Registered unemployment peaked first around 1992 and over 1996–7 it rose again; with the exception of the Czech Republic and Romania it had two digits across Central and South-eastern Europe in 1997. Benefits tend to redistribute towards the low-wage groups, who are also overrepresented among the unemployed. This redistribution is clear also in OECD countries (Scarpetta and Reutersward 1994). In Central and Eastern Europe it is underlined by the fact that more and more unemployed people are drifting towards the social assistance component of the unemployment compensation system and/or are compelled to turn to means-tested benefits or participate in workfare (Boeri 1996: 46; Council of Europe 1999). However, there is also evidence that the share of those who are unemployed and do not receive any benefit is on the rise (Micklewright and Nagy 1996: 127). As Scarpetta and Reutersward have noted, possibilities to redistribute in favour of the unemployed with dependants, either through an increase in replacement rates or through fixed additional payments, are missing from Eastern European systems, although these are frequent in OECD countries (Scarpetta and Reutersward 1994).

Unemployment compensation remained parsimonious in Russia and other CIS countries, where the number of registered unemployed tends to represent only a small fraction of those who are out of work and looking for a job. Not infrequently, employers are still the main providers of welfare services and benefits; as Manning concludes, in Russia the old and the new systems co-exist in the more dynamic urban and the slowly moving rural areas (Manning 1998).

Disability benefits and sick pay

The worsening of adult mortality in many countries makes it probable that the incidence of disability and sickness grew in the region with soaring poverty and poor or even deteriorating lifestyles (including inadequate nutrition, smoking, alcohol and drug abuse, and exposure to sexually transmitted diseases). Moreover, it also could have been expected that people will increasingly declare themselves sick—or bribe doctors to be declared sick—in order to have access to disability and sickness transfers (including in-kind benefits) as part of their strategies to cope with poverty and unemployment. Often the state made it easier to have access to disability pensions so as to reduce the size of the labour force. However, not all types of benefits show greater uptake rates; in particular sick-pay declined partly because of less employment but also because employers became keenly interested in reducing the uptake rates of sick-pay as many countries shifted costs almost fully to employers (Rein and Friedman 1997).

In the Czech Republic, for example, the number of newly awarded disability pensions peaked in 1993 and the new pension law of 1996 made partial disability pensions more appealing; in fact these were swollen by sharply worsening employment prospects from 1997 (Council of Europe 1999). In 1994, 41 per cent more disabled children were newly registered than in 1990 (UNICEF 1997: 47). In Russia there were four children registered with disabilities out of a thousand in 1990; five years later there were more than three times as many. In Poland the number of children under 5 years old hospitalized for general health reasons has increased between 1989 and 1994 by 30 per cent. On the other hand, during the same period the use of sick leave for childcare almost halved (UNICEF 1997).

Child-related benefits and social assistance

One important outcome of the transition-related early adjustments in social security was that family allowances generally became universal in the region. For example, in Russia and other Former Soviet Union states, the price compensation benefits introduced around 1991–3 represented the first time in those countries that most families with children were awarded cash benefits as a matter of right. However, in more recent times these entitlements have mostly been withdrawn or transformed into a means-tested benefit (UNICEF 1997, 1999a). Maternity and parental leave was similarly strengthened around 1990 in the light of the privatization of state-owned enterprises that had provided most pre-school care; moreover, these measures were also seen as useful as the economic crises had reduced the need for high female labour-force participation rates (Fajth 1994). Shrinking female employment rates and other factors reduced the uptake of maternity leave and benefits while some countries, like Hungary, have restricted parental leave to low-income families, and others such as Armenia or Georgia have dropped leave programmes entirely. However, the system of maternity and parental leave as introduced around 1990–1 was basically maintained in the majority of countries (UNICEF 1999a: 55–7).

Although many countries, from the Czech Republic to Bulgaria, from Lithuania to Albania, have introduced a social assistance programme separate from unemployment or child-rearing, these remained mostly of marginal importance even for the poor. There is, however, an increasing synergy between poverty, work and child-related programmes: unemployment and child-related programmes are transferred into systems that aim at poverty alleviation rather than income-smoothing over the life cycle, correcting for the family wage or for gender discrimination. Moreover, as countries reform their revenue systems, personal income taxes are generally becoming more important than in the past. A review provided by UNICEF concluded that current income tax systems "are friendly to women's labour force participation and mostly offer concessions to families with children. However, it appears that concessions benefit mainly middle-income rather than low-income households and that the tax systems do little to help single parents" (UNICEF 1999a: 52).

Conclusions

The evidence reviewed allows some broad conclusions on the usefulness of having a comprehensive social security system in the case of countries undergoing deep economic crises and far-reaching political and institutional changes, with a range of problems that occur as these systems are being adapted to the new conditions. The existing social security network—even though not fully tailored to a market economy—has played an effective role in buffering the welfare impact of losses in output and sudden impoverishment of full countries. This experience is important especially in light of the vulnerability of many countries to the economic and institutional change associated with the emergence of a global economy (UNDP 1999) and efforts of international organizations to alleviate the human costs of such rapid, still not necessarily short-term, transformations (Deacon 1998).

Countries in the region did not start the transition from similar human development levels (UNICEF 1999a) and the chapter highlighted the fact that countries do not necessarily follow the same paths when reforming their institutional arrangements; even within the same country different welfare regimes co-exist. Nevertheless, there are some general trends: albeit to a varying degree, most countries appear to be moving away from collective to individualized solutions as they are re-emerging from the crisis and new institutions are consolidated. This main thrust of the reform is fully justified in the economic field but is less generally applicable to the social field, where concessions (or using the language of the rights-based literature, "special measures") are necessary to counter discrimination, disadvantage and investment potential in human capital, prevented by market failure from being fully explored and utilized.

In this respect there is good reason for taking care that, when moving away from "over-employing" the principle of solidarity and making complex systems more simple and transparent, the interests of some important parts of the population (who, for one reason or another fail to form a powerful interest group) are not overlooked. From the social security perspective it is the middle-aged male breadwinner who now appears as the ultimate winner of the transition, while women, children and young people systematically show up among the losers. The evidence reviewed in the chapter suggests that a more comprehensive approach to social security might help to correct such a trend by making the cumulative social and long-term economic implications of system reforms clearer for all—an important precondition to reforms that claim transparency and sustainability in the long term.

Acknowledgement

I am indebted to Nick Manning for his comments on the draft chapter. Any remaining errors are mine.

Parts of the chapter draw on information collected through the "MONEE project" at UNICEF International Child Development Centre (ICDC), which is concerned with monitoring social conditions and public policy in the transition countries. (Further details of the project and its public-use database "TransMONEE" are availavble from the ICDC home page at www.unicef-icdc.org.)

References

Ahmad, E. (1992), Poverty, inequality and public policy in transition economies, *Public Finances/Finances Publiques*, 47: 94–106.

Atkinson, A. B., and Micklewright, J. (1992), *Economic Transformation in Eastern Europe and the Distribution of Income*, Cambridge: Cambridge University Press.

Barr, N. (1994), Income transfers: social insurance. In Barr, N. (ed.), *Labor Markets and Social Policy in Central and Eastern Europe: The Transition and Beyond*. Washington: World Bank.

Barr, N., and Harbison, R. W. (1994), Overview: hopes, tears, and transformation. In Barr, N. (ed.), *Labor Markets and Social Policy in Central and Eastern Europe: The Transition and Beyond*, Washington: World Bank.

Baskakova, M. (1999), Gender Aspects of Pension Reform in Russia. Paper presented at the Conference "Making the Transition Work for Women in Europe and Central Asia", World Bank, Washington 7–9 June.

Bobeva, D. (1994), Labour market policy in Bulgaria. In OECD, *Unemployment in Transition Countries: Transient or Persistent?*, Paris: OECD CCET: 92.

Boeri, T. (1996), Unemployment outflows and the scope of labour market policies in Central and Eastern Europe. In OECD, *Lessons from Labour Market Policies in the Transition Countries*, Paris: OECD CCET.

Bradbury, B., and Jäntti, M. (1999), *Child Poverty across Industrialized Nations*, Innocenti

Occasional Papers, Economic and Social Policy Series, no. 71, Florence: UNICEF International Child Development Centre (forthcoming).

Bruinooge, G., Grubben, B., Éltetö, Ö., and Fajth, G. (1990), Income distribution in an international perspective: the case of Hungary and the Netherlands, *UN Statistical Journal*, 7.

Commander, S., and Jackman, R. (1997), Firms and government in the provision of benefits in Russia. In Rein, M., Friedman, B.L., and Worgotter, A. (eds), *Enterprise and Social Benefits After Communism*, Cambridge: Cambridge University Press.

Commander, S., and Lee, U. (1998), How does public policy affect the income distribution?: evidence from Russia, 1992–1996. London: European Bank for Reconstruction and Development and World Bank. Mimeo (12 August).

Cornia, G.A. (1995), *Ugly Facts and Fancy Theories: Children and Youth during the Transition*, Innocenti Occasional Papers, Economic and Social Policy Series, no. 47, Florence: UNICEF International Child Development Centre.

Cornia, G. A. (1998), Labour Market Shocks, Psychosocial Stress and the Transition's Mortality Crisis. Paper presented at the "Arena Meeting I", Verona Initiative, Verona, 14–17 October, sponsored by Regional Office for Europe, World Health Organization, Copenhagen.

Cornia, G. A., and Stewart, F. (1993), *Two Errors of Targeting*, Innocenti Occasional Papers, Economic and Social Policy Series, no. 36, Florence: UNICEF International Child Development Centre.

Cortezar, R. (1997), The new Chilean pension system: lessons after 15 years. In United Nations, Department for Economic and Social Information and Policy Analysis, *Sustaining Social Security*, New York: United Nations.

Council of Europe (1999), *Social Security Systems and their Operation in a Difficult Economic Context: A Social Security Resource Book*, Committee on Social Security Systems and their Operation in a Difficult Economic Context (D-CED), Strasbourg: Council of Europe.

Csontos, L., Kornai, J., and Tóth, I. Gy. (1998), Tax awareness and reform of the welfare state: Hungarian survey results, *Economics of Transition*, 6, 2: 287–312.

Deacon, B. (1998), *Globalization and Social Policy*, London: Sage.

EBRD (1998), *Transition Report 1998: Financial Sector in Transition*, London: European Bank for Reconstruction and Development.

Esping-Andersen, G., and Micklewright, J. (1991), Welfare state models in OECD countries: an analysis for the debate in Central and Eastern Europe. In Cornia, G. A., and Sipos, S. (eds), *Children and the Transition to the Market Economy: Safety Nets and Social Policies in Central and Eastern Europe*, Aldershot: Avebury.

Fajth, G. (1994), *Family Support Policies in Transitional Economies: Challenges and Constraints*, Innocenti Occasional Papers, Economic and Social Policy Series, no. 43, Florence: UNICEF International Child Development Centre.

Fajth, G. (1996), Family Support Policies in Central and Eastern Europe. Paper presented at the workshop "Economic Transformation, Institutional Change and Social Sector Reform", Task Force on Economies in Transition, National Research Council, Washington DC, September.

Fajth, G. and Lakatos, J. (1994), Unemployment in Hungary. In OECD, *Unemployment in Transition Countries: Transient or Persistent?* Paris: OECD CCET: 170–5.

Ferge, Zs. (1991), Social security systems in the new democracies of Central and Eastern Europe: past legacies and possible futures. In Cornia, G. A., and Sipos, S. (eds), *Children and the Transition to the Market Economy: Safety Nets and Social Policies in Central and Eastern Europe*, Aldershot: Avebury.

Gillion, C. (1997), Issues in the reform of social security: a perspective from the International Labour Office. In United Nations, Department for Economic and

Social Information and Policy Analysis, *Sustaining Social Security*. New York: United Nations.

Gora, M. (1994), Labour market policies in Poland. In OECD, *Unemployment in Transition Countries: Transient or Persistent?*, Paris: OECD CCET: 205.

Gora, M., Lehman, H., Socha, M., and Sztanderska, U. (1996), Labour market policies in Poland. In OECD Proceedings, *Lessons from Labour Market Policies in the Transition Countries*, Paris: OECD CCET: 152.

Gordon, M. (1988), *Social Security Policies in Industrial Countries: A Comparative Analysis*, Cambridge: Cambridge University Press.

Harwin, J., and Fajth, G. (1997), Child poverty and social exclusion in post-communist societies, *IDS Bulletin*, 29, 1, January: 66–76.

Johnson, S., Kaufman, D. and Schleifer, A. (1997), *Politics and Entrepreneurship in Transition Economies*, Working Paper Series, no. 57. Ann Arbor MI: William Davidson Institute, University of Michigan.

Kopits, G. (1991), *Fiscal Reform in European Economies in Transition*, IMF Working Paper 91/43, Washington DC: International Monetary Fund.

Kornai, J. (1992), *The Socialist System: The Political Economy of Communism*, Princeton NJ: Princeton University Press.

KSH (1990), *A Természetbeni Társadalmi Jövedelmek És a Dotációk Rétegeloszlása 1989 (The Incidence of Subsidies and Incomes in Kind in 1989) ben*, Budapest: KSH (in Hungarian).

KSH (1991), *Magyar Statisztikai Évkönyv 1990 (Hungarian Statistical Yearbook 1990)*, Budapest: KSH (in Hungarian).

Kupa, M., and Fajth, G. (1990), *Incidence-Study 90: The Hungarian Social-Policy Systems and Distribution of Incomes of Households*, Budapest: Central Statistical Office and Ministry of Finance.

Manning, N. (1998), Social policy: labour markets, unemployment, and household strategies in Russia, *International Journal of Manpower*, 19, 1–2: 48–67.

Micklewright, J., and Nagy, G. (1996), Evaluating labour market policies in Hungary. In OECD, *Lessons from Labour Market Policies in the Transition Countries*, Paris: OECD CCET: 127.

Micklewright, J., and Nagy, G. (1997), *The Implication of Exhausting Unemployment Insurance Entitlement in Hungary*, Innocenti Occasional Papers, Economic and Social Policy Series, no. 58. Florence: UNICEF International Child Development Centre.

Noncheva, T. (1995), *The Winding Road to the Market: Transition and the Situation of Children in Bulgaria*, Innocenti Occasional Papers, Economic and Social Policy Series, no. 51. Florence: UNICEF International Child Development Centre.

OECD (1996), *Social Expenditure Statistics of OECD Member Countries*, Labour Market and Social Policy Occasional Papers no. 17, Paris: OECD.

Preker, A. S., and Feachem, G. A. (1994), Health and health care. In Barr, N. (ed.), *Labor Markets and Social Policy in Central and Eastern Europe: The Transition and Beyond*, Washington: World Bank.

Rein, M., and Friedman, B. L. (1997), in Rein, M., Friedman, B. L., and Wörgötter, A. (eds), *Enterprise and Social Benefits After Communism*, Cambridge: Cambridge University Press.

Scarpetta, S., and Reutersward, A. (1994), Unemployment benefit systems and active labour market policies in Central and Eastern Europe: an overview. In OECD, *Unemployment in Transition Countries: Transient or Persistent?*, Paris: OECD CCET.

Simonovits, A. (1998), Az új magyar nyugdíjrendszer és problémái (The new Hungarian pension system and its problems), *Közgazdasági Szemle*, XLV, évf: 689–708 (in Hungarian).

Sipos, S. (1992), *Poverty Measurement in Central and Eastern Europe before the Transition to the*

Market Economy, Innocenti Occasional Papers, Economic and Social Policy Series, no. 29, Florence: UNICEF International Child Development Centre.

Sipos, S. (1994), Income transfers: family support and poverty relief. In Barr, N. (ed.), *Labor Markets and Social Policy in Central and Eastern Europe: The Transition and Beyond*, Washington: World Bank.

Szalai, J. (1986), *Az egészségügy betegségei* (*The Diseases of the Health Care System*), Budapest: KJK (Közgazdasági és Jogi Könyvkiadó, Economics and Legal Publishing House) (in Hungarian).

UNDP (1999), *Human Development Report 1999*, New York: Oxford University Press: 134–6.

UNICEF (1994), *Crisis in Mortality, Health and Nutrition*, Regional Monitoring Report, no. 2, Florence: UNICEF International Child Development Centre.

UNICEF (1995), *Poverty, Children and Policy: Responses for a Brighter Future*, Regional Monitoring Report, no. 3, Florence: UNICEF International Child Development Centre.

UNICEF (1997), *Children at Risk in Central and Eastern Europe: Perils and Promises*, Regional Monitoring Report, no. 4, Florence: UNICEF International Child Development Centre.

UNICEF (1998), *Education for All?*, Regional Monitoring Report, no. 5, Florence: UNICEF International Child Development Centre.

UNICEF (1999a), *Women in Transition*, Regional Monitoring Report, no. 6, Florence: UNICEF International Child Development Centre.

UNICEF (1999b), *TransMONEE Database*, Florence: UNICEF International Child Development Centre (www:\\unicef-icdc.org).

World Bank (1993), *Poland: Income Support and the Social Safety Net during the Transition*, Washington DC: World Bank.

World Bank (1994), *Averting the Old-Age Crisis*, New York: Oxford University Press.

World Bank (1996), *From Plan to Market, World Development Report 1996*, New York: Oxford University Press.

6

Employment, Industrial Relations and Social Policy: New Life in an Old Connection

Colin Crouch

In most Western European societies the equivalent term for "social policy" refers to both the welfare state and industrial relations, a usage that sounds strange to British ears. This is so much so that, in order to make the distinction, the English word "welfare" is used in French and Italian discussion to denote the specific part of social policy that has to do with pensions, social security, various social assistance programmes, and sometimes health services too.[1] Historically, both institutionalized industrial relations and the provision of various social benefits were seen as a response to the predicament of the growing new industrial working class, protected from the insecurities of the capitalist labour market by neither the wealth of the bourgeoisie and aristocracy nor the institutions of family, church, community and *noblesse oblige* that were thought, rightly or wrongly, to provide some protection to rural populations.

This is not just a matter of concepts and ways of thinking, but of hard policy too. Trade unions are usually involved in the administration of national systems of pensions and social insurance, which are in turn closely related to status as an employee, often as an employee in a specific occupation or economic branch. British exceptionalism here is something that developed over the years. British unions originally doubled as industrial relations actors and as the organizers of rudimentary providers of contributory, occupation-related social insurance schemes. When government began to establish a state system, in the National Insurance Act 1911, trade union and other voluntary schemes were given a role alongside the new state provision, and unions could participate in the administration and distribution of benefits even if they had not previously organized their own voluntary scheme. Had this been maintained, this aspect of the British welfare state, like several others, would have resembled those of Scandinavia.

However, the unions' own schemes took a severe beating as they tried to cope with the extraordinary increase in unemployment of the late 1920s. Gradually the unions reached the conclusion that this was not an area where they wanted to be directly involved. They continued to lobby for the strengthening of welfare benefits and took up policy stances on issues like the means test, but by the time of the major advance in British welfare policy thinking in the mid-1940s, they had decided to shed their involvement in administration in favour of a pure state-run scheme (Finlayson 1994: 264–70).

This proved very useful in the construction of the particular British form of the postwar compromise and welfare state enlargement. Lazy thoughtways led to anything specifically British within the European context being dubbed "liberal", with reference to both the nineteenth-century legacy of English liberalism and the increasing tendency of the British during the 1980s and 1990s to remodel their institutions on a version of US economic liberalism. Not only is the latter rather anachronistic for an account of the 1940s, but it omits a fundamental compromise, or more accurately a convergence, between two forces in the Britain of that time. One of these was social democracy, or socialism. Following the experience of how the country had been organized during the Second World War, this was full of a new confidence in the planning and steering capacities of the central state. The other was the "mandarin" tradition of the civil service: elitist, always self-confident, imbued with a genuine concept of public service, and reinforced in its sense of the capacity of the central state by both the war and the colonial experience, especially the government of India. In the wake of the war these two forces, coming though they did from very different, often opposed, classes within society, had much in common: a belief in the capacity of the state to do public good, but also in its almost Jacobin lack of a need to consult with or embed itself within the wider population.

This latter might appear to be the price the Labour Party had to pay to win the former, but it must have seemed a cheap price at the time. The Labour Party was inclined to feel that it itself constituted the voice of the relevant part of the wider population and therefore required no wide consultation. ("Socialism is what the Labour Government does," as Herbert Morrison famously remarked.) And the unions had demonstrated clearly that they did not want to be involved in running the welfare state, just as they had renounced any ambitions for worker participation in managing either nationalized industries or private firms.

Meanwhile, in much of continental Western Europe unions had become firmly installed in the governing bodies of national or specific occupational social insurance and similar systems, with a particular moment of consolidation coming in the reconstruction years immediately following the Second World War. For many years after that the diverse national developments which had created these systems seemed to be of minimal interest outside those concerned with the minutiae of administrative arrangements. In Austria, Belgium, Germany, the Netherlands, and above all in Switzerland, union participation in running social insurance seemed all of a piece with the neo-corporatist and codeterminative models of the industrial relations system, but a very uninteresting part of it. These institutions were rarely if ever engaged in any interesting issues of coordination or inflation-avoidance. They possibly just added some of the cement that held together a structure, the main business of which was steering collective bargaining outcomes and changes in working conditions. Things seemed more interesting in Scandinavia, where such participation seemed even more fully part of the tripartite character of the state.[2] Sometimes, especially in Sweden, these had important macro-economic effects, when government, advised by social partners, used to steer pension fund accumulations into industrial investment.

In France and Italy formal union involvement in the management of pension and social security schemes seemed totally at odds with the prevailing industrial relations context. This involvement had developed fitfully from the late nineteenth century onwards, and had been consolidated in the participatory consensus institutions with which those countries had equipped themselves in the solidaristic atmosphere of 1944–7. Then had followed the Cold War, the exclusion of the majority Communist wings of the labour movement from national respectability, and the marginalization of the weakly representative and internally divided non-Communist minority. Industrial relations became, as they had been in the 1920s and 1930s, a nonexistent arena, or one of uncompromising conflict, with codeterminative and tripartite institutions of the immediate postwar years being reduced to residual status. The continuation of union involvement in the management of social insurance schemes seemed just an aspect of the last of these alternatives, its very survival in such an otherwise hostile environment serving as a testimony to its lack of seriousness.

Today matters look very different. Given a widespread belief that welfare states, and especially their social insurance components, must be reformed, union participation in the reform process has become fundamental in all systems where unions and employer organizations have a formal role of the kind we are discussing. Unless governments are willing to risk the conflict that would ensue from expelling unions from social insurance management, they have to win union agreement jointly to make the reforms. As we shall see below, the Dutch and Italian cases show that this can be achieved. The French and German ones suggest that it can be very difficult (Ebbinghaus and Hassel 1999). From this flow a number of rather diverse consequences.

First, no matter how weak they might become in terms of the main indicators of union strength (membership, resources, engagement in collective bargaining), unions with this kind of institutionalized role in an arena high on the policy agenda at the present time cannot be easily marginalized or excluded from national respectability. This can be seen from a comparison between the UK and France. Unions in the former country retain a considerably higher membership and material resource base than their French colleagues, and they are engaged more effectively in serious collective bargaining. They have, however, been effectively excluded from serious participation in national events. Following the poor experiences of the 1970s, no major political party is interested in their cooperation in the management of wage inflation. During the 1980s Conservative governments either expelled union representatives from national consultative bodies or closed down the bodies themselves. The Labour government elected in May 1997 made important improvements in union workplace rights, but showed no inclination to treat them as serious participants in national economic or social policy. Although this exclusion can be partly explained by the specific policies of governments in the 1980s, the prior, earlier unnoticed, specificity of British unions' voluntary exclusion from administration of the welfare state has contributed further to their weakness in these years when elsewhere the national political role of unions is being intensified.

Although French unions now have barely 7 per cent of the private-sector workforce in membership, and only 12 per cent of the public sector, and though they are too divided among themselves to engage in any concerted action, successive governments seek to cultivate their participation in national policy-making. One reason is that the French unions retain an extraordinary capacity for social disruption irrespective of their formal strength. Another, however, is the government's realization that no reforms can be achieved in the welfare arena without their support and preferably their active cooperation.

From a governmental point of view, the British case demonstrates the advantages of the British elitist model of welfare state development, of not having to bother with consultation with groups in the population affected by a policy area: the British social insurance system has presented far fewer barriers to employment flexibility than those in most of the rest of Western Europe, and reform of the system is fairly easily achieved. This is a judgement which will not necessarily be shared by British workers and pensioners, but meanwhile the reform capacity of systems embodying greater employer rights has in fact varied quite considerably. A major purpose of this chapter is to explore what might be some of the conditions for this reform capacity, and therefore for the nexus between industrial relations and social policy, to move to the forefront of employment policy initiatives. First we must examine the background logic of various different arrangements in this arena.

Social Insurance and Forms of Citizenship

Original conceptions of an intrinsic link between industrial relations and social policy in nearly all countries, including the UK, included the concept of bipartite employment-based contributions to the social insurance funds from which unemployment benefit, sickness and accident benefit, and retirement pensions were paid. The insurance is against risks which might prevent a person from working and thus earning money; the contributions therefore constituted a setting aside (mutually by employer and employee) of part of the earnings that, notionally, would otherwise be paid, so that they could be enjoyed by the worker when facing any of these risks.[3] This conception has had a number of consequences.

Occupational versus universal citizenship

First, as a number of authors has pointed out (e.g. Daly 1996; Esping-Andersen 1996a; Lewis 1993), given the male breadwinner concept of the workforce embedded in late nineteenth- and early twentieth-century ideas of industrial work, social insurance developed as an essentially male system, with non-working women gaining only widows' rights. Ideas of family dependants (wife and children) were often built into benefit scales. Second, rights were tied to years of participation in the employed workforce. Those finding it difficult to join the workforce, or those spending periods as self-employed, often had access only to inferior systems of social assistance. Third, especially in countries with strongly developed systems of occupational training and therefore of occupational identity (e.g. Austria, Germany, Switzerland, to a lesser extent Denmark), the social insurance systems of different occupations were kept very separate from each other, with little or no cross-financing or general government subsidy. As a result levels of benefit varied sharply according to different occupations.

If welfare-state entitlements are a kind of citizenship right, these systems constituted citizenship based on participation in the workforce rather than as a generalized right based on adult status (as in the case of legal and political citizenship in the model famously developed by T. H. Marshall, 1963). This is citizenship as an exchange of rights and duties. There is nothing odd about this; the original Athenian concept that has inspired virtually all subsequent ideas of citizenship was based on the duty to bear arms. Its implications have been interesting, as it has led to general and occupational citizenship developing along different lines. Long after they had won the vote, married women were underprivileged in social insurance schemes. Since it was originally introduced to ease the social exclusions and deprivations of employee status, the self-employed also initially found themselves excluded. On the other hand, occupation-based rights have been of great assistance to foreign immigrants, who have often been able to acquire welfare citizenship before, or even in the face of exclusion from, political citizenship. This has been particularly prominent in Germany, where there has been a combination of high levels of immigration, strict political citizenship laws, and generous occupational welfare citizenship rights (Guiraudon 1998).[4]

Subsequent developments have been complex. On the one hand the rigid occupational derivation of rights was eroded in face of the demands of democratic citizenship. Increasingly generous systems of social assistance, extensions of women's rights, and other innovations all reduced the stark contrast between those with rights earned at work and those without them.

Some systems moved more fully towards political or universal citizenship rather than an occupational citizenship base for welfare-state entitlements, principally the Scandinavian countries and the UK. In all the Nordic countries, however, social partners, especially the unions, remained important in the management of the social insurance systems, so there was always scope for interlock between it and the industrial relations system, retaining an occupational and representative component within a universalist framework (Hippe and West Pedersen 1996; Øverbye 1996). There were then two developments which reinforced the occupational link. First, initially in Scandinavia in the 1950s and later and more weakly in the UK, an income-related component was added to the basic social insurance entitlement, so that some connection was retained between an individual's pay level in the workforce and that while retired or otherwise out of employment (Øverbye 1996; Kangas and Palme 1996). The departure from strict egalitarian principles involved in this was accepted by social democratic parties as the price for sustaining the loyalty of middle-income groups to the national public system. In theory, an occupation-based scheme implied the maintenance of occupational inequalities within social policy, while a universalist scheme implied redistribution and equality. In practice, government subsidy of the former introduced an element of redistribution while earnings-related benefits in the latter introduced inequality.

Work and welfare states: the double relationship

Second, the rapid development of the Scandinavian and to a lesser extent the British welfare states, not just as sets of transfer payments, but as providers of substantive services, produced a major expansion of predominantly female employment in delivering these services themselves (Hassel, forthcoming). This was then accompanied by a more general growth in female employment. *De facto*, therefore, systems which had been based on universalistic rather than occupational citizenship came to acquire the latter characteristics as the majority of adults, and not just of males, worked. Esping-Andersen (1996a; 1999) has demonstrated how the viability of the Scandinavian welfare states came to depend on this cyclical process of female employment generating both an enlarged taxation base and reduced dependency on transfer payments, which in turn increased the resources available to the welfare state for the development of substantive services, which in turn increased female employment, and so on . . .

Even more generally, the Scandinavian welfare states had both depended on, and been used for the generation of, a high level of labour-force participation by both men and women. Compared with virtually all other countries, Sweden in particular consistently spent a higher proportion of its budget on active rather than passive labour market policies. By active policies are denoted such measures as help with job search, assistance with geographical mobility, and occupational training, all designed to enable people to find work, at which point they cease to require state assistance because they have incomes of their own. Passive policies are those which provide unemployment benefit, disability pensions, early retirement and other transfer payments that keep people out of the workforce.

Under the pressure of rising unemployment, by the late 1980s this had ceased to be so clear. Active labour market policy sometimes became a means for keeping people out of the unemployment statistics, the schemes in which they were enrolled often not having much chance of leading to serious employment. At the same time the more passive policies of such countries as Italy, the Netherlands and France were making an equivalent response, retiring people from the labour force at lower ages and at lesser levels of disability or sickness than in the past.

The important point is that social policies developed primarily by labour-movement parties and trade unions in Scandinavia were as heavily linked to participation in employment as those of the Bismarckian tradition, albeit in different ways. It was certainly not part of their design to enable able-bodied men or women of working age to lead comfortable lives without working. While Scandinavian welfare rights were more rooted in universal than in occupational citizenship, this was the universal citizenship of a community which worked for its living, men and women alike. When the British Labour government of the late 1990s began to stress the role of welfare policy as a means of increasing people's capacity to work and to argue that participation in work was a citizenship duty, it was neither adopting neo-liberal arguments nor inventing a "third way" of social policy, but speaking from the heart of the social democratic social policy tradition.

Social insurance contributions and labour costs

A third aspect of the link between industrial relations and welfare policy which has today acquired a new and problematic importance is the role of employment-based contributions. Originally this was simply an obvious part of the logic of the insurance principle. While contributions and benefits remained small, there was little need to consider any implications for unit labour costs in the employer's contributions. In any case, in a true labour market, any rise in non-wage labour costs should lead to a reduction in wages, with a neutral net effect for unit labour costs. In fact, if one assumes that employers in this way pass on the costs of insurance schemes to employees, while employees themselves also make compulsory contributions, the economic functions of social insurance are to increase savings ratios, to impose prudence on workers, making them reduce their current consumption by putting aside contributions against income-reducing risks, and to help them organize mutual risk-sharing through the state insurance system. The only redistribution that takes place is from those in work to the unemployed, sick and old—often only within the particular occupational group. Vertical redistribution takes place only if the state subsidizes the schemes from general taxation levies, and then only if the taxation involved is progressive.

This labour-cost neutrality ceases to function if there are institutional mechanisms which sustain actual wage levels irrespective of social insurance contributions. These include: legal minimum wages based on current subsistence needs; collective agreements which similarly tie wage levels to some function of subsistence levels; or the knock-on effect of social security programmes which sustain the subsistence standards of the unemployed, and therefore raise the level of income required to induce people into employment. Some version of these mechanisms has existed in virtually all industrial societies since the late nineteenth or early twentieth centuries. However, in earlier decades the implications for employment were restricted by the fact that, except in the smallest nation states, most trade took place within a country, often protected by a framework of tariffs. A national system of employers' and employees' contributions therefore created a level playing field for inter-firm competition, which gave employers an incentive to support such schemes rather than develop company-level ones. Even then, the German government in the 1880s was sufficiently worried about the effect, on the export of German goods, of the lead the country had taken in developing compulsory social insurance with employers' contributions to try to persuade other national governments to imitate it.

Employment, Industrial Relations and Social Policy: New Life in an Old Connection

In the decades after the Second World War the size of employer and employee contributions grew steadily as the advanced welfare states that we know today developed; levels of benefit rose, not only proportionally with wages, but absolutely as newly prosperous populations generated higher expectations of the standard of living they could maintain during periods of absence from the workforce and in retirement, and as longevity also rose. At the same time industrial relations institutions placing a floor under, if not a ratchet on, actual wage costs also developed. These contributions therefore became an increasingly important cost component. Employers were unlikely to be able to offset increases in contributions with reductions in wages, while employees were likely to seek wage increases to offset increases in their own contributions. If, as was the case during these decades, real wages were rising anyway, there need be nothing so dramatic as a wage reduction, merely a smaller rise than might have been granted in the absence of social security payments. But the main factor preventing any crisis of contribution burdens in these years was something else.

These were years of male full employment and a growing labour shortage, while productivity levels in even the most efficient European economies still trailed behind those of the USA. By accident, employers' contributions to social insurance schemes came to serve a positive economic function. Employers had an incentive to economize on the use of labour, to install labour-saving technologies and working methods. European productivity rose; employment levels remained high because expansion continued to be so rapid. At the same time, and also as a consequence of the general labour shortage, the more prosperous countries attracted large numbers of immigrants. At least in the initial stages, immigrants come disproportionately from the population of working age. They contribute taxes to finance the welfare state, but make few demands on it. In Scandinavia and to a lesser extent the UK, the relationship between welfare state and female employment already discussed was also set in motion. Overall, the labour market, the welfare state, and economic efficiency were related to each other through a series of benign cycles.

The story of how various parts of this model came unstuck has been told several times (Esping-Andersen 1996b, 1999). In summary, the following problems developed. First, the capacity of the manufacturing sector to employ low-skilled workers peaked, partly because skill requirements were rising, partly because automation had replaced much unskilled labour, and partly because industries still needing such workers were tending to migrate to countries with very low labour costs. To a considerable extent the growth of social and community services, particularly but not solely within the welfare state, replaced manufacturing in this role, though the overall employing capacity of these services was more weighted to the upper end of the skill hierarchy. However, by the late 1980s growth in this sector too had peaked, especially in countries where it was primarily public employment. Low-skilled workers were coming increasingly to depend for employment opportunities on low-paying private services sectors (the distributive trades, food outlets of various kinds, and other personal services) (Hassel, forthcoming; Scharpf 1997). These low-productivity sectors could only grow if

107

their unit labour costs were low, but this was being prevented by the size of social insurance contributions. The incentives of the social security contributions systems to economize on labour were now having perverse welfare effects.

Initially the link between co-determinative social insurance systems and industrial relations now acquired a new usefulness. Union and employer representatives, who had in their industrial relations work seen a need for exit from the workforce by some low-productivity groups, were encouraged in their social insurance management roles to introduce early and disability retirement schemes (Hassel, forthcoming). However, in so doing they were storing up trouble for the future.

Meanwhile, in most countries declining birth rates, increased longevity, and a tendency to earlier retirement through special schemes and increasingly generous disability pensions were producing a sharp change in the balance between declining contribution-paying and growing benefit-receiving populations. In particular, it was very tempting to employers to get rid of redundant workers by offering them early retirement or a generous assessment of disability; the social insurance system could take over the cost of their subsistence. While in the long run this would only raise the costs of the scheme to employers themselves through higher contributions, for those getting in early on the idea there was a major gain in at least the short term as the generality of employers and employees would share the cost. However, these tendencies combined dangerously with a certain growing tax resistance among electorates and an amount of tax-regime shopping by firms.

The early retirement tendency had itself initially been benign and economically wise. In countries with rapidly expanding education systems it makes good economic sense to encourage a less well educated and notionally lower-productivity older workforce to retire and make way for a better educated younger generation. This seemed particularly important for countries with major problems of youth unemployment. However, this practice not only coincided with demographic and tax-resistance factors creating problems in the balance between contributions and benefits, but it often failed to have the expected effect on youth employment. Sometimes (as particularly, it seems, in France) employers developed a preference for older workers and did not expand employment in order to employ the young, despite a major expansion in educational achievements.

In Italy, where government policy in the 1980s encouraged retirement among some people in their forties or even younger,[5] there was also little effect on youth employment. This was partly because one of the main deficiencies in Italian employment is the great regional cleavage which leaves much of the south of the country outside the economic growth of the northern and central regions. In addition to the well-known problems of the *Mezzogiorno* which cause this, there is a particular absence of opportunities for women in the south, despite the fact that young southern women are, on average, better educated than either men in the south or both men and women in the rest of the country. The main reason is an absence in that region of the main employment source for women of all education levels: social and community services.

This is itself related to the problems of the distinctive form taken by the welfare state. In most of Western Europe apart from Scandinavia and the UK, the emphasis of social policy has been on transfer payments, as embodied in the social insurance systems which are here our main concern (Esping-Andersen 1990). As the costs of these grew, they tended to crowd out possibilities for spending on direct services (health, education, social services). In southern Europe this is further intensified by two factors. First, this general bias of welfare spending patterns is reinforced by and in turn reinforces strong traditional family patterns, which assign caring roles to female family members. Relatively little nursing care is provided in southern Europe. It is assumed that a mother, sister, wife or female cousin will look after the sick, whether by visiting them in hospital or caring for them at home. Second, the clientelism of local politics in the region means that local governments tend to use the resources at their disposal to make direct payments to individuals rather than to provide services. The net result of this bias against service provision is that fewer women find employment, which reduces the social insurance contributions they would make if they were working.

The benign role of contributory social insurance systems from the 1950s to the 1970s therefore become highly perverse by the 1980s. In principle, and technically, it is not difficult to see ways out of the impasse. Most obviously, employers' contributions to the funds could be redesigned in various ways to stop them giving disincentives to employ labour. The employment-based part of employers' contributions *stricto sensu* could be reduced to a small proportion of the total, and taxes levied on firms on the basis of turnover, profits, assets or some other variable to compensate for the deficiency. Far more than in the past the net worth or level of economic activity of a firm bears little relation to its number of employees. Particularly in manufacturing, very high value added can be achieved by a small workforce equipped with advanced technology. Basing firms' contributions to social insurance schemes on their numbers of employees, while entirely rational in the first instance and strictly speaking entirely just, is almost by definition shifting the burden more and more to the low-productivity sectors, precisely those which are vital to the provision of new employment but which are highly sensitive to labour costs (Hassel, forthcoming). More controversially and either alternatively or additionally, the balance of contributions can shift from the strict 50 : 50 basis usually embodied in policy to place a larger share on employees.

More controversially still, the trend to earlier retirement can be not only arrested—that is tending to happen in most countries now—but actually reversed. If we now live longer and stay healthier during that old age, it seems perverse that we should be leaving the labour force younger. These possibilities are limited by the fact that labour productivity arguments against an ageing workforce still apply in many, though by no means all, occupations. However, the growth of part-time work and its very gradual spread to men as well as women can be helpful here. It can also enable people to make a gradual adjustment to retirement, instead of the shock of one day suddenly ceasing to have life guided by the work rhythm of the past 40 years. The idea of elderly people staying on at work might seem inhumane, especially if, as is often the case with part-time work, they have to move to jobs of a lower status than that to which they have become accustomed. But that needs to be set against the inhumanity of sudden retirement. The balance of inhumanity of the two scenarios varies from situation to situation.

It is frequently objected that it is irrational to combat a shortage of job opportunities among those with low-productivity labour by an expansion in the supply of such labour. This is, however, only true if the social insurance system is employment-neutral. In most contemporary economies it is in contrast highly relevant (Hassel, forthcoming). Those in work both contribute to its cost and do not call on its benefits, reducing the overall burden that falls on employers and therefore enabling them to expand employment. In economies with employment-related welfare costs, employment can produce employment; the supply of labour can increase its own demand. These paradoxical effects can hold true even without considering any deregulation of the labour market.

The Governance of Social Insurance and Labour Market Reform

If reforming the perverse tendencies of the social insurance system is in principle possible, what are the political obstacles which prevent it from taking place rapidly everywhere? In the first instance the finger points to the involvement of social partners in management of the systems. If they are primarily concerned with protecting the interests of those within the system, they will not be concerned with expanding opportunities for those outside, and may even see such an expansion as threatening those for whom they are concerned. Surely, if the social partners are not involved, there is nothing to prevent governments—who in theory are responsible to insiders and outsiders alike—from reallocating costs and expenditures in order to produce the benign effects that it is possible to achieve.

The British case presents both the demonstration of this point and its limitations. After the initial world-leading character of its postwar reforms, the elite-led character of the British welfare state seemed to make it rather proof against subsequent democratic demands for expanding generosity. The idea of income replacement hardly developed at all; instead a subsistence model of benefits remained dominant, and by the 1990s the income replacement rate of British unemployment benefits was the lowest in Western Europe apart from Greece and Italy (OECD 1994; 1997). When an element of earnings-relatedness was introduced in the 1960s it was rather minor; an alliance between the egalitarianism of the socialists and the desire of the private pensions industry to have a public system that left a lot of scope for private provision and occupational schemes.

True to its status as a social insurance system without social partner participation, the British system became one of weak universal (as opposed to occupational) citizenship. It was, however, a citizenship model rather than a residual one, because all except the wealthiest expected to make some use of it. This had ambiguous consequences. While it produced one of the meanest benefit systems in Western Europe, it did produce a far less gender-differentiated system than many others. Further, benefits not being tied closely to occupational contributions, it did not discourage part-time work or periods of temporary participation in the labour force—two further factors which considerably assisted female employment. Because the level of benefits, and therefore contributions, has been low, the latter do not constitute a severe barrier to the employment of low-productivity labour, enabling the lower end of the labour market in private services to grow, by the mid-1990s offsetting the decline in manufacturing employment.[6]

The British social insurance system and general welfare state are currently undergoing a reform wave, just as elsewhere in Europe. Part of the agenda is the same as elsewhere: trying to use the benefit system to re-equip people for employment rather than simply support their absence from it. As everywhere else, this is a stick and carrot policy: criteria of eligibility for benefit become tougher and rougher; opportunities for retraining and for assistance with obstacles to taking on work become more creative and helpful. What, however, seems distinctive about the current British debate over pensions reform is that there is virtually no public debate at all. The whole issue is dealt with in private discussions between government representatives and the handful of pensions firms which dominate the private sector. There is no involvement by the generality of employers, by the unions, or by representatives of pensioners themselves. This is a distinctiveness that stems clearly from the absence of any representative component in the management of British social insurance institutions.

If these are the mixed consequences of the absence of a social partnership model, the presence of social partnership should give us the opposite characteristics: generous benefits related to income replacement; based on occupational citizenship and therefore tied to male breadwinner interests; discouraging part-time or non-continuous labour-force participation (Hemerijck and Manow, forthcoming; Esping-Andersen 1996b); associated with weak development of low-productivity employment; difficult, blocked, but open and public debate over reform.

This stereotype does seem to characterize the German and French social insurance reform debates. As noted above, both countries have strong models of co-determination in the welfare system—running with the grain of general industrial relations in the German case, rather incongruous with it in the French. There are differences in the outcomes of the two cases. France does not so much exhibit the low female labour-force participation anticipated by the model, though French women do share the dislike of working part-time that one would expect from a social insurance system based on the accumulation of time served in the workforce. Quite separate aspects of social policy have somewhat eased the position of working mothers in France. For many years French policy-makers were obsessed with the country's low birth rate; since republican rather than Catholic groups dominated policy-making, the result was a series of natalist policies which did not at the same time try to keep women in a home-making role.

The German manufacturing model remains extremely strong, so that country has less need than many others to move into new service sectors in order to protect its economic performance. It is also not a system which protects existing workers at the expense of the young. As a result of the vocational education system, the German economy remains almost alone in the advanced world in having youth employment levels below those of the adult population. However, partly for these very reasons, the German case does show even more clearly than the French the way in which a social insurance system moulded to the interests of full-time males in manufacturing and governed by co-determination mechanisms is slow to adapt to the encouragement of female and part-time working and services sector development. Until now, representatives of workers in the core sectors have had little incentive to reform their system, because their members are doing very well. Their numbers are being reduced as productivity in the export sectors continues to rise, and this must soon have an effect in threatening opportunities for their sons. They have, however, little reason to accept changes which might threaten the security of their own anticipated benefits in order to get their wives and daughters into part-time jobs. The German *collective bargaining* system still functions more or less as "responsibly" as it did in the 1970s and 1980s; it was probably always the dominant role of the price-sensitive export sector and the stern stance of the Bundesbank rather than "encompassingness" as such which ensured non-inflationary wage behaviour. Within *social insurance*, however, the system has had fewer disincentives to protect its insiders at the expense of those outside (Hemerijck and Manow, forthcoming).

In fairness to these insiders, one must also point out the major issue that all German institutions have had to face following unification in 1990: no other advanced society has faced a comparable task to that of absorbing 16 million people who had experienced a far lower standard of living and completely different working patterns, but who had strong expectations of rapidly moving to the lifestyle of their new fellow citizens. Ensuring that the whole existing workforce of the eastern *Länder* did not become a mass of outsiders was in itself a major institutional challenge. It has been achieved with some success, but has probably absorbed and even exhausted much of the capacity of the system for strategic action and change.

However, this very point reminds us that it can be factors and institutions outside the strict terms of a system itself which can affect its behaviour. While one can demonstrate that the internal conditions of codeterminative occupational insurance systems make them resistant to reform, exogenous or partly exogenous elements might provide incentives for change, to which the system can respond. Indeed, the fact that these systems do have a clear representative arrangement for their governance means that they are capable of responding strategically when the incentive for change is sufficiently strong. Two cases which can be set against the French and German are the Dutch and Italian.

The Dutch reforms

As is now well known, largely thanks to the detailed study by Jelle Visser and Anton Hemerijck (1997), the Dutch collective bargaining and welfare state system has been subject to an extraordinary reform wave during the 1990s, which considerably increased the country's employment participation rate, especially among women, where it had previously been exceptionally low (see also Hemerijck and Manow, forthcoming). Further, the country's extraordinarily heavy dependence on removing people from the labour force with disability pensions is gradually being reduced. There is not space here to dwell on the details of the reforms, not all of which have been successful and which follow quite a diversity of political paths. Elements of the emerging Dutch system closely resemble a British model of gradually privatized welfare; others seem to match a more Scandinavian approach. Rather distinctive is the particularly high level of part-time work, including among males. We can, however, ask why this system, which shared the characteristics of a model which enables us accurately to predict lack of change in the French and German cases, eventually demonstrated a capacity for reform.

One answer is that the government took decisive action, clearly threatening a major dismantling of the codetermination structure of the social insurance system if the social partners did not respond (Ebbinghaus and Hassel 1999). One can also add two further factors. First, the Dutch unions had been becoming progressively weaker, with dramatic and continuing membership losses. Related to this, and in contrast with Germany, the Dutch economy was not a strong industrial power. Rather like the British economy, the Dutch has long had major commercial and financial services sectors which reduced the priority of manufacturing industry in both public policy and the approaches of the social partners. There was therefore little to compare with such German unions as IG Metall and IG Chemie in fostering and protecting the manufacturing model.[7] The Dutch industrial relations system was therefore vulnerable to very serious threat of collapse; the position of its insiders was not therefore necessarily much stronger than that of the outsiders. This served as a disincentive to rent-seeking behaviour and an incentive among employer and employee representatives alike to listen seriously to plans for reform.

By themselves, however, vulnerability and fear of collapse do not induce action to reform; they can simply cause collapse. The second important characteristic here was that the relevant Dutch organizations had not lost their institutional position and therefore potential strategic capacity (Ebbinghaus and Hassel 1999; Hemerijck 1992; Hemerijck and Kloostermans 1995; Visser and Hemerijck 1997). In the 1980s their combination of formal institutional security and drastic membership loss was making Dutch labour-market organizations seem like a group of abandoned and broken-down vehicles blocking a roadway while being incapable of any movement. The combination of government threat, looming existential crisis, but continued potential steering capacity, seemed to be enough to bring drivers and passengers back to the vehicles, to repair them, and to start them moving, often in a decisive way.

In comparison with the Germans, Dutch labour-market institutions have had to face both the determination of government and the weakness of the manufacturing sector: vulnerabilities which provided paradoxical advantages. Although observers usually place more stress on the former (Ebbinghaus and Hassel 1999), I suspect the latter was not only important in its own right but a factor determining government behaviour. While it is true that German federal governments are subject to a number of constitutional limitations, its coalitions are usually considerably more focused than the multi-party groupings of the Netherlands; it cannot be taken for granted that Dutch governments would be more decisive than German ones.

The French would seem to share the Dutch vulnerabilities: a manufacturing sector that has not been functioning anything like as well as the German one; and trade unions with problems of declining membership, indeed, in the private sector a considerably worse situation than in the Netherlands. Also, while electoral calculations and subsequent *cohabitation* had blunted the usual confidence and autonomy of the French state, the centre-right government did go so far as to change the constitution of the governing bodies of the social insurance system, reducing the role of the unions (Ebbinghaus and Hassel 1999). Also, there must always be a strong expectation that at some point the French state will act in a tough manner. I believe that the fundamental factor preventing French imitation of the Dutch lies not so much in state capacity as in the lack of strategic capacity among the social partners, especially the unions. As noted, the codetermination of the social insurance system is very much at odds with the dominant traditions of French industrial relations, which remain deeply conflictual. There is therefore little support for action in the social insurance sector from the wider industrial relations system. One aspect of this, which also stems directly from the low membership level, is the lack of resources at the disposal of the unions. This makes it very difficult for them to develop the expertise that something like social insurance reform requires, and inclines them to take up general ideological stances instead.

Perhaps more important for lack of strategic capacity, the French labour movement remains deeply divided. The religious differences among Dutch unions had long ago been submerged in an overall commitment to cooperation, and in any case today the two main wings (socialist and Catholic) have merged into a common organization. The main French union confederation, the Communist Confédération Générale de Travail (CGT), remains opposed to reaching agreements with employers or governments, and this defiance seems to increase as the organization's relative position within the labour movement declines. The other four or five organizations are all willing to participate in collective agreements and codetermination, but since they are rivals they are likely to try to outsmart each other in any major bargaining event. Therefore, any union going down the road of cooperation with government plans for reform, or even broaching its own proposals for change, will immediately be accused by the CGT of betrayal of workers' interests, and will probably not be able to construct a coalition with other unions either. The crucial characteristic here is not so much the ideological colour of one or another union, but the complete lack of strategic capacity which is imparted to the labour interest as a whole by the extent and character of the divisions.

The Italian reforms

Italian unions demonstrated from the 1993 wage structure reform onwards a capacity to overcome the divisions among themselves ostensibly similar to those of the French. On the other hand, problems of vertical coordination remain a major hazard for any Italian organization trying to achieve strategic capacity. Italian shop-floor militant movements, unlike the old shop-steward organizations in the UK, do not even formally form part of the official union structure but are quite autonomous associations. There is therefore a severe challenge for any Italian organization engaging in shared reform initiatives with government and employers. Nevertheless, in both collective bargaining itself and pension reform the Italian experience during the 1990s has been more similar to the Dutch than to the French or even to the German. How can we explain this most unlikely case of divergence from what, on the basis of the German evidence, we might expect from a codeterminative social insurance system?

To some extent there has been the same shared economic vulnerability as in the Netherlands and France, though in fact the industries of the northern and midlands regions of the country have proved more resilient and adaptable to the new competitive environment than their opposite numbers in either of those countries. There has also been government determination to see reform, and following the collapse of the Christian Democratic Party Italy faces the theoretical possibility of periods of government by a more or less neo-liberal right. However, the main autonomous neo-liberal reform initiative that tried to bypass social partnership, by the Berlusconi government in the early 1990s, led to the fall of the government. Meanwhile, in reality the political system remains as fragmented and incapable of delivering decisive majorities as ever. It is difficult to see Italy having a higher level of governmental capacity than either France or Germany.

One answer might lie in the sheer absurdity that had been reached by the pension system, enabling able-bodied people in their early forties to leave the workforce on pensions that were not being funded by anything other than unsupportable public debt. The situation was similar to, though more problematic even than, the Dutch disability pensions. However, it is doubtful whether this would have been enough to force a concentration on reform without the final, crucial component of the Italian context of the 1990s: the widely shared determination of virtually all elites and a large proportion of the general population to see Italy remain at the core of the European Union and in particular to enter the single European currency. The reasons for this exceptional commitment to the European Union and the euro can be variously interpreted: a desire to see the country achieve the status that its size and the strength of its economy seemed to deserve, but which its political and bureaucratic practices seemed so often to let down; a desire to be rid of the constantly weakening lira; a preference for rule by foreigners in Brussels over rule by a political class that had been publicly demonstrated to be corrupt.

Whatever the combination of motives social research might reveal to us, the outcome was not in doubt and was fully, even exceptionally, shared by the labour movement and the business community: Italy must qualify for entry to the euro. If this meant a tough central line on wage restraint in order to meet the Maastricht inflation criterion, so be it; if it meant a major onslaught on the early retirement scheme in order to meet the public deficit criterion, that too must be done. There were organizational costs for this assertion of a slender strategic capacity by labour leaders. The unofficial movement seems to have grown in strength. Other social partners seem to expect that it is enough if the unions deliver their own consent to an agreement; they cannot be expected to keep the unofficial movements in line too.

Keeping the energy of the reform wave moving now that euro entry has been achieved and cannot be reversed has proved more difficult. Meanwhile, the system has not really been adapted to meet the needs of a multi-sector, two-gender workforce; the main achievement of reform has been getting rid of an early retirement system that had become impossible to maintain. However, the activities of the 1993–7 period show how only partially exogenous pressures can disturb what seems like the irresistible path-dependency of the social insurance model.

Conclusions

One could examine other cases: for example, the way in which a prior strong employment and unionization of women (mainly in the welfare state itself) prevented Danish social insurance ever developing the full-time, industrial male bias, despite very strong union involvement in the management of the unemployment system (Clasen, forthcoming; Due *et al.* 1995; but see also the more pessimistic view of von Nordheim Nielsen (1996), who sees the relationship between the pension system and industrial relations leading to a fragmentation of the Danish pension system).

We have, however, seen enough to be able to draw some central conclusions. These concern the importance of examining agency as well as structure, of politics as well as sociology, of the micro- as well as the macro-level of action. Setting out the core characteristics of system types is not enough to enable us to predict how the actors in an individual case will respond. This is partly because real cases are extremely unlikely ever to be pure examples of one model, or of one ideal type. Empirical social structures are not only highly complex, but they embody a diversity of interests, legacies of past periods, and even some attributes which do not follow any organizational logic at all but just happen to be there. It is therefore possible for a component of a case that does not follow the logic of what we might have discerned as its core model suddenly to have an importance and determine change. Dutch departure from the German model of a primarily manufacturing-based economy would be one example; the priority of the single European currency for the Italians another.

Also, while all but the most determinist models will accept the notion of what economists call external shocks, it is only partially exogenous elements that have featured strongly in the above account. A determination to enter the euro was not an external shock to the Italian system, but something which imparted a particular character to the normal interest calculations of the endogenous actors.

Identification of path dependency has become a favourite device of comparative policy analysts in recent years. It originates in Douglass North's highly successful use of the concept in his study of the history of capitalist institutional development. This has encouraged the search for "lock-in", when social actors pursue a path which, initially offering advantages, eventually becomes a trap. It draws further strength from the popular comparative research methodology, whereby cases are allocated to theoretical boxes, and the behaviour of the inhabitants of the boxes is then statistically compared. (For example, welfare states are labelled "liberal", "social democratic" or "corporatist", and the unemployment performance of the different groups compared.)

These procedures lead to exaggeration and even reification of core characteristics. The import of the Northian path-dependency model is that once a group of actors have enjoyed some success moving along a particular path, they lose the capacity to try alternative approaches, generate institutions which lock them in, and eventually lose the capacity to change. North derived the idea from studies of scientific and technological methodology, where researchers following a particular design paradigm would become unable to cope with challenges that were not anticipated by the logic of that paradigm. But transferred to something as incoherent as a social institution this analogy can be only partial and eventually deceptive. It leaves out of account the mixed character of real as opposed to ideal-typical institutional legacies, and the importance of different weighting of calculations of action induced by the partial exogeneity that we have noted above. Similarly, the research method of testing statistically the behavioural outcomes of characteristics which have been used as labels of cases misses the fact that most cases are mixes of types, and actors within them will at certain points switch from following one of the logics available to them, to another, perhaps lying latent in their potential repertoire, or in a state of disrepair as in the case of the Dutch labour-market institutions, thereby frustrating the analyst's attempt to pigeonhole them.

Followers of these methodologies are likely to miss much of what is going on in actual policy-making and dilemma-facing. The point is a very general one, but it has particular application to the topic here under debate. We have been observing a set of institutions (those of codeterminative social insurance), which for a long time were not called upon to perform any strategic tasks of note, suddenly being faced with some urgent new challenges (to reform in order to facilitate certain labour market changes). At the same time these institutions are rediscovering their connections to a different field (industrial relations) with which they have always been linked but which often developed in different ways. This is happening during a period of quite diverse changes, embodying often very different logics: globalization, the decline of manufacturing, the feminization of the labour force, European integration, the dominance of neo-liberalism. We should not expect to be able to make hand-me-down predictions of how whole classes of cases will react without precise observation of the forces at work in individual instances.

Notes

1. This is not a result of a linguistic deficiency; *bien-être* and *benessere*, while literally corresponding more closely to well-being than to welfare, convey the latter meaning adequately. They are occasionally used, though the idea of welfare state is more likely to be rendered as *la protection sociale* or *lo stato sociale*. The word "welfare" having a Germanic rather than a Latin root, the German language—normally so ready to use foreign borrowings—is for once content with *Wohlfahrtsstaat*. When it comes to industrial relations, *relations professionnelles* makes perfectly good French, but *relazioni industriali* and *industrielle Beziehungen* betray an English borrowing. Outside the English language, words related to industry and its derivatives refer strictly to manufacturing and cannot easily be extended to other areas of economic activity.

2. In Belgium, Denmark, Finland and Sweden there is the additional element of the so-called Ghent system, whereby state unemployment insurance schemes are administered by the unions, who feel a strong identification with the schemes. Although it is not necessary to belong to the union in order to participate in the schemes, either workers do not know this, or it is simply easier to recruit and sustain their membership when they are having regular contact of this kind with the union organization. Either way, the Ghent system seems to explain why union membership in Norway (which does not have such a system) is rather lower than in the other Nordic lands; and why Belgium has a considerably higher membership level than either of its neighbours (France and the Netherlands).

3. "Risk" might seem an odd concept to use in the case of retirement pensions. However, as Ferrera (1997) somewhat callously explains, in the late nineteenth century when these concepts were being developed, the life expectancy of a manual worker extended little beyond the age when one was considered as no longer of any use in the workforce; there was, however, a "risk" that one might go on living for rather longer than that. Ferrera goes on from there to argue that, now that life expectancy has extended considerably beyond the point of ending normal working life, the whole idea of a risk of excessively long survival has been lost; indeed, people actually plan how they will enjoy their years of retirement. This leads him to advocate the scrapping of the idea of compulsory state pensions beyond a subsistence level and the privatization of provision for more generous retirement income.

4. In acquiring welfare citizenship before political, German immigrants are re-enacting the experience of Germans themselves. The Bismarckian state developed its welfare system before its democracy, thereby reversing Marshall's (1963) evolutionary scheme of first legal, then political, then welfare citizenship.

5. The *pensione di anzianità* or seniority pension, for some reason colloquially called "baby pension", in English, though it was a distinctly Italian invention.

6. There continues to be a net decline in male and full-time work, but strong increases in part-time female jobs.

7. It was perhaps in awareness of the vulnerability of an industrial relations system which lacks sensitivity to export prices that Dutch unions in the manufacturing sector merged to form a single union, regaining a weight within the main federation that they had lost to public service unions.

References

Clasen, J. (forthcoming), Unemployment insurance and varieties of capitalism. In Ebbinghaus and Manow (forthcoming).

Daly, M. (1996), The gender division of welfare: the British and German welfare states compared. PhD thesis, Florence: European University Institute.

Due, J., Madsen, J. S., Jensen, C. S., and Petersen, L. K. (1995), *The Survival of the Danish Model*, Copenhagen: DJØF.

Ebbinghaus, B., and Hassel, A. (1999), The role of tripartite concertation in the reform of the welfare state, *Transfer*, 1–2: 64–81.

Ebbinghaus, B., and Manow, P. (forthcoming), *The Varieties of Welfare Capitalism: Social Policy and Political Economy in Europe, Japan and the USA*, London: Routledge.

Esping-Andersen, G. (1990), *The Three Worlds of Welfare Capitalism*, Cambridge: Polity Press.

Esping-Andersen, G. (ed.) (1996a), *Welfare States in Transition. National Adaptations in Global Economies*, London: Sage.

Esping-Andersen, G. (1996b), Welfare states without work: the impasse of labour shedding and familialism in continental European social policy. In Esping-Andersen (1996a).

Esping-Andersen, G. (1999), *Social Foundations of Postindustrial Economies*, Oxford: Oxford University Press.

Ferrera, M. (1997), *Le Trappole del Welfare*, Bologna: Il Mulino.

Finlayson, G. (1994), *Citizen, State, and Social Welfare in Britain 1830–1990*, Oxford: Clarendon Press.

Guiraudon, V. (1998), Citizenship rights for non-citizens: France, Germany, the Netherlands. In Joppke, C. (ed.), *Challenges to the Nation State: Immigration in Western Europe and the United States*, Oxford: Oxford University Press.

Hassel, A. (forthcoming), The governance of the employment-welfare relationship: the cases of Germany and the UK. In Ebbinghaus and Manow (forthcoming).

Hemerijck, A. (1992), The historical contingencies of Dutch corporatism. DPhil thesis, University of Oxford.

Hemerijck, A., and Kloostermans, R. C. (1995), Der postindustrielle Umbau des korporistischen Sozialstaats in den Niederländern. In Fricke, W. (ed.), *Jahrbuch Arbeit und Technik*: 287–96.

Hemerijck, A., and Manow, P. (forthcoming), The experience of negotiated social policy reform in Germany and the Netherlands. In Ebbinghaus and Manow (forthcoming).

Hippe, J. M., and West Pedersen, A. (1996), The Labour movement, social policy and occupational welfare in Norway. In Shalev (1996).

Kangas, O., and Palme, J. (1996), The development of occupational pensions in Finland and Sweden: class politics and institutional feedbacks. In Shalev (1996).

Lewis, J. (ed.) (1993), *Women and Social Policies in Europe: Work, Family and the State*, Aldershot: Edward Elgar.

Marshall, T. H. (1963), *Sociology at the Crossroads and Other Essays*, London: Routledge.

North, D. C. (1990), *Institutions, Institutional Change and Economic Performance*, Cambridge: Cambridge University Press.

OECD (1994), *The OECD Jobs Study: Evidence and Explanations*, Paris: OECD.

OECD (1997), *The OECD Jobs Strategy: Making Work Pay. Taxation, Benefits, Employment and Unemployment*, Paris: OECD.

Øverbye, E. (1996), Public and occupational pensions in the Nordic countries. In Shalev (1996).

Scharpf, F. W. (1997), *Employment and the Welfare State: A Continental Dilemma*, Cologne: Max-Planck-Institut für Gesellschaftsforschung.

Shalev, M. (ed.) (1996), *The Privatization of Social Policy? Occupational Welfare and the Welfare State in America, Scandinavia and Japan*, Basingstoke: Macmillan.

New Risks, New Welfare: Signposts for Social Policy

Visser, J., and Hemerijck, A. (1997), *"A Dutch Miracle": Job Growth, Welfare Reform and Corporatism in the Netherlands*, Amsterdam: Amsterdam University Press.

von Nordheim Nielsen, F. (1996), Danish occupational pensions in the 1980s: from social security to political economy. In Shalev (1996).

7

Culture: The Missing Variable in Understanding Social Policy?

John Baldock

Is Culture Relevant to Social Policy?

This, relatively brief, chapter explores a large but rarely addressed question: to what extent are a country's social policies the product of its culture? In industrial societies welfare systems constitute a large part of the national economy. Public welfare is also an expression of values in so far as it redistributes resources from those it defines as capable of contributing to those it defines as in need. But how far are these arrangements consistent with the people's values? These questions have been made more acute at the turn of the century by the frequent observation that economic and social changes, particularly in the organization of work and the family ("post-industrialism"), are leading to substantial cultural shifts ("postmodernism"). It is suggested that populations are becoming increasingly differentiated in terms of the risks they face and the values they hold, and that these changes have profound implications for public welfare systems. For example, in a review of problems of social policy, Gosta Esping-Andersen suggests that "Contemporary welfare states . . . have their origins in, and mirror, a society that no longer obtains . . . Welfare regimes are built round a set of egalitarian ideals and risk profiles that predominated when our parents and grandparents were young" (Esping-Andersen 1999: 5).

When I first thought about this chapter, I hoped it would assert the importance of culture as an explanation of how social welfare systems emerge, develop, and then impact on the people that use them. It is intuitively obvious that social policies must be profoundly affected by the wider cultures that surround them and into which they are delivered. The role of religion in affecting the character of welfare systems is important. In so far as social policies are an expression of a community's values they are likely to reflect the established or dominant religion, and possibly conflict with the religious beliefs of minorities. It is widely observed that within predominantly Catholic societies the detailed texture of social welfare institutions differs from that in Protestant communities (Wilensky 1981). It is also often suggested, and contested, that the welfare systems of the industrialized countries of the Far East, while they may appear quite similar to Western arrangements in terms of purely legal forms, are deeply different in their daily operation because of the effect of Confucian, Buddhist and other religious cultures (Ka 1999; Esping-Andersen 1997). These initial thoughts on the chapter have, not surprisingly, turned out to be impossibly wide in scope. Before explicating the impact of religion on social policy it is necessary to be clear about what would count as a causal connection. This chapter is therefore no more than an exploration of how far "culture" and "social policy" might be linked, the ways in which others have described those links and the implications for social policy at the turn of the century.

"Culture" and the Social Policy Literature

If one defines culture in its broadest sense—as the unorganized and largely implicit values and norms represented in the behaviour of a community or nation—then for the last fifty years academic social policy studies have almost entirely avoided the issue of its effects on welfare development. As a result there is no established corpus of theory or data for a chapter like this to use.

At first glance this will appear to be an extraordinary line to take. Looking only at the British case, there is surely a vast range of material describing the culture and considerable literature dealing with its links to welfare? Across most of the century there have been numerous polls of public values—aside from commercial and political polls there are the "Mass Observation" data for the mid-century, which described what people thought, felt and did, through to the more recent series of Social Attitudes Surveys which have often tracked welfare issues. In addition, regular large-scale surveys like the Family Income Survey and the General Household Survey are a measure of changing values and behaviour. The literature on the history of ideas and of social philosophies is voluminous, as is that examining every aspect of popular and mass culture. None the less, the argument here is that very little of all this work links the values and behaviour of ordinary lived life to the structure and nature of state welfare. In the UK the two major exceptions to this rule have been, first, studies of how social policy has reflected false and patriarchal views of women's and family lives. Second, there is the literature on the ways social policy can reproduce or counter the dominant culture's discrimination against minorities and disabled people. However, even in these two cases the focus is not essentially on how a culture is translated into the goals and form of the public welfare system but rather on how it is at odds with them. Indeed, the main argument here is that there is no direct link between culture and state welfare systems. There is no literature on how a nation's culture leads to its particular forms of welfare because there is no such causal linkage. The integrated welfare states of the second half of the twentieth century were not produced by their cultures but despite them. Indeed this is one reason they are unlikely to survive.

The study of social policy, particularly as it has been conducted in Britain, has paid little attention to the concept of culture. In this it is unlike the other social sciences with the significant exception of economics. In political science the idea of culture is used to capture the behaviour of both specific groups (class culture, the culture of elites, bureaucratic and administrative cultures) and of whole political systems (particularly the study of political culture established by Almond and Verba 1963). In anthropology and sociology, culture plays a fundamental analytical role as the repository of meaning and thus plays a similar role to "class" and "society" as one of the overarching categories that is central to the very operation of the disciplines. Similarly in history, particularly social history, and more widely in the arts and humanities, "culture" appears not only in many specific ways as a source of explanation, but, in its broader senses, it is the fundamental object of study.

One reason why academic social policy has ignored culture may be due to its links with economics. Both disciplines have their academic roots in the eighteenth-century study of political economy, and much modern social policy analysis is carried out by economists. The exception of economics to the general rule, that culture is a core explanatory variable and object of study, is rooted in the very nature of that discipline. For economic analysis, in all its variations, culture is defined as taste and preference and it is fundamental that these are treated as given. The focus of economic analysis is not on understanding how tastes and preferences are formed but on what happens once they exist: the consequences they have for demand and thus the production and distribution of resources. Thus culture is not unimportant to economic analysis but it remains deliberately unexplored.

There is of course a substantial literature that seeks, in various ways, to account for the development of welfare systems but this has focused on almost every conceivable variable other than culture. Instead explanations for the expansion of social policy are cast in terms of such factors as political competition and party politics, industrialization and economic growth, the expansion of bureaucracy and the state, the effects of war and of recession. There is also a large social philosophy literature on the principles and arguments that have been used to justify the expansion of the state into welfare provision. This is largely about "the idea of welfare in political thought" (Barry 1999) and is concerned with the explicit and deliberate development of social theory rather than with the implicit and inchoate realm of norms and values that constitutes culture. Only relatively recently, with the growth of a debate about the nature of postmodern society, have questions about the fit between social policies and the wider culture been taken up.

What is Culture?

The "definition" of culture presented here claims no greater validity than that it will serve as a foundation for the arguments that follow. However, a brief exploration of writings on culture, particularly in the social sciences, reveals a surprisingly substantial consensus about what is meant by the word itself. A culture is made up of the shared beliefs, values and behavioural norms of a community. The span of beliefs and values entailed is therefore almost infinitely wide—from those concerning political and social issues to those that determine what is good or evil, beautiful or ugly. Thus culture is a much broader concept than "ideology" which is generally understood to refer to a coordinated set of beliefs about specific aspects of social organiza-tion (Plamenatz 1970). Indeed, culture generally refers to so huge a range of inherited belief and taste that it is far beyond any cataloguing or description. Frazer's vast multi-volume *The Golden Bough: A Study in Magic and Religion* (1922) is often presented as a classic attempt. Even so, a culture is not generally defined as containing all the knowledge of a society; technical knowledge is not normally considered central but rather the values and aspirations that sustain and develop it. Perhaps the most distinctive aspect of the idea of culture is that it is not to be observed directly but only through the signs and behaviour that demonstrate it at one or more removes. Thus the art, the literature, the religious books and even the daily routines of a society reveal its culture; they are the products of the culture rather than the culture itself. In this sense culture's status is like that of the emotions. As Gilbert Ryle (1973) most famously pointed out we deduce another's happiness from a smile or other behaviour; we do not have access to the emotion itself. Similarly, a culture is revealed by its outward manifestations and cannot be directly observed or measured—a characteristic that reduces its appeal to the empirical tradition of social policy research.

The relationship between values and action is so evidently fundamental to our understanding of the social world that it was often tackled by the founders of social science, though not specifically in relation to social policy. Both Durkheim, in his work on the sources of social solidarity (1984) and of suicide (1952), and Weber, in *The Protestant Ethic and the Spirit of Capitalism* (1958) and in his analysis of religion in China (1964), regarded the connection between culture in its broadest sense and action as the essence of social explanation.

Durkheim's conception of the *"conscience collective"* was developed in his book *The Division of Labour in Society* and first published in 1893 (Durkheim 1984). Durkheim was concerned to account for the forces that gave a society its communality and solidarity; what did its members share that was different from their individual psychologies? He defined the *conscience collective* as "the set of beliefs and sentiments common to the average members of a single society . . . it is independent of the particular conditions in which individuals are placed; they pass on and it remains" (quotations taken from Lukes 1973: 4). It consisted of shared moral and religious beliefs and of less explicit preferences which he called "sentiments". Durkheim, in developing this idea, was seeking to capture the link between the "living culture" that exists in the heads of those presently alive and the "dead culture" of the past; to define what gives a society its continuity. What is also particularly relevant to the analysis proposed in this chapter is that he was principally concerned with the relationship of the *conscience collective* to the division of labour in a society. The concept was created to account for the unity of societies in which the division of labour was undeveloped. However, as the organization of labour became more complex, dividing into the large solidaristic blocks that were typical of late nineteenth-century France that Durkheim observed, he argued that the *conscience collective* was replaced by the *"representations collectives"* of the industrial and agrarian classes creating social classes each linked by their distinctive "cultures" rather than a society-wide *conscience collective*.

Thus, it is not inappropriate to argue that Durkheim might well have suggested that the changes to the division of labour entailed by the decline of large-scale industrial employment (post-Fordism) would have profound implications for the organization of a society's cultural formations. Lastly, in this inevitably hurried and cavalier résumé, it is important to notice that almost any social unit can be said to share its own distinctive culture—a family, a school, a workplace—in addition to those it shares in some wider context such as a nation or even a larger geographical entity like Europe.

This attempt at a quick definition of culture will probably by now have confirmed for most readers of this journal that it is not a concept with much to offer students of social policy and administration. It is surely too vague to have any operational or analytic use? In particular, if it can refer to almost any beliefs, values and norms, how is it to be contained, let alone be measured, for any descriptive or analytical account of the design or working of social policy? The answer to this, pursued throughout this chapter, is to reverse the objection. It is not that accounts of social policy can readily be strengthened by the use of the concept of culture, but rather that if it is left out altogether they are often greatly weakened by its absence.

Culture as Context: A Spanner in the Social Policy Works

British academic social policy writing has been much more ready to treat culture as context than as cause, and that context is often seen as a negative one. There have been many studies of the provision of public benefits and services that have portrayed culture as a "spanner in the works", preventing the fulfilment of the proper intention of social policies. Titmuss, in particular, saw some popular values both as obstacles to the effective operation of public welfare and as reasons for expanding social services. He was particularly influenced by Irving Goffman's analysis of stigma (Goffman 1963) and the tendency of all societies to ascribe to some people lesser and "spoiled" identities on the basis of their poverty, their race or other physical or social characteristics. Titmuss argued that universal social welfare provision could play an important role in reducing stigma, but that wherever services were allocated according to some sort of selection they risked exacerbating the problem or even creating new forms of stigma. He believed that welfare services designed only for the poor would recruit "the worst rather than the best" professionals and generate a culture of "less freedom of choice and more felt discrimination".

> We cannot now, just because we are getting richer, disengage ourselves from the fundamental challenge of distributing social rights without stigma . . . Nor can we solve the problems of discrimination and stigma by recreating poor law or panel systems of welfare in the belief that we should thereby be able to concentrate state help on those whose needs are greatest. (Titmuss 1976: 143)

These quotations, from the book of essays called *Commitment to Welfare*, demonstrate Titmuss's now academically unfashionable view that social policy could and should be used to change social values. They also typify the way in which he saw social policy very much in the modernist sense of a project in social improvement, even in social engineering.

Many studies of welfare implementation have pointed to ways in which some local, institutional or professional culture threatened to undermine policy intentions: Hill's studies of the organization of work in benefits offices (1976); Prottas's accounts of how street-level bureaucrats control the flow of their work (1979); studies of status and power in medical care (Strong 1979); of how social workers value different goals to their managers (Pithouse 1987); and of how local authority staff discriminate against some housing applicants (Henderson and Karn 1987); and many accounts of how "total institutions" can generate undesirable values. In all these studies culture tends to be the context and the problem rather than the source of welfare values.

People who manage, deliver and use welfare services will often be unaware of their original driving principles. Managers, service workers and service users integrate welfare work into the ongoing texture of their lives. A new social policy is absorbed into and mediated by the ongoing cultures into which it is directed. This is not to say that a policy does not have at least some of the intended effects but that there are also degrees of failure and unintended effects.

Some of this is captured by the substantial literature on organizations and implementation, particularly those studies that concentrate on "implementation deficits". A good deal of this research has focused on central–local relations and on how the intentions of legislators become "corrupted" by more parochial interests and cultures. The seminal source in this literature is Philip Selznick's (1949) study of the Tennessee Valley Authority and its representation of the ideals of the Roosevelt New Deal. More recently, the focus of this research tradition is well captured by possibly the longest book title in social science, Jeffrey Pressman's and Aaron Wildavsky's *Implementation: How Great Expectations in Washington are Dashed in Oakland, or, Why It's Amazing that Federal Programs Work at All, This Being a Saga of the Economic Development Administration as Told by Two Sympathetic Observers who Seek to Build Morals on a Foundation of Ruined Hopes* (1973). In the UK a steady flow of empirical studies have documented how the culture of local authority officialdom mediates and changes the political agendas of elected councillors (Swartz 1969; Dearlove 1973; Newman 1996).

However, important as this analytical tradition is, as an understanding of culture in social policy, it is limited in two ways. First, its focus is usually restricted to the values and behavioural norms of officials at various levels in the implementation chain. Rarely is much said about the nature of the wider culture into which policies are delivered and why that responds in varied ways. This is partly because this research tradition developed from within the policy sciences and therefore has an institutional focus, and partly because researchers have found ways to study and describe the practices and culture of bureaucrats and professionals but not to account for behaviour of users and consumers. The second limitation is of a different kind. It is remarkable how little impact the sociology of organizations has had on social policy design and implementation. It seems that politicians and policy managers do not want to learn from, or at best simply cannot use, the voluminous literature about how they behave and "go wrong". This blindness appears to be an integral part of organizational culture and extends widely amongst institutions; consider how frustrating it must be for public administration academics as they watch the managers of their own universities work through the well-documented book of errors.

The Irrelevance of Social Policy Studies to Social Policy Making

The refusal of much contemporary social policy analysis to engage with the cultural values of welfare users has greatly weakened its impact on policy-making. At the end of a century amongst whose key features must be counted a huge increase in the role of the state in people's lives—measured both quantitatively and qualitatively—it is startling how little influence and weight academic social policy studies carry both in government and amongst the citizens of Britain. This has not always been so. A century ago, following a period of severe economic recession in the 1890s, and in the events leading to the first social insurance legislation and a fundamental inquiry in the form of the Royal Commission on the Poor Laws, academic commentators played an influential part. Half a century later they were actively involved when the coming to power of the Labour movement in the form of the first majority Labour government was reaching its legislative fulfilment with the creation of the postwar welfare state and its promise of security "from cradle to grave". Now, soon after the 1997 election of a Labour government explicitly seeking to revive social policy after eighteen years of Tory administrations that did not hide their antipathy to state welfare, one might have expected to see social policy academics playing a full and vigorous part in developments. But, unlike some earlier periods, academic social policy now finds itself largely in a reactive or oppositional role and, often, just ignored.

On the last occasion that Labour was returned to power after a substantial absence, in 1964 with the election (twice in the same year) of Harold Wilson's government, social policy academics quickly became habitués of Whitehall. During its time in opposition Labour's National Executive Committee had appointed members of the Social Administration Department at the LSE to its working parties on welfare reform. At least during the early years of government, cabinet ministers routinely consulted both formally and informally with academics (Titmuss, Abel-Smith, Townsend, Donnison) on social policy issues. (Much about these contacts is still only to be learnt of by talking to those with memories of the time, but some accounts appear in Crossman 1966, Heclo 1974, Banting 1979, Deakin 1987 and Crossman 1977.) Even quite junior members of the LSE department found themselves on government committees, surrounded by ready listeners. However, by 1970 social policy academics had begun to write strong critiques of Labour's record, particularly on poverty, and from then on they appear to have lost their entrée through the portals of power. The Labour administrations of 1974–9 turned to specialist civil servants for advice ("The Central Policy Review Staff") while from 1979 onwards politicians have preferred to use political "think tanks" of both the right and left. Only very recently, with direct government support for the "Social Exclusion Unit" at the LSE and the special relationship between Tony Blair and Anthony Giddens, may we be seeing a renaissance of direct academic inputs into social policy-making.

How Has Public Policy Analysis Cut Itself off from the Public's Preoccupations?

As the volume of policy analysis has grown, so its influence has declined. In seeking academic rigour and respectability, the study of social policy has paradoxically cut itself off from contemporary political debate and rendered itself rather irrelevant to politicians and policy managers. In a recent series of seminars funded by the Brookings Institution some of the leading figures in American public policy analysis sought to understand why at the end of the century "a peculiar and distressing gulf separates scholarly from popular discussions of many social issues" (Aaron *et al.* 1994). The way in which the organizers of the seminars state the problem is worth quoting at length:

> Ask an economist or a sociologist why families go on welfare and stay there, and you are likely to get a learned disquisition on how declining wages have contributed to an increase in welfare, on how payment formulas drain the economic gain from employment and make staying on welfare easier than leaving it, and on how welfare rules undermine family stability. Ask an ordinary citizen the same question and you are likely to get an earful on sloth, shortsightedness, and lack of morality in welfare recipients . . . Ask educators why test scores are falling, and you had better be ready for a discourse on why student performance is sensitive to curriculum, teacher skills and school management and organization. Ask ordinary citizens and you may hear judgmental remarks . . . about parents who care too little to make their children do homework, about the distractions of television, and about peer pressures. (Aaron *et al.* 1994: 1)

Aaron and colleagues go on to analyse why academics are unwilling to confront the issues of value that preoccupy "ordinary citizens" and which are therefore relevant to the politicians who seek their votes. First, values, and the cultures they are part of, are hard to characterize and quantify in ways that will be readily accepted by other scholars. It is also methodologically difficult to construct models which relate values to behaviours in systematic and testable ways (Van Deth and Scarbrough 1995). Second, the few scholars who do enter this territory can quickly find their academic legitimacy under attack. Unfortunately, a fair proportion of those who use academic cover to discuss other people's values are no more than propagandists and even extremists. Some of the most shameful episodes in the history of social science have occurred when it became associated with a particular political ideology.

But for practitioners of public policy analysis, the most important reason for not examining the content of values and culture is that the theoretical frameworks they use do not encourage it. It has already been mentioned that as public policy analysis has developed in methodological sophistication it has also increasingly adopted economistic models that treat values and culture as a given. "Personal utility, tastes or values have traditionally occupied a position in policy analysis similar to postulates in Euclidian geometry—fundamental properties to be accepted as they are and not themselves subject to analysis" (Aaron *et al.* 1994: 2). Thus, while many politicians seek ways to change behaviour by directly influencing values, policy analysts assume values will remain fixed. For example, asked to recommend what will work to reduce crime, prevent children growing up in poverty or raise levels of employment, policy analysts are more likely to suggest relatively expensive and slow-working remedies that assume people will retain their preferences. They are unlikely to suggest increased imprisonment, taking single young mothers off welfare or reducing public assistance. It is not simply that policy analysts are wedded to value-neutrality as a methodological principle—though that is an important factor. All the evidence is that the sources of culture and preference are both very complex and, particularly in the short term that counts for policy-making, relatively immutable. Social scientists "know" that culture and values cannot easily be changed by planned interventions, indeed if at all. But with this professional insight they cut themselves off from the public and politicians who continue to believe in the power of cultural persuasion. This was not always so.

Social Policy and the Second World War

The paradigm case of cultural change having a direct effect on social policy is that of increased social solidarity amongst the British people during the Second World War, leading fairly directly to the legislative foundations of the postwar welfare state. This is a "truth" taught to many social policy undergraduates. The argument contains at least two propositions: first, that the experience of war, particularly of bombing and other disruptions amongst the civilian population, led to more communitarian, altruistic and even redistributive values; second, that these new values drove the politicians of both the wartime coalition and of the Labour administration from 1945 to design and pass major social reforms. As soon as one begins to unpack the causal processes of even this classic case the difficulties in specifying just how culture may affect social policies come into focus. Robert Page has carefully reviewed the arguments and debates (1996: 60–94) and shows how varied and complex were the mechanisms involved.

It is not clear that the supposedly more generous and egalitarian values were widely shared or much more than temporary. There were indeed the well-known examples of generosity and solidarity: many people of all classes agreed to accept evacuees and to foster children from the cities; people of all classes shared cramped and uncomfortable shelter in the underground stations. However, Page lists numerous examples of wartime inequality, unfairness and even scapegoating: some better-off families avoided being drawn into the evacuation scheme and the owners of larger houses were sometimes not asked to billet soldiers; many middle-class women avoided civilian "call-up" for war duties; despite rationing there were numerous ways in which the better-off could use their money to buy more food in restaurants or better clothes in the shops; publicly provided health care became more readily available to bomb victims and those of working age but at a price for the aged and infirm who were literally turned out of hospitals and into a system of "benign neglect"; there were cases of minority groups being singled out as "cowardly or selfish"—Jewish people "were accused of all manner of anti-social acts" (1996: 68–70). Wartime also witnessed increased levels of crime and of industrial action. There now appears to be a broad consensus amongst social historians that "the war changed some ideas and habits, in the long term, though probably not so many or so much as had been supposed . . . There were few signs of any urge to share once an immediate threat was past. There were as many fresh disputes and frictions as new fellowships" (Harrison 1978: 311).

In this ambivalent context, the wartime social reforms which laid some of the foundations of postwar social policy—for example the Determination of Needs Act of 1941 which reduced means-testing, the 1944 Education Act and the 1945 Family Allowances Act—can be understood less as expressions of social solidarity and more as politically necessary to retain the support of a suspicious working class. The subsequent 1945 election of a party whose manifesto explicitly promised the implementation of the Beveridge plan required just 48 per cent of the vote and was as much the product of dissatisfaction with the Conservative plans as it was an endorsement of Labour's. Page's overall conclusion is that, while the wartime "commitment to fairer shares was based on something more than crude instrumentalism", the social reforms of the time owed more to the exigencies of running a war requiring mass support and subsequently to the particular workings of the British electoral system which allowed ideas of a small number of welfare reformers to be introduced to a British public that previously had little conception of them (1996: 83–4). It was less a case of the wider culture requiring reform than a unique historical moment in which a few committed reformers were able to begin changing the culture by institutionalizing its welfarist ideology. The source of the received wisdom in social policy studies, that the value changes of the war came first and the reforms followed, is in large part due to the work of one of that elite, Richard Titmuss. The ideas about the primacy of value changes can be traced to his monumental history of wartime social change, *Problems of Social Policy* (1950), in which he argued,

> The mood of the people changed, and in sympathetic response, values changed as well. If dangers were to be shared, then resources should also be shared . . . dramatic events on the home front served only to reinforce the war-warmed impulse of the people for a more generous society. (1950: 508)

Titmuss not only had a profound influence on, and access to, reforming politicians but in later essays was often to argue that welfare services, particularly the NHS, could create "islands of collectivism" in an individualistic market society and that these could then, through growth, gradually change the overall inegalitarian culture (Titmuss 1974). More recent policy analysis has tended to either ignore Titmuss or suggest he was more propagandist than academic. The last accusation may sometimes have been true and not one that Titmuss himself would have rejected. Where he essentially differed from contemporary social policy academics was in his readiness to admit to a particular view of human nature. He believed that both the wider culture and individuals carried within themselves competing values, both selfish and altruistic. It does not require a very close reading of his work to discover that this led to a more complex view of the relationship between social values and policy-making. By choosing to meet social needs through collaborative non-market institutions, Titmuss believed, and sought to demonstrate, social policies could define and strengthen "generous" parts of the culture and weaken the "selfish" ones (Titmuss 1970). Though cast in different terms, this is an analysis quite similar to forms of institutional path analysis used today.

Social Policy as a Modernist Enterprise

Today, with the benefit of hindsight, it is clearer that creation of state social welfare systems during the twentieth century has been a typical modernist enterprise. The "idea of social policy", as Robert Pinker (1979) so aptly called it, is not a populist one but is of a piece with Bauhaus, the social architecture of Le Corbusier, the urban planning movement and the conception of "new towns". These in their turn are all classic representations of the wider modernist movement represented in art, literature and, in different forms, in the ideas of socially responsible natural science and in utopian socialism. Twentieth-century modernism was the apogee of rationalism, the triumph of human knowledge over nature and of humane sentiments over brutishness and base instinct. The ideals of modernist social policy were not the product of the existing culture, as represented in established religion, mass politics or the accepted tastes and manners of the day. Modernist thought, in all its forms, has always been elitist and self-consciously progressive—seeking to triumph over the limiting culture and prejudices of the present. Modernism, in so far as it was an ideology, was very much the province of intellectuals and their attempts to understand and control the modernity they saw developing around them.

> Modernity . . . means a social order which has turned from the worship of ancestors and past authorities to the pursuit of a projected future—of goods, pleasures, freedoms, forms of control over nature, or infinities of information. This process goes with a great emptying and sanitizing of the imagination. Without ancestor-worship, meaning is in short sup-ply—[in the sense of] agreed on and instituted forms of value and understanding, implicit orders, stories and images. (Clark 1999: 7)

Clark, like many historians of art and literature, argues that the modernity which modernists believed they could foresee, never actually arrived. Popular and everyday culture continued to evolve in terms of "irrational", religious, nationalist, superstitious and discriminatory forms of thought. That is why "modern" art has still not achieved popular acceptance, why a Corbusier block of flats is "misunderstood and ill-used" by its occupants, and why most people find new towns rather odd and an acquired taste. Modernist thought, in all the fields in which it has appeared, has sought to deny and overturn orthodox, established and traditional culture rather than to reflect it.

The integrated state welfare systems of postwar Western Europe (and of a few other nations elsewhere such as New Zealand) could be counted the most startling success of the modernist project. The fortuitous historical coincidence of universal suffrage, recession followed by total war, and the brief hegemony of a small elite wedded to social democracy led to the secure taxfunding of collective welfare provision. In no sense were blueprints for complex and novel arrangements like family allowances, unemployment insurance and national health systems to be found within the dominant cultural formations. Their specific structures and designs can much more readily be traced to the ingenuity of a few individuals. The social philosophies that justified them may have been quite widely understood by the politically literate but again were articulated by relatively few individuals (the Webbs, Tawney, Beveridge, Myrdal, Keynes) and explicitly to counter the dominant and conventional wisdoms of the time.

It is arguable that comprehensive welfare states are historical exceptions rather than the historical rule. Comparative studies of the evolution of welfare systems are preoccupied with exploring relatively subtle distinctions between different, usually European, models. In global terms this is a very ethnocentric preoccupation. They rarely ask the much more difficult question of why the vast majority of the world's population lives in societies where systematic social welfare is neither provided nor expected, despite the fact that many of these societies support economies quite as affluent as Germany in the 1880s, Britain in the 1910s or Sweden in the 1930s, and populations as literate and urbanized. Industrialization and a degree of democracy may be prerequisites for social welfare provision; they certainly do not entail it. As the postwar welfare states of Western Europe are increasingly constrained and frayed by global economic competition it has become more possible that history will look back upon them as the rather eccentric products of a particular epoch. Already a key academic focus is the sustainability of state welfare rather than its reform and expansion—rather like the focus of art historians on issues to do with the conservation of rare paintings.

The "Third Way", or Eclectic Social Policy

It has been argued here that the character and design of the postwar welfare states cannot be derived in any direct sense from the values and habits (the cultures) of the citizens who inhabited them. Rather they were the products of distinct welfarist social philosophies developed by relatively small coteries of influential thinkers. But, once constructed, the new welfare systems did depend on popular acceptance and voters' willingness to continue paying taxes to fund them. The modernist social policy project required strong economic growth and continuity in the pattern of risks it was designed to meet. Once economic growth slowed and, simultaneously, began to generate forms and patterns of diswelfare that the established social policies could not remedy, public acquiescence began to fracture (e.g. Carter 1998; Giddens 1998). One option is to seek to reform and adapt the existing welfare institutions in ways that more nearly meet the new patterns of risk. However, in the context of a politics that will not allow incremental growth in public expenditure, such reforms require voter support. To some degree this has been forthcoming in smaller and more homogeneous societies such as the Scandinavian countries (Stephens 1996). But in Britain and the United States particularly, the traditional and reliable voting blocks based on class, geography or ethnicity have crumbled and been replaced by shifting issue-based majorities. Broad social policy projects which require sustained agreement and compromise in support of a spectrum of social policy interventions do not succeed.

Some core values continue to retain mass support (Yankelovich 1994), but at the same time sharpening differences in people's economic fortunes have created a political environment where electoral success often depends upon patching together temporary majorities based on support for unsystematic lists of policy positions. This route to re-election was particularly clearly demonstrated by President Clinton's second-term victory in 1996 in the context of a political climate that was producing majorities for his Republican opponents in both houses of Congress. Clinton's re-election was achieved quite literally by finding out what voters wanted and promising to provide it. Often this "serendipity" approach shocked the president's policy advisers and cabinet members who still thought in terms of sets of policies ordered in terms of core principles. The re-election strategy was therefore devised in secret by the political strategist Dick Morris, who continuously polled voters in key states and tested the findings by monitoring the response to relatively unnoticed (in Washington and New York) television advertisements.

> The core of the strategy that emerged was to embrace parts of the Republican initiative and reject others. We would work to eliminate the deficit, require work for welfare, cut taxes, and reduce federal bureaucracy . . . But we would reject . . . the efforts to cut Medicare benefits, to eliminate Medicaid guarantees, weaken environmental-protection laws, and reduce federal aid to schools. (Morris 1997: 93)

> We identified and spelled out [a] consensus in our polling . . . Massive majorities consistently rejected the doctrinaire views of both the left and the right and embraced an amalgam of conservative and liberal positions:
> On abortion: keep it legal and safe, but regulate it, require parental involvement . . .
> On welfare: require recipients to work, limit the time on the rolls, but provide day care, job opportunities, education and training . . .
> On the deficit: balance the budget . . . , but don't violate core priorities,

like Medicare, Medicaid, education . . . , the environment . . .
> On crime: mandate tough sentences, capital punishment, more policy
> and controls on handguns . . . but not on hunting rifles . . .
> Consensus was apparent in virtually every poll on all these issues. The
> American rejection of politics today is largely rooted in the government's
> failure to implement these common beliefs. (1997: 208)

Dick Morris is recognized as a brilliant strategist but his methods still shock the political establishment. They are accustomed to a politics dependent upon consistent programmes, defined by recognizable political philosophies. His approach is indeed to discover what the mass culture wants and to promise, if not deliver, it. In the UK at the turn of the century a similarly eclectic approach to welfare reform is being practised by the Blair government. It focuses above all on values: "a central vision based around principle but liberated from particular policy prescriptions that become confused with principle" (Blair 1994: 7). It is democratic in that it pursues the changes that majorities support. But it often offends those, increasingly called "Old Labour", who still think in terms of a coherent welfare project. One might even suggest that Frank Field's mistake in toiling over his Green Paper, *A New Contract for Welfare* (DSS 1998) was to try to construct, like Beveridge, an internally consistent welfare framework. He too was seeking to change culture rather than reflect it. He might have found it far easier merely to have compiled a list of policy changes each of which was likely to command a value majority.

Conclusion

The mass culture of a society, its broad values and tastes, is not a foundation for the construction or systematic reform of the welfare state. These can only take place at times of exceptional political or economic crisis. A nation's culture, particularly in the context of "post-industrial" break-up of the large constituencies based on occupation, is riven with particularistic, contradictory, shifting, sometimes bigoted, often exclusive value positions. Culture is neither a likely cause nor a supportive context for the welfare state.

References

Aaron, H. J., Mann, T. E., and Taylor, T. (eds) (1994), *Values and Public Policy*, Washington, DC: Brookings Institution.

Almond, G. A., and Verba, S. (1963), *The Civic Culture, Political Attitudes and Democracy in Five Nations*, Princeton, NJ: Princeton University Press.

Banting, K. (1979), *Poverty, Politics and Policy*, London: Macmillan.

Barry, N. (1999), *Welfare* (2nd edn), Concepts in the Social Sciences Series, Buckingham: Open University Press.

Blair, T. (1994), *Socialism*, Fabian Pamphlet no. 565, London: Fabian Society.

Carter, J. (ed.) (1998), *Postmodernity and the Fragmentation of Welfare*, London: Routledge.

Catanese, A. J. (1974), *Planners and Local Politics: Impossible Dreams*, Aldershot: Sage.

Clark, T. J. (1999), *Farewell to an Idea: Episodes from a History of Modernism*, New Haven and London: Yale University Press.

Crossman, R. H. S. (1966), *Socialism and Planning*, London: Fabian Society.

Crossman, R. H. S. (1977), *Diaries*, ed. J. Morgan, London: Fontana Books.

Deakin, N. (1987), *The Politics of Welfare*, London: Methuen.

Dearlove, J. (1973), *The Politics of Policy in Local Government, the Making and Maintenance of Public Policy in the Royal Borough of Kensington and Chelsea*, Cambridge: Cambridge University Press.

Department of Social Security (DSS) (1998), *New Ambitions for Our Country: A New Contract for Welfare*, Cm 3805, London: The Stationery Office.

Durkheim, E. (1952), *Suicide: a Study in Sociology* [1897], ed. G. Simpson, London: Routledge and Kegan Paul.

Durkheim, E. (1984), *The Division of Labour in Society* [1893], tr. W. D. Halls, intro. Lewis Coser, Basingstoke: Macmillan.

Esping-Andersen, G. (1997), Hybrid or Unique? The Japanese Welfare State between Europe and America, *Journal of European Social Policy*, 7, 3: 179–89.

Esping-Andersen, G. (1999), *Social Foundations of Postindustrial Economies*, Oxford: Oxford University Press.

Giddens, A. (1998), *The Third Way: the Renewal of Social Democracy*, Cambridge: Polity Press.

Goffman, I. (1963), *Stigma: Notes on the Management of Spoiled Identity*, Englewood Cliffs, NJ: Prentice Hall.

Harrison, T. (1978), *Living Through the Blitz*, Harmondsworth: Penguin.

Heclo, H. (1974), *Modern Social Politics in Britain and Sweden, from Relief to Income Maintenance*, New Haven, CT: Yale University Press.

Henderson, J., and Karn, V. (1987), *Race, Class and State Housing: Inequality and the Allocation of Public Housing*, Aldershot: Gower.

Hill, M. J. (1976), *The State, Administration and the Individual*, London: Fontana.

Ka, L. (1999), *Confucian Welfare Cluster: a Cultural Interpretation of Social Welfare*, Acta Universitatis Tamperensis 645, Tampere.

Lukes, S. (1973), *Emile Durkheim: His Life and Work*, London: Allen Lane The Penguin Press.

Morris, D. (1997), *Behind the Oval Office: Winning the Presidency in the Nineties*, New York: Random House.

Newman, J. (1996), *Shaping Organisational Cultures in Local Government*, London: Pitman, in association with Institute of Local Government Studies.

Page, R. M. (1996), *Altruism and the British Welfare State*, Aldershot: Avebury.

Pinker, R. A. (1979), *The Idea of Welfare*, London: Heinemann.

Pithouse, A. (1987), *Social Work: the Social Organization of an Invisible Trade*, Aldershot: Avebury.

Plamenatz, J. (1970), *Ideology*, London: Pall Mall.

Pressman, J. L., and Wildavsky, A. (1973), *Implementation: How Great Expectations in Washington are Dashed in Oakland, or, Why It's Amazing that Federal Programs Work at All, This Being a Saga of the Economic Development Administration as Told by Two Sympathetic Observers who Seek to Build Morals on a Foundation of Ruined Hopes*, Berkeley: University of California Press.

Prottas, J. M. (1979), *People Processing, the Street-level Bureaucrat in Public Service Bureaucracies*, Lexington, MA: Lexington Books.

Ryle, G. (1973), *The Concept of Mind*, Harmondsworth: Penguin.

Selznick, P. (1949), *TVA and the Grass Roots, a Study of Politics and Organization*, Berkeley: University of California Press.

Stephens, J. D. (1996), The Scandinavian Welfare States: achievements, crisis and prospects. In Gosta Esping-Andersen (ed.), *Welfare States in Transition: National Adaptations in Global Economies*, London: Sage.

Strong, P. M. (1979), *The Ceremonial Order of the Clinic, Parents, Doctors, and Medical Bureaucracies*, London, Boston: Routledge and Kegan Paul.

Swartz, M. (ed.) (1969), *Local-level Politics: Social and Cultural Perspectives*, London: London University Press.

Titmuss, R. M. (1950), *Problems of Social Policy*, London: Longmans, Green and Co.

Titmuss, R. M. (1970), *The Gift Relationship*, London: Allen and Unwin.

Titmuss, R. M. (1974), *Social Policy*, London: Allen and Unwin.

Titmuss, R. M. (1976), *Commitment to Welfare* (2nd edn), London: Allen and Unwin.

Van Deth, J. W., and Scarbrough, E. (1995), The concept of values. In J. W. Van Deth and E. Scarbrough (eds), *The Impact of Values, Beliefs in Government Volume Four*, Oxford: Oxford University Press.

Weber, M. (1958). *The Protestant Ethic and the Spirit of Capitalism*, tr. Talcott Parsons, foreword by R. H. Tawney, New York: Scribner's.

Weber, M. (1964), *The Religion of China: Confucianism and Taoism*, tr. H. H. Gerth, London and New York: Collier-Macmillan.

Wilensky, H. (1981), Leftism, Catholicism and democratic corporatism: the role of political parties in recent welfare state development. In P. Flora and A. J. Heidenheimer (eds), *The Development of Welfare States in Europe and America*, London and New Brunswick, NJ: Transaction Books.

Yankelovich, D. (1994), How changes in the economy are reshaping American values. In Aaron *et al.* (1994): 16–53.

8

"Risk Society": The Cult of Theory and the Millennium?

Robert Dingwall

By comparison with sociology, social policy has only occasionally worshipped at the shrine of social theory. Although some of its founders had a serious interest in the philosophical aspects of the subject, social policy has conventionally been caricatured, especially by sociologists, as an empiricist discipline, obsessively collecting facts to be assembled into a relatively unquestioned narrative of progress towards Fabian enlightenment. Like all caricatures, this has elements of both truth and falsity. Although it is probably correct that social policy students receive less formal training in social theory than their counterparts in sociology, it is also undeniable that social policy scholars have shown an increasing awareness of social theory over the last twenty years as the postwar normative consensus has broken up and both the means and the ends of social policy have become more contested. The titular movement from "social administration" to "social policy" may be an index of this: the focus has widened from the fine-tuning of accepted institutions to embrace the intellectual frameworks which generate and challenge those institutions. Sometimes the result seems like a "cultural cringe" in the face of those writers from the humanities or other social sciences who do this very special and difficult thing called "theory". However, it is important that the discipline does not lose its comparative advantage in asking questions about the empirical foundation of theoretical analyses: if the deformation of social policy is empiricism, that of sociology is ungrounded abstraction.

This chapter pursues its argument about the relationship between theory and empirical knowledge in social policy through a discussion of the increasingly fashionable proposition that we now live in something called a "risk society". Although its popularization owes much to the rhetorical skills of Tony Giddens (1990, 1991, 1994; see also Franklin 1997), its coinage by the German sociologist, Ulrich Beck (1992), is fully acknowledged within the social science community. Beck's *Risk Society: Towards a New Modernity* was first published as *Risikogesellschaft: Auf dem Weg in eine andere Moderne* in 1986. Translated into English in 1992, five reprintings were recorded by 1998, the date of the copy used by the present author. Few contemporary monographs yield such returns, whether in economic capital for the publishers or symbolic capital for the author. In this chapter, *Risk Society* stands for a genre of theoretical writing which argues that, at some point in the last 20–30 years, traditional capitalist societies, which could still be analysed largely in the terms set by the nineteenth-century founders of sociology, began to change in some rather fundamental way—towards "late modernity", "post-modernity", "high modernity", "post-capitalism" or whatever. These books have had an increasing influence on thinking about social policy and its response to that society—however we choose to label it. We enter the new millennium with an apparent consensus on the change, even if we cannot quite agree what to call it.

Before accepting this analysis, however, its central theoretical and empirical propositions should be rigorously tested. In the space of a journal essay, this cannot be comprehensively accomplished. However, by taking *Risk Society* as a case study, it may be possible to assess the claim that the new century will be very different from the last—the millennium may be left to chiliasts. Are we simply looking at intellectual *fin de siècle* or is a different world really emerging, with dimensions that challenge both social theory and social policy?

The Social Context of "Risk Society"

Risk Society is a profoundly German book. Most of the citations are to other German authors, the acknowledgements are to German colleagues and the book's drafting "in the open on a hill above the Starnberger See" (p.15) is lovingly recorded.[1] This is not xenophobic criticism but a conventional observation that sociology is itself a social product and, as such, needs to be understood in the same way as any other cultural artefact. French writing on postmodernity cannot be separated from the competitive arena of the Parisian intellectual TV chat show, which has no equivalent in the English-speaking world. Ritzer's (1996) McDonaldization thesis is indelibly marked with the experience of the unification of American cultures by the mass market. The circumstances of production must be considered to evaluate any book's claim to analyse the contemporary world in general. It is easy to assume that which should properly be demonstrated, that the condition of capitalism and the alleged movement towards its successor society are always and everywhere broadly the same.

Three features of the German experience seem important in under-standing where the analysis in *Risk Society* comes from. One, obviously, is the history of fascism, of the war and of complicity in the Holocaust. A second is the postwar economic miracle and the wide political consensus between Christian and social democracy about the management of society and the economy over that period. This ideological closure is often held to have played a particular role in the rise of urban political terrorism and so-called "extra-parliamentary opposition" in the late 1960s and 1970s. These movements laid the foundations for a Green constituency in the politics of the 1980s and 1990s whose nature and scale have not been reproduced elsewhere in Europe. Finally, there is a particular conception of the role of intellectuals. Although this is derived in part from these social conditions, it also reflects a longstanding tradition in German thought, where critique has been valued over constructive engagement. Practical schools like Cameralism (Small 1909) have been less central, and less translated, than the line from Kant and Hegel through Marx, Freud and Frankfurt Marxism, which has sought to define the Good Society and to chart the failure of any contemporary example to match that Utopian ideal. The struggle has continued in the postwar period, where the *Positivismusstreit*, the quarrel about positivism, which split the German Sociological Association in the 1960s, was as much an argument about politics, the social engagement of sociology with the processes of policy and government, as it was about method (Adorno *et al.* 1976). Many contemporary German sociologists, and Beck is no exception, dwell in the massive shadow cast by Jürgen Habermas and his renewal of critical theory. A core theme is the assertion that modernity has failed to deliver the freedom that it promised but has simply created new forms of enslavement, new obstacles to authentic communication. Empirical evidence rarely figures in these arguments: the response of many in the critical theory tradition can be summed up by Poulantzas's reply to a question about the extent to which his position could be changed by evidence, namely that his theory did not provide for the possibility that it could be (Bell and Newby 1977: 25). A concern for evidence is located within an entirely different and incommensurable discourse.

However, a concern for evidence may be a reasonable concern for those who are asked to translate critical theory into measures of policy and practice. In reading *Risk Society* as a text for social policy, as well as for social theory, the foundation of its assertions must constantly be questioned. Often, it will be argued, this seems to derive far more from "what as a matter of commonsense any German intellectual knows to be true" rather than any specific social or historical study.

Risk Society is divided into three main sections: an introduction of the main thesis and its contrast with traditional analyses; the application of this thesis in the context of class, family and work; and the discussions of its implications for the place of science and technology and their relation to the political sphere. Each of these will be reviewed before a general appraisal of the book and its impact is offered.

Living on the Volcano of Civilization

Beck's own title for the first part sets a metaphorical tone for his book. We are invited to imagine ourselves in the place of the farmers on Vesuvius, peacefully tending our gardens and vineyards while, beneath our feet, immense and unimaginable forces are at work which can at any unpredictable moment bring catastrophe, death and destruction upon us. *Risk Society* is a wake-up call. More formally, the book's argument is summed up in its opening lines:

> In advanced modernity the social production of *wealth* is systematically accompanied by the social production of *risks*. Accordingly, the problems and conflicts relating to distribution in a society of scarcity

overlap with the problems and conflicts that arise from the production, definition and distribution of techno-scientifically produced risks. (p. 19)

This can be unpacked into a series of underlying or implied claims: first, that we live in a condition called "advanced modernity" or, elsewhere in the text, "late modernity" which is somehow different from "modernity" *tout court*, which is in turn different from whatever went before; second, that distribution in "a society of scarcity"—whose relationship to "modernity", let alone "advanced modernity", is unspecified—poses problems and conflicts; third, that these problems and conflicts overlap—but are not identical to—the problems and conflicts associated with techno-scientifically produced risks; fourth, that techno-scientific risks are in some sense different from other, as yet adjectivally unspecified, risks.

The two chapters which make up the first part of *Risk Society* extend and develop these claims. The first claim is dealt with largely by implication and it will be convenient to postpone discussion of it until the case studies in the second part of the book are reviewed. The second is dealt with fairly sketchily by reference to the traditional concern of sociology for the problem of order and the ways in which wealth could be distributed in ways which were simultaneously unequal and perceived to be legitimate. Beck's real interest is in the third and fourth claims.

Risk distribution is replacing wealth distribution as a core issue—Beck's third claim—because the growth of productivity and state welfare has meant that "genuine material need" can be significantly reduced and confined to marginalized groups and that the productive forces responsible for this have thrown up new and previously unknown hazards. These hazards, however, fall unequally and the problem of legitimating this inequality has yet to be solved. The faster productive development eliminates material need, the more hazards appear: in effect, modernization compounds its own problems. In one of Beck's core concepts, modernization becomes the problem in the form of *reflexive modernization*, the dog which chases its own tail and can never catch it. This is most obvious in the welfare states of the West, where the end of the struggle for subsistence has removed the prop of legitimacy from modernization and technological development as a crusade against scarcity. The beneficiaries of technical and economic development come to perceive themselves as its victims.

Beck considers the objection, to the fourth claim, that risk is not a new phenomenon. However, he argues that contemporary techno-scientific risk is qualitatively different. It is not *personal* in the way that Columbus and his crew volunteered for the hazards of a voyage of discovery. It is *global*, in the sense that the destruction of forests results from pollution rather than direct exploitation. It is *imperceptible*, in contrast to the stink of the nineteenth-century River Thames. It derives from an *oversupply* rather than an *undersupply* of technology, as in waste disposal. These diffuse collective risks challenge the bases of the probabilistic calculations of scientific risk management which proceed without reference to the human beings affected by them. The result is an irruption of the political into a domain which has been technocratic and naturalistic. Risk management is an impersonal metric which conceals a range of social and moral judgements. This revelation challenges trust in governments, expertise and science. The rationalities of scientists, technocrats and citizens collide. However, the responsibility for risks becomes increasingly elusive. The interdependence of productive forces characteristic of modern societies dissolves personal responsibility into that of a diffuse "system", apparently an elaboration of an argument within German sociology where Luhmann (1984: for a useful summary discussion see Munch 1994: 271–305) and his followers have proposed a particularly strong version of systems theory.

> Everyone is cause *and* effect, and thus *non*-cause. The causes dribble away into a general amalgam of agents and conditions, reactions and counter-reactions, which brings social certainty and popularity to the concept of system. This reveals in exemplary fashion the ethical significance of the system concept: *one can do something and continue doing it without having to take personal responsibility for it.* (Beck 1992: 33)

Paradoxically, those societies which have solved the visible problem of wealth are those which have come to face the invisible problem of risk. However, those societies which are preoccupied with the problem of wealth and the elimination of tangible need—in the Third World—are, in the process, piling up problems of risk. The race for wealth may suppress the perception of risk but cannot suppress the risk itself. In the end, risk society always wins.

The risk society is the environment for new political alliances and new social movements. The proletariat is replaced by the mass of citizens as the political subject. The proletariat and its organizations have been the great winners in the move from scarcity to wealth. This places them among the conservative forces in a risk society precisely because of their investment in the class society which is being superseded. In a risk society, everyone is a potential victim—not just those who have nothing to sell but their labour power. The basis of solidarity shifts from need to anxiety, something which is unrelated to wealth. Money cannot buy insulation from risk. Modern civilization is a collective enemy of all.

In the original, of course, this argument is stated with qualifications and complexities to which a summary essay cannot do justice. It is difficult to avoid creating a straw figure with which to do combat rather than the thesis itself. Nevertheless, to the extent that core elements of the case shake under scrutiny, this may create some reasonable doubt about the parts which cannot be examined in the same detail.

Focusing for a moment on the third claim, there seems to be a fundamental problem with Beck's insistence on the meeting of "objective material need". The concept of "need" has, of course, been a traditional difficulty within the academic discipline of social policy (Smith 1980; Doyal and Gough 1991). Beck appears to be adopting what one might call the "Rowntree approach" of equating need with subsistence. This raises two further problems. One, which might be identified with the work of Sahlins (1974) and, to some extent, Sen (e.g. Drèze and Sen 1989) is that of whether subsistence becomes a problem only within a capitalist order at a particular stage of development.

Sahlins, for example, argues that few people in traditional indigenous societies would ever have gone to bed hungry, except in the wake of unpredictable natural catastrophes—droughts, storms, earthquakes, etc. The view that they are poor and on the margins of subsistence is one that anthropologists have taken over uncritically from colonial observers. To the extent that their way of life can be recovered from historical records and contemporary observations, hunter-gatherers do not have to work particularly hard to obtain sufficient food and to be able to possess those goods which their own culture considers to be of value. Poverty, Sahlins suggests, is the creation of an industrial civilization which measures what we have against limitless possibility.

Natural catastrophes and their incidence have, of course, many of the characteristics of the risks described by Beck—invisible, random, collective in their impact and essentially uncontrollable by individual actors. This has, however, never prevented attempts to propose explanations and control measures within local systems of rationality, whether these have involved attempts at predicting events, perhaps by divination or oracles, or placating the forces or entities believed to be responsible, by prayer, say, or sacrifice. (The differences between these traditional rationalities and Western science will be discussed later.) Techno-economic development became possible as a result of squeezing a margin of surplus from people living at subsistence level. The accumulating inequalities led ultimately to the situation described by Drèze and Sen (1989) in their study of the Bengal famine of 1974, now a commonplace of development economics, namely that starvation in the contemporary world is rarely a matter of lack of food but is crucially the result of a lack of purchasing power. Arguably, for example, the success of the Green Revolution in Asia has had less to do with the specific increase in rice crop yields and more to do with the way in which the farmers' production of larger surpluses has enhanced their ability to participate in the market economy and to invest for the future through the market rather than, say, through large families. The meeting of subsistence needs remains an important distributional issue and cannot be assumed quite as lightly as Beck does from his position in one of the world's most affluent societies.

Although Beck makes some acknowledgement of this, it is puzzling that he does not extend his generally constructionist position to the analysis of need itself. Social policy has moved on from the "Rowntree approach" to seeing need as in large measure relative to societal context, much as Sahlins argued. In his classic study of poverty, for example, Townsend (1979) argued that goods like televisions, telephones and holidays should be seen as needs, in the sense that those who do not have access to them are significantly excluded from participation in the society in which they live. Whatever the force of Beck's argument in relation to objective need, it is implausible to argue that these relative needs can be met without a concern for wealth distribution which he rejects as a phenomenon of a disappearing past. We may accept that the rich will always have more than the poor: on the other hand, many of the things which the rich have today—Internet access, for example—will come to be seen as necessities of civilized life tomorrow. The widening economic inequalities seen in many societies do not suggest that the problem of distribution can be treated as closed, even if the bases for mobilization are less immediately obvious than to the observers of nineteenth-century industrial work.

Risk Society seems uncertain about whether it is posing a new social distribution of risk or treating risk as a collective threat. If the emphasis is on distribution, then it may be very hard to disentangle from the distributional issues around wealth. Poverty also brings an increased exposure to risks of accidents, morbidity and premature death. Hazardous occupations do not pay the risk premium that neo-classical economics would predict (Felstiner *et al.* 1989). To a considerable extent, the rich can buy insulation from risk. It is no accident that better-off people have tended to live to the South and West of British industrial cities where the prevailing wind takes the pollution in the opposite direction. Beck suggests that the risks of the contemporary world are not susceptible to this kind of avoidance. It may be more accurate to argue, however, that the rich have simply not yet discovered how to avoid them. An important counter-example to Beck's thesis is that of epidemic disease. It is widely accepted by social historians that an important influence on the effort to clean up British cities in the nineteenth century was the recognition by the wealthy that diseases like cholera were a threat to their own health as much as to the health of the poor, just as Beck describes for radiation or atmospheric pollution. The theoretical basis for these interventions was miasmatic and non-specific, that disease generally resulted from foul odours, rather than bacterial and specific, but the interventions were nevertheless effective. The actual impact of these diseases was just as associated with the distribution of wealth as any modern disease—the poor died from cholera in greater numbers than the rich, just as it is still the poor who die earlier from myocardial infarctions and most other causes. However, everyone was exposed to miasmas and any move to reduce these would benefit the rich, even if it actually gave an even greater benefit to the poor in terms of absolute reductions in mortality. The paradox of scientific advance in medicine is that it has in some respects become easier for the rich to insulate their health from that of the poor. If we know that cholera is caused by a bacterium, which is transmitted only through contaminated water supplies, can be resisted by vaccination and successfully treated by specific therapy, we can buy our own supply of clean water and our own medical facilities and cut ourselves off from other social groups who remain exposed to this hazard. Education about health may increase rather than diminish inequality, as those least at risk lead the way in changing their environment and lifestyle further to reduce this—a new twist on the "Inverse Care Law", that those least in need of health services tend to receive more of them (Tudor Hart 1971).

As an example, cholera has its limitations because of the "obviousness" of the miasma, although Beck stands back again from his own constructionism. Did the River Thames really smell any worse when Parliament was obliged to suspend its sittings on hot days in the summer of 1858 or was it that sensibilities had changed? Even today cities have characteristic smells which pass all but unnoticed to their own residents but strike directly at visitors. Plague may be a better example, a peril which stole up on Europe from time to time for a period of five hundred years. Again, the rich could not consciously buy insulation, except by flight, which was only a limited guarantee of security. In a comparison of responses to epidemic disease from the Black Death to AIDS, Strong (1990) has shown a characteristic pattern of societal reaction from fear, insecurity, a manic casting around for explanations, and a sense of panic that civilization itself was under threat, to a recognition that one of life's nuisances had come around again but that enough of us would survive to carry on. All risks were eventually routinized.

If it is arguable that neither the nature of risk nor its association with the distribution of wealth is particularly new, then doubt must be cast on Beck's fourth claim. Is it simply the case, as Strong's argument suggests, that the contemporary risks which he identifies have yet to be absorbed by the historic processes of risk management which seem to recur widely across human time and space, even if it is too grand and unverifiable a claim to suggest that they characterize all human societies? Perhaps there is, at most, a particular congestion of risks which has placed these processes under an unfamiliar strain? The term "risk management" is, of course, used here in a wider sense than Beck employs it, to acknowledge that the mathematical technologies of insurance or risk assessment are not the only means by which humans seek to manage risk. The Aztec captive sacrificed to manage the risk that the sun will not rise tomorrow is the functional equivalent of an insurance policy for the parish fete to cover losses due to rain. In fact, the encounter of pre-Columbian America with the *conquistadores* is a helpful model for the loss of trust in government and expertise. These societies fell apart less as a result of the superior military technology of the Spanish than from the sight of absolute rulers and their priest class simply being unable to sustain claims to control relations between the human, divine and natural worlds. There are clearly differences between the theologically-based claims of the Inca or Aztec emperors and priests and the claims of modern governments to manage the risks of life by techno-economic means: however, the sociological question is surely whether these are really more important than the similarities.

The wider politics of Beck's analysis recur as themes throughout, and it will be more convenient to deal with them later when the general thesis has been more fully tested.

The Individualization of Social Inequality

The second part of *Risk Society* focuses on the distributional logic of the risks held to be associated with advanced modernity. Reflexive modernization is destroying the social forms of industrial society—class, family, gender, marriage, parenthood, occupations—in the shapes we have known them. There is a surge of individualization so that the ascribed fate of classes and their members becomes the achieved fate of individuals. The dissolution of classes forces people into a narcissistic preoccupation with planning and managing their own lives. Social crises such as mass unemployment are reduced to aggregates of individual failures. The family becomes "nego-tiated", an assembly of individuals who will stay together only as long as self-interest dictates. Individualization is, though, deceptive: it works only so long as it matches the standards imposed upon it by institutions, most notably those associated with the labour market. This contradiction may form the basis of new social movements, a search for the reality of individualism and freedom from control which is always vulnerable to colonization by the very institutions it opposes—think of the use of street music to sell mass-produced soft drinks or the development of "ethnic" burger products by international franchises.

These issues are explored through discussions of class, gender, families and labour markets. Given the space available, only the issues around families will be examined here. Beck's analysis of these may be less distinctive than some other parts of his argument but this may allow it to serve better as a case study.

He begins by asserting what is at one level an uncontroversial proposition among sociologists, that discussions of the organization of the family and of gender relations cannot be wholly separated from discussions of the organization of work, occupations and the market. Traditional gender roles are dissolving, although the legitimacy of distinction is changing faster than the reality. Men and women are not fully equal but discrimination is no longer publicly acceptable. However, these are not changes as a result of processes in the private sphere alone but the result of the reconstruction of the private sphere by the public. The version of family life which served an earlier phase of modernity is no longer viable and is being destroyed by reflexive modernization.

According to Beck, this process has three aspects. First, the gendered division of labour "is the *basis* of industrial society" (p.104). The separation of male and female roles by nineteenth-century capitalism is the foundation of the nuclear family and of women's dependence upon men. Wage labour presupposes housework. The contractual nature of market relationships presupposes the communality of marriage. One's place in the division of labour is ascribed from birth according to gender. However, the advance of industrial society throws up increasing contradictions, comparable to those described by Marx for social classes. Relationships of dependency and statuses of ascription, located outside the market, are increasingly anachronistic. Men and women cannot be equalized within structures that assume their difference and inequality. As women are brought into the market and achieve economic independence by their own merits, the traditional industrial family is less and less attractive.

Second, the onward march of individualization creates a need for partnership which it simultaneously undermines. To introduce Durkheim's language, as men and women are released from the predetermined roles and status fates of mechanical solidarity, they are driven to search for an emotional community of organic solidarity. That dream is, however, always undercut by the assertion of individualism, that the relationship must satisfy each member's self-interest. The lives of men are less affected directly by this: economic individualization joins directly to masculine behaviour. The lives of women are in tension between the demands of career and of homemaking. Women's individualization turns them against men's "failures" as homemakers, as it turns men against women's "selfishness". This is compounded by the third aspect—the culture of choice. If we choose our fates, then we are responsible for them, and it is increasingly difficult to avoid choosing in a market where everything is held to be open. Beck points to the tensions around the labour market's demand for personal mobility, the notion that both spouses have a right to an individual career and their desire for an affective relationship which can satisfy their individual desires. These are aggravated by the presence of children: indeed, the market society is ultimately a childless one, unless the children are associated with single, mobile parents. The point might be added that even this is questionable if one accepts the argument that children are also individuals with individual rights. For the present, though, parenthood is the last primary relationship and absorbs all the emotions and commitments that can no longer be poured into marriage.

Beck speculates about three possible futures: the reconstitution of the nuclear family by mass unemployment and social security arrangements which reinstate women's dependency on men; the acceptance of a "fully mobile society of singles" which fails to meet the affective needs of both sexes and is sustainable only by heavy investment in friendships; and a rather vaguely specified third way of seeking to provide stronger institutional supports for *families*—in employment opportunities, housing, day care and social security—while allowing *individuals* more freedom to work out their own division of labour as a matter of choice. Beck is pessimistic about the likelihood of any of these solutions emerging or being wholly satisfactory. However, there may be some consolation in recognizing that the troubles with which men and women reproach each other are a matter of social structures rather than individual failings.

This has some echoes of the ways in which systems theory undermines individual responsibility, which Beck criticized in an earlier chapter of *Risk Society*. However, there are two more fundamental problems with his analysis. One relates to the implied history and the other to the evidence of a collision between individual rights and human needs.

The first of these returns to Beck's claim that modernity is somehow different from previous forms of society. Here it is allied to a specific assertion that the nuclear family is an invention of modern industrial societies. The notion that the modern world is very different to its predecessors is fundamental to sociology. It is the explicit or implicit contrast at the heart of all the classical writers—Marx, Spencer, Weber, Durkheim. The problem is that this opposition is formulated as a matter of vague generalities and, in many cases, as a contrast between an Arcadian past and an inhuman future. If it is reduced to a series of more specific propositions, as contemporary social and economic historians have sought to do, then its empirical validity becomes seriously questionable. The idea that a new form of family emerged during the nineteenth century is a good example (see the general discussion in Dingwall and Eekelaar 1988). The evidence to support this claim is not very convincing for England—although it may be defensible for Germany and other parts of the European mainland (Flandrin 1979; Anderson 1980). The English have tended to live in relatively small family groups for as long as anyone can record (Wrigley and Schofield 1981). For most ordinary people, marriage was a voluntary relationship regulated mainly by community sanctions, certainly until the arrival of civil registration in 1836 and arguably well beyond (Parker 1990). Extensive provision was still required after the First World War for the payment of pensions to dependants of servicemen killed in action who were recognized as their spouses but not joined in a legal relationship. Conversely, in a society before computers, people who wanted to leave a marriage could and did literally walk away. The English were a remarkably mobile people from the earliest times (Clark 1979). They had a strong sense of individualism, even under a pre-capitalist economy (Macfarlane 1979) and a strong sense of romantic attachment (Macfarlane 1970). Ordinary women always worked in large numbers, in household production or agriculture and enjoyed considerable *de facto* economic independence. This was stimulated by the industrialization of employment: Anderson (1971) records the complaints of early nineteenth-century Lancashire mill towns about the behaviour of young women earning good wages in the textile factories.

To be sure, Beck makes his argument in relation to what he describes as the bourgeois model of the family. In doing so, however, he disregards both the remarkable persistence of alternative forms, and the extent to which the so-called nuclear industrial family is evident well before the dominance of that mode of production, at least in England. It should, perhaps, be conceded that England always presented a problem for European mainland sociologists because of the difficulty of fitting it to their models of capitalist development—as in Weber's argument for the necessity of formally-rational law, which England did not have, as a precondition for the emergence of a capitalist economy (Weber 1954). However, the classic thesis is stated as a general proposition and its inapplicability to the English case is a serious methodological problem, even if we do not adopt a strict falsificationist position and demand its entire rejection. This problem should also encourage us to look more closely at the contrast between modern and pre-modern societies and the extent to which a fictionalized past is used either as a basis of criticizing the present, as in the work of Marx, Weber and other German contemporaries, or celebrating it, as in the case of Spencer and, to a lesser extent, Durkheim. We might also ask why the former lives as a tradition so much more strongly than the latter.

The second problem with Beck's argument about the family is the source of his assertions about a fundamental human need for certain kinds of relationships. The more individualized we become, the more we are driven to seek a shared inner life, he argues. There is no citation that supports this claim or allows it to be traced back to some empirical study. In effect, its only authority is its location within a particular chain of philosophical anthropology, which reflects upon the human condition in a quasi-theological fashion. Indeed, God is never very far away in this chapter and Beck is clearly concerned about what might replace the Divine as the foundation of morality and ethical human interrelations. This type of argument is not testable in any sense that an Anglo-Saxon empiricist would recognize: it cannot be specified in ways that make it either falsifiable or verifiable. Either the story is persuasive or it is not. Its persuasiveness depends upon an interaction in which the author and the text meet a reader who brings his or her own framing to both the medium and the content. Read within a tradition of critical theory, it evokes many echoes—of Habermas, of Fromm and Marcuse, or of a theologian like Buber and his search for authentic community in "I–Thou" relationships.

Read outside that hermetic and self-referential tradition, it may seem empty, particularly as the effect is to exclude the obvious fourth possibility, that people may choose commitment over individual rights. If the essence of social order is cooperation and negotiation, as many microsociologists would argue, why should family life be any different? Clearly new family forms in new structural environments may impose new contingencies on the negotiation. However, if hunter-gatherers, or gatherer-hunters, could, without the help of professional sociologists, work out divisions of labour consistent with the reproduction of their societies, it .seems strange to suppose that contemporary men and women cannot do the same. There are dangers in the drift towards a rights-oriented society, which may be seen as a version of reflexive modernization in the way that the unregulated pursuit of rights undercuts the possibilities of community, but these are well recognized and do not seem to be insoluble (e.g. Friedman 1987; Selznick 1992; Etzioni 1996).

Science and Politics

The third part of *Risk Society* aims to pull together the argument about reflexive modernization, as expressed in the logic of risk distribution and the advance of individualization, through a study of science and technology and their relationship to politics. Individualization has destroyed the traditional bases of authority in the industrial society, traditional in the sense that they are the replacements for the forms of authority that held sway in the feudal agrarian society that industrialization itself destroyed. One of these is the prestige of science and technology, which are seen merely as particular belief systems rather than as windows on truth. This view is reinforced by the role of science and technology both in wealth creation and in revealing the risk associated with that process. One of the paradoxes of reflexive modernization is that the scientists' work in the discovery and delineation of risk becomes the basis for the discrediting of science as a risk-generating exercise.

In the interests of brevity, this discussion will again focus on one part of the development of this argument, Beck's discussion of medicine, which he himself presents as "an extreme case study". Beck professes himself agnostic on whether medicine has actually improved the well-being of humankind. However, he argues, it is indisputable that it has contributed to the increase of population through "improvements in hygiene which would have been unthinkable without the results of medical research" (p. 204). In advanced modernity, medicine produces more diseases than it can treat, in the sense that the advance of diagnosis allows the labelling of chronic illnesses without the means to cure them. Medicine has taken illness away from people and systematically increased their ignorance. Professionalization has gone hand in hand with the medicalization of everyday life as power has been removed from the public arena by the profession to act without the consent of the public who are the objects of its technology. Beck quotes the example of *in vitro* fertilization, where a technology is introduced because of its possibility and a cultural revolution (of fatherless motherhood) made possible, without anyone other than genetic specialists choosing this. The foundations of the family, marriage and intimate relationships are being destroyed without challenge or question. The profession's control of the cognitive development of medicine gives it the opportunity both to create risks and to profit by their management. At the same time, the awareness of those risks undermines its credibility as individuals choose the systems of health theory which appeal to them. Medicine is one of the great monopolies of industrial society which will break up unless it can institutionalize self-criticism and diversity.

The account of medicine given here probably has more in common with the polemics of Ivan Illich (1977) than with anything that a medical sociologist or social historian of medicine would regard as evidentially justifiable. Although the pure form of the "McKeown thesis"—that medicine had virtually nothing to do with the reduction in mortality in industrial societies from 1840 to the 1950s—now has few supporters, even his critics accept that clinical intervention played a minimal part in this process. Beck's argument may be partly a matter of different historical experiences and institutional structures. Critics of McKeown (1976, 1979), like Winter (1982) and Szreter (1988), have argued convincingly that he understates the role of public health doctors in the promotion of hygienic measures. However, under English government structures, doctors could only act with the support of local civic leaders and in partnership with sanitary engineers and other urban technologists. Arguably, the situation in Prussia, where social medicine developed a more central role, would justify Beck's statement—which underlines the earlier point about not mistaking a particular national experience for a general feature of modernization.

The centrality of nosology in medicine goes into the mists of antiquity. The starting point of any system of medicine—allopathic, complementary or traditional—is the naming of problems. Correct naming is the foundation of correct therapy. In that process, there have always been conditions for which there are names but no unique and effective therapy. To the extent that one can still talk about progress, much of this has involved the dissection of categories, so that those which do not respond to some therapy are taken out and become a starting point for new investigations. The historical dynamic of medicine involves a constant movement from loosely specified and empiri- cally treated problems to differential diagnosis and specific therapy. There is no reason to think that what we are seeing today is fundamentally different. The empirical problems of the medicalization thesis were well established by Strong (1979) when he pointed out the error of taking the pronouncements of moral entrepreneurs within the medical community as representative. The discussion of *in vitro* fertilization takes no account of the speed with which the UK government at least moved to regulate the technology, and the assertion that it uniquely permits fatherless motherhood overlooks the simple and widespread use of the turkey-baster, a low-technology, popularly controlled intervention said to be much favoured by lesbians seeking to conceive. The monopoly theory of professionalization has come under increasing criticism since the mid-1980s and the extent to which this rests on a conjunction of occupational, market and state interests in the supply of regulation, rather than on the capture of the state by a well-organized group demanding favourable regulation, has been identified as an important issue for investigation (Dingwall 1999). Again, Beck may have been misled by the national differences: the German medical profession has a tighter legal monopoly than in the UK or the USA and has been notoriously resistant to state intervention in its affairs—partly because of the shadow of the Nazi experience and the consequences of that intervention for the profession and its patients.

Arguably, it is in the conclusion that *Risk Society* demonstrates most crucially the limits of its author's approach to science and technology. On the one hand, the proposal that self-criticism needs to be institutionalized seems to accept far too much of the constructionist critique of scientific knowledge and practice. The issues are well discussed in Horton's (1967) comparison of African traditional thought and Western science, which draws out the importance of the institutionalized commitment to the testing of knowledge that distinguishes the latter. The Azande do not systematically investigate the correctness or otherwise of their oracles. Of course it is important not to over-idealize Western science—it is well documented that much work is essentially routine, that paradigms are not easily shifted and that much of the time both scientists and the users of science think in a commonsense way about it. Nevertheless, the ideal is a regulator of practice and there are few sectors where it is as firmly entrenched as medicine. The "evidence-based medicine" project—that only therapies proven to be effective by the best available tests should be employed—has many fundamental philosophical flaws, but its critical spirit cannot be denied. Beck's unhappiness with systems thinking also seems to lead him away from the importance of competition as a check. This functions at many levels: from the interaction between medicine and law in regulation and tort litigation (Dingwall 1994), to the rivalry between corporations to secure markets, to that between governments, as in the allegations that the German government pressed for strict regulation of genetically-modified food trials to rein back the technological lead of the British biotechnology industry over its German counterpart. Beck sees a corporatist world of monopolies where others might be more struck by the long-term power of creative destruction. Would a scholar in 1500 have seen the potential break-up of the monopoly of the Catholic Church any more than a scholar in 1970 would have foreseen the decline of IBM?

On the Place of Grand Theory

Although this chapter has been a critique of one book, its objective from the outset has been to treat this as representative of a genre. *Risk Society* stands in a line which stretches back to the classical theorists who founded the discipline at the end of the nineteenth century. In this sense, sociology is also an expression of modernity. There are frequent complaints that such books are now rarely written, although greatly valued. If one considers the source of these complaints, however, they seldom come from working sociologists, who observe the profusion of attempts to market oneself as the new Max Weber—ironically, of course, it is only the selective bias of the market for translations that has obscured the scale of Weber's activity as an empirical sociologist. More commonly, these complaints seem to come from people schooled in a humanities tradition, where critical theory has found a ready home in recent years, whether in universities, in intellectual magazines or the review sections of the broadsheet press. The complainants start from an *a priori* hostility to the contemporary world—consider the neglect of Spencer or Parsons, for example, although both had strong arguments that the ends of liberty, justice and equality would be better served by the spontaneous order of a market society than by one which reflected the imposition of the economic and moral preferences of some philosopher-monarch. All that is required to feed their demands is a well-stuffed armchair—or an open hillside above the Starnberger See exposed to the play of the light, the wind and the waves and protected from the intrusions of children and animals—and a sufficiently gloomy disposition. It was not for nothing that Philip Strong used to call sociology a "glum science", convinced that all change was for the worse and that contemporary civilization was doomed. With the added incitement of the eve of the millennium, much of this work is more reminiscent of cultic books and other popular expressions of *fin de siècle* weariness than with the challenges of a difficult century.

Perhaps, however, there is a chance to take an alternative turn and to declare our indifference to the judgement of the humanities. At the beginning of the seventeenth century, Francis Bacon saw that science and technology would not advance while they remained obsessed with high levels of abstraction and generalization:

> The understanding must not . . . be allowed to jump and fly from particulars to remote axioms and of almost the highest generality (such as the first principles as they are called of arts and things), and taking stand upon them as truths that cannot be shaken, proceed to prove and frame the middle axioms by reference to them; which has been the practice hitherto . . . we hope well of the sciences, when in a just scale of ascent, and by successive steps not interrupted or broken, we rise from particulars to lesser axioms; and then to middle axioms, one above the other; and last of all to the most general. For the lower axioms differ but slightly from bare experience, while the highest and most general (which we now have) are notional and abstract and without solidity. But the middle are the true and living axioms, on which depend the fortunes and affairs of men . . . (Bacon 1858: 97)

Almost four hundred years later, Glaser and Strauss (1967) tried to define a similar programme for sociology out of the traditions particularly associated with the University of Chicago from the early 1900s until the 1950s, a call reinforced at the very end of his life by Goffman (1983) in offering, at the close of his ASA Presidential Address, to trade the whole of sociology for some decent conceptual distinctions and a cold beer. Social policy scholars should not need to be reminded of their discipline's traditional virtue of empirical work. Unfortunately this takes time, costs money, requires cooperation from others and does not get the author invited to deliver the Reith lectures or appear on chat shows. It may also lead to an unfashionable respect for the resilience of institutions, cultures and people and a scepticism about the possibilities or benefits of revolutionary change. Remedying some local problems may seem a modest goal but it may make a more valuable contribution to human welfare in the new millennium than any mega-treatise that tries to set the whole world to rights at one go.

Acknowledgement

I am grateful to Alan Aldridge, Paul Martin and Elizabeth Murphy for their comments and suggestions on earlier drafts.

Note

1. The Starnberger See is a large lake just south of Munich.

References

Adorno, T.W., Albert, H., Dahrendorf, R., Habermas, J., Pilot, H., and Popper, K. (1976), *The Positivist Dispute in German Sociology*, London: Heinemann.
Anderson, M. (1971), *Family Structure in Nineteenth Century Lancashire*, Cambridge: Cambridge University Press.
Anderson, M. (1980), *Approaches to the History of the Western Family 1500–1914*, London: Macmillan.
Bacon, F. (1858), *The works of Francis Bacon, Baron of Verulam, Viscount St Albans and Lord High Chancellor of England*, London: Longman.
Beck, U. (1992), *Risk Society: Towards a New Modernity*, London: Sage.
Bell, C., and Newby, H. (eds) (1977), *Doing Sociological Research*, London: Allen and Unwin.
Clark, P. (1979), Migration in England during the late seventeenth and early eighteenth centuries, *Past and Present*, 83: 57–90.
Dingwall, R. (1994), Law and medicine. In Gabe, J., Kelleher, D., and Williams, G. (eds), *Challenging Medicine*, Routledge: London: 46–64.
Dingwall, R. (1999), Professions and social order in a global society, *International Review of Sociology* 9, 1: 131–40.
Dingwall, R., and Eekelaar, J. M. (1988), Families and the state: an historical perspective on the public regulation of private conduct, *Law and Policy*, 10, 4: 341–61.
Doyal, L., and Gough, I. (1991), *A Theory of Human Need*, Basingstoke: Macmillan.
Drèze, J., and Sen, A. (1989), *Hunger and Public Action*, Oxford: Clarendon Press.
Etzioni, A. (1996), *The New Golden Rule: Community and Morality in a Democratic Society*, New York: Basic Books.
Felstiner, W. L. F., Siegelmann, P., and Durkin, T. (1989), Consumers as workers: the problems of complacent theory, *Journal of Consumer Policy*, 12: 381–97.
Flandrin, J.-L. (1979), *Families in Former Times: Kinship, Household and Sexuality*, Cambridge: Cambridge University Press.

Franklin, J. (ed.) (1997), *The Politics of Risk Society*, Cambridge: Polity Press.
Friedman, L. M. (1987), *Total Justice*, Boston: Beacon Press.
Giddens, A. (1990), *The Consequences of Modernity*, Cambridge: Polity Press.
Giddens, A. (1991), *Modernity and Self-Identity: Self and Society in the Late Modern Age*, Cambridge: Polity Press.
Giddens, A. (1994), *Beyond Left and Right: The Future of Radical Politics*, Cambridge: Polity Press.
Glaser, B. G., and Strauss, A. L. (1967), *The Discovery of Grounded Theory: Strategies for Qualitative Research*, New York: Aldine.
Goffman, E. (1983), The interaction order, *American Sociological Review*, 48, 1: 1–17.
Horton, R. (1967), African traditional thought and Western science, *Africa*, 37: 155–87.
Illich, I. (1977), *Medical Nemesis*, Harmondsworth: Penguin.
Luhmann, N. (1984), *Soziale Systeme: Grundriss einer allgemeinen Theorie*, Frankfurt am Main: Suhrkamp.
Macfarlane, A. (1970), *The Family Life of Ralph Josselin, A Seventeenth Century Clergyman*, Cambridge: Cambridge University Press.
Macfarlane, A. (1979), *The Origins of English Individualism*, Oxford: Blackwell.
McKeown, T. (1976), *The Modern Rise of Population*, London: Edward Arnold.
McKeown, T. (1979), *The Role of Medicine*, Oxford: Blackwell.
Munch, R. (1994), *Sociological Theory Volume Three: Developments since the 1960s*, Chicago: Nelson-Hall.
Parker, S. (1990), *Informal Marriage, Cohabitation and the Law 1750–1989*, London: Macmillan.
Ritzer, G. (1996), *The McDonaldization of Society* (rev. edn: first published 1992), Thousand Oaks: Pine Forge Press.
Sahlins, M. (1974), *Stone-Age Economics*, London: Tavistock.
Selznick, P. (1992), *The Moral Commonwealth: Social Theory and the Promise of Community*, Berkeley: University of California Press.
Small, A. (1909), *The Cameralists: Pioneers of German Social Polity*, Chicago: University of Chicago Press.
Smith, G. (1980), *Social Need*, London: Routledge and Kegan Paul.
Strong, P. M. (1979), Sociological imperialism and the practice of medicine, *Social Science and Medicine*, 13A: 199–215.
Strong, P. M. (1990), Epidemic psychology: a model, *Sociology of Health and Illness*, 12, 3: 249–59.
Szreter, S. (1988), The importance of social intervention in Britain's mortality decline c1850–1914: a reinterpretation of the role of public health, *Social History of Medicine*, 1, 1: 1–37.
Townsend, P. (1979), *Poverty in the United Kingdom: A Survey of Household Resources and Standards of Living*, Harmondsworth: Penguin.
Tudor Hart, J. (1971), The inverse care law, *Lancet*, 1(7696): 405–12.
Weber, M. (1954), *On Law in Economy and Society*, Cambridge, MA: Harvard University Press.
Winter, J. M. (1982), The decline of mortality in Britain 1870–1950. In Barker, T., and Drake, M. (eds), *Population and Society in Britain 1850–1980*, London: Batsford.
Wrigley, E. A., and Schofield, R. (1981), *The Population History of England 1541–1871: A Reconstruction*, London: Edward Arnold.

NOTES ON CONTRIBUTORS

Peter Abrahamson is Associate Professor, Ph.D. in the Department of Sociology, University of Copenhagen.

John Baldock is Reader in Social Policy at the University of Kent, Canterbury.

Colin Crouch is Professor of Sociology at the European University Institute, Florence, and External Scientific Member of the Max Planck Institute for Society Research, Cologne.

Robert Dingwall is Professor of Sociology and Director of the Genetics and Society Unit, University of Nottingham.

Gáspár Fajth is the Co-ordinator of the project "Public Policies and Social Conditions: Monitoring the Transition in Central and Eastern Europe (MONEE)" at UNICEF's Innocenti Research Centre, Florence.

Bob Jessop is Professor in the Department of Sociology, Lancaster University.

Nick Manning is Professor of Social Policy and Sociology and Head of the School of Sociology and Social Policy, University of Nottingham.

Ian Shaw is Deputy Director of the Centre for Research in Medical Sociology and Health Policy, University of Nottingham.

Nicola Yeates is a Lecturer in Social Policy in the School of Sociology and Social Policy, Queen's University of Belfast, Northern Ireland.

Index